KRISHNAMURTI'S NOTEBOOK

KRISHNAMURTI'S NOTEBOOK

by

J. KRISHNAMURTI

With a foreword by
MARY LUTYENS

HARPER & ROW, PUBLISHERS

New York, Hagerstown, San Francisco, London

FIRST UNITED STATES EDITION

ISBN: 0-06-06-4793-6

LIBRARY OF CONGRESS CATALOG CARD NUMBER: 76-9952

76 77 78 79 80 10 9 8 7 6 5 4 3 2 1

FOREWORD

In June 1961 Krishnamurti began to keep a daily record of his perceptions and states of consciousness. Apart from about fourteen days he kept up this record for seven months. He wrote clearly, in pencil, and with virtually no erasures. The first seventy-seven pages of the manuscript are written in a small notebook; from then until the end (p. 323 of the manuscript) a larger, loose-leaf book was used. The record starts abruptly and ends abruptly. Krishnamurti himself cannot say what prompted him to begin it. He had never kept such a record before, nor has he kept one since.

The manuscript has received the minimum amount of editing. Krishnamurti's spelling has been corrected; a few punctuation marks have been put in for the sake of clarity; some abbreviations, such as the ampersand he invariably used, have been spelt out in full; some footnotes and a few interpolations in square brackets have been added. In all other respects the manuscript is presented here as it was written.

A word is needed to explain one of the terms used in it—"the process". In 1922, at the age of twenty-eight, Krishnamurti underwent a spiritual experience that changed his life and which was followed by years of acute and almost continuous pain in his head and spine. The manuscript shows that "the process", as he called this mysterious pain, was still going on nearly forty years later, though in a much milder form.

"The process" was a physical phenomenon, not to be confused with the state of consciousness that Krishnamurti variously refers to in the notebooks as the "benediction", the "otherness", "immensity". At no time did he take any-pain-killing drugs for "the process". He has never taken alcohol or any kind of drug. He has never smoked, and for the last thirty years or so he has not so much as drunk tea or coffee. Although a life-long vegetarian, he has always been at great pains to ensure a plentiful and well-balanced diet. Ascetism is, to his way of thinking, as destructive of a religious life as over-indulgence. Indeed he looks after "the body" (he has always differentiated between the body and the ego) as a cavalry officer would have looked after his horse. He has never suffered from epilepsy or any of the other physical conditions that are said to give rise to visions and other spiritual phenomena; nor does he practise any "system" of meditation. All this is stated so that no reader should imagine that Krishnamurti's states of consciousness are, or ever have been, induced by drugs or fasting.

In this unique daily record we have what may be called the well-spring of Krishnamurti's teaching. The whole essence of his teaching is here, arising from its natural source. Just as he himself writes in these pages that "every time there is something 'new' in this benediction, a 'new' quality, a 'new' perfume, but yet it is changeless", so the teaching that springs from it is never quite the same although often repeated. In the same way, the trees, mountains, rivers, clouds, sunlight, birds and flowers that he describes over and over again are forever "new" because they are seen each time with eyes that have never become accustomed to them; each day they are a totally fresh perception for him, and so they become for us.

On June 18th, 1961, the day Krishnamurti started writing this record, he was in New York staying with friends in West 87th Street. He had flown to New York on June 14th from London where he had spent some six weeks and given twelve talks. Before going to London he had been in Rome and Florence, and, before that, for the first three months of the year, in India, speaking in New Delhi and Bombay.

M. L.

ITINERARY

June 18th [1961 New York.]
In the evening it was there : suddenly it was there, filling the room, a great sense of beauty, power and gentleness. Others noticed it.

19th   LIMITS OF THE BRAIN
All night it was there whenever I woke up. The head was bad going to the plane [to fly to Los Angeles].—The purification of the brain is necessary. The brain is the centre of all the senses; the more the senses are alert and sensitive the sharper the brain is; it's the centre of remembrance, the past; it's the storehouse of experience and knowledge, tradition. So it's limited, conditioned. Its activities are planned, thought out, reasoned, but it functions in limitation, in space-time. So it cannot formulate or understand that which is the total, the whole, the complete. The complete, the whole is the mind; it is empty, totally empty and because of this emptiness, the brain exists in space-time. Only when the brain has cleansed itself of its conditioning, greed, envy, ambition, then only it can comprehend that which is complete. Love is this completeness.

20th
In the car on the way to Ojai,* again it began, the pressure and the feeling of immense vastness. One was not experiencing this vastness; it was simply there; there was no centre from which or in which the experience was taking place. Everything, the cars, the people, the bill-boards, were startlingly clear and colour was painfully intense. For over an hour it went on and the head was very bad, the pain right through the head.

The brain can and must develop; its development will

* The Ojai Valley, some eighty miles north of Los Angeles.

always be from a cause, from a reaction, from violence to non-violence and so on. The brain has developed from the primitive state and however refined, intelligent, technical, it will be within the confines of space-time.

Anonymity is humility; it does not lie in the change of name, cloth or with the identification with that which may be anonymous, an ideal, a heroic act, country and so on. Anonymity is an act of the brain, the conscious anonymity; there's an anonymity which comes with the awareness of the complete. The complete is never within the field of the brain or idea.

21st

Woke up about two and there was a peculiar pressure and the pain was more acute, more in the centre of the head. It lasted over an hour and one woke up several times with the intensity of the pressure. Each time there was great expanding ecstasy; this joy continued.—Again, sitting in the dentist's chair, waiting, suddenly the pressure began. The brain became very quiet; quivering, fully alive; every sense was alert; the eyes were seeing the bee on the window, the spider, the birds and the violet mountains in the distance. They were seeing but the brain was not recording them. One could feel the quivering brain, something tremendously alive, vibrant and so not merely recording. The pressure and the pain was great and the body must have gone off into a doze.

Self-critical awareness is essential. Imagination and illusion distort clear observation. Illusion will always exist, so long as the urge for the continuation of pleasure and the avoidance of pain exist; the demand for those experiences which are pleasurable to continue or be remembered; the avoidance of pain, suffering. Both these breed illusion. To wipe away illusion altogether, pleasure and sorrow must be understood, not by control or sublimation, identification or denial.

Only when the brain is quiet can there be right observation. Can the brain ever be quiet? It can when the brain, being highly sensitive, without the power of distortion, is negatively aware.

All the afternoon the pressure has been on.

22nd

Woke up in the middle of the night and there was the experiencing of an incalculable expanding state of mind; the mind itself was that state. The "feeling" of this state was stripped of all sentiment, of all emotion, but was very factual, very real. This state continued for some considerable time.— All this morning, the pressure and the pain has been acute.

Destruction is essential. Not of buildings and things but of all the psychological devices and defences, gods, beliefs, dependence on priests, experiences, knowledge and so on. Without destroying all these there cannot be creation. It's only in freedom that creation comes into being. Another cannot destroy these defences for you; you have to negate through your own self-knowing awareness.

Revolution, social, economic, can only change outer states and things, in increasing or narrowing circles, but it will always be within the limited field of thought. For total revolution the brain must forsake all its inward, secret mechanism of authority, envy, fear and so on.

The strength and the beauty of a tender leaf is its vulnerability to destruction. Like a blade of grass that comes up through the pavement, it has the power that can withstand casual death.

23rd

Creation is never in the hands of the individual. It ceases entirely when individuality, with its capacities, gifts, techniques and so on, becomes dominant. Creation is the movement of the unknowable essence of the whole; it is never the expression of the part.

Just as one was getting to bed, there was that fullness of

*il L.** It was not only in the room but it seemed to cover the earth from horizon to horizon. It was a benediction.

The pressure, with its peculiar pain, was there all the morning. And it continues in the afternoon.

Sitting in the dentist's chair, one was looking out of the window, looking past the hedge, the TV antenna, the telegraph pole, at the purple mountains. One was looking not with eyes only but with one's whole head, as though from the back of the head, with one's entire being. It was an odd experience. There was no centre from which observation was taking place. The colours and the beauty and lines of the mountains were intense.

Every twist of thought must be understood; for all thought is reaction and any action from this can only increase confusion and conflict.

24th

The pressure and the pain was there all day yesterday; it is all becoming rather difficult. The moment one's by oneself, it begins. And desire for its continuance, any disappointment if it does not continue does not exist. It is simply there whether one wants it or not. It's beyond all reason and thought.

To do something for its own sake seems quite difficult and almost undesirable. Social values are based on doing something for the sake of something else. This makes for barren existence, a life which is never complete, full. This is one of the reasons of disintegrating discontent.

To be satisfied is ugly but to be discontented breeds hatred. To be virtuous in order to gain heaven or the approval of the respectable, of society, makes of life a barren field which has been ploughed over and over again but has never been sown. This activity of doing something for the sake of something else is in essence an intricate series of escapes, escapes from oneself, from what is.

* A house above Florence where he had stayed in April.
Without experiencing the essence there is no beauty.

Beauty is not merely in the outward things or in inward thoughts, feelings and ideas; there is beauty beyond this thought and feeling. It's this essence that is beauty. But this beauty has no opposite.

The pressure continues and the strain is at the base of the head and it's painful.

25th

Woke up in the middle of the night and found the body perfectly still, stretched out on its back, motionless; this position must have been maintained for some time. The pressure and the pain were there. The brain and the mind were intensely still. There was no division between them. There was a strange quiet intensity, like two great dynamos working at great speed; there was a peculiar tension in which there was no strain. There was a sense of vastness about the whole thing and a power without direction and cause and so no brutality and ruthlessness. And it continued during the morning.

During the past year or so, one would wake up, to experience, in wakened state, what had been going on while asleep, certain states of being. It is as though one woke up merely for the brain to register what was going on. But curiously, the particular experience would fade away quite soon. The brain was not putting it away in its scrolls of memory.

There is only destruction and no change. For all change is a modified continuity of what has been. All social, economic revolutions are reactions, a modified continuation of that which has been. This change does not in any way destroy the roots of ego-centric activities.

Destruction, in the sense we are using the word, has no motive; it has no purpose which implies action for the sake of result. Destruction of envy is total and complete; it implies the freedom from suppression, control, and without any motive whatsoever.

This total destruction is possible; it lies in seeing the total structure of envy. This seeing is not in space-time but immediate.

26th

The pressure and the strain of it was there, very strongly, yesterday afternoon and this morning. Only there was a certain change; the pressure and the strain were from the back of the head, through the palate to the top of the head. A strange intensity continues. One has to be quiet only for it to begin.

Control in any form is harmful to total understanding. A disciplined existence is a life of conformity; in conformity there is no freedom from fear. Habit destroys freedom; habit of thought, habit of drinking and so on makes for a superficial and dull life. Organized religion with its beliefs, dogmas and rituals denies the open entry into the vastness of mind. It is this entry that cleanses the brain of space-time. Being cleansed, the brain can then deal with time-space.

27th

That presence which was at *il L*. was there, waiting patiently, benignly, with great tenderness. It was like the lightning on a dark night but it was there, penetrating, blissful.

Something strange is happening to the physical organism. One can't exactly put one's finger on it but there's an "odd" insistency, drive; it's in no way self-created, bred out of imagination. It is palpable when one's quiet, alone, under a tree or in a room; it is there most urgently as one's about to go off to sleep. It's there as this is being written, the pressure and the strain, with its familiar ache.

Formulation and words about all this seem so futile; words however accurate, however clear the description, do not convey the real thing.

There's a great and unutterable beauty in all this.

There is only one movement in life, the outer and the inner; this movement is indivisible, though it is divided. Being divided, most follow the outer movement of knowledge, ideas, beliefs, authority, security, prosperity and so on. In reaction to this, one follows the so-called inner life, with its visions, hopes, aspirations, secrecies, conflicts, despairs. As this movement is a reaction, it is in conflict with the outer. So there is contradiction, with its aches, anxieties and escapes.

There is only one movement, which is the outer and the inner. With the understanding of the outer, then the inner movement begins, not in opposition or in contradiction. As conflict is eliminated, the brain, though highly sensitive and alert, becomes quiet. Then only the inner movement has validity and significance.

Out of this movement there is a generosity and compassion which is not the outcome of reason and purposeful self-denial.

The flower is strong in its beauty as it can be forgotten, set aside or destroyed.

The ambitious do not know beauty. The feeling of essence is beauty.

28th

Woke up in the middle of the night shouting and groaning; the pressure and the strain, with its peculiar pain, was intense. It must have been going on for some time and it went on for some time after waking up. The shouting and groaning take place quite often. These do not take place from indigestion. Sitting in the dentist's chair, while waiting, the whole thing began again and is going on, in the afternoon, as this is being written. It is more noticeable when one is alone or in some beautiful place or even in a dirty, noisy street.

That which is sacred has no attributes. A stone in a temple, an image in a church, a symbol is not sacred. Man calls them sacred, something holy to be worshipped out of complicated urges, fears and longings. This "sacredness" is still within the field of thought; it is built up by thought and in thought there's nothing new or holy. Thought can put together the intricacies of systems, dogmas, beliefs, and the images, symbols, it projects are no more holy than the blue-prints of a house or the design of a new aeroplane. All this is within the frontiers of thought and there is nothing sacred or mystical about all this. Thought is matter and it can be made into anything, ugly—beautiful.

But there's a sacredness which is not of thought, nor of a feeling resuscitated by thought. It is not recognizable by thought nor can it be utilized by thought. Thought cannot formulate it. But there's a sacredness, untouched by any symbol or word. It is not communicable. It is a fact.

A fact is to be seen and the seeing is not through the word. When a fact is interpreted, it ceases to be a fact; it becomes something entirely different. The seeing is of the highest importance. This seeing is out of time-space; it's immediate, instantaneous. And what's seen is never the same again. There's no again or in the meantime.

This sacredness has no worshipper, the observer who meditates upon it. It's not in the market to be bought or sold. Like beauty, it cannot be seen through its opposite for it has no opposite.

That presence is here, filling the room, spilling over the hills, beyond the waters, covering the earth.

Last night, as it has happened once or twice before, the body was just the organism and nothing else, functioning, empty and still.

29th

The pressure and the strain of deep ache is there; it's as though, deep within, an operation was going on. It's *not* brought on through one's own volition, however subtle it might be. One has deliberately and for some time gone into it, deeply. One has tried to induce it; tried to bring about various outward conditions, being alone and so on. Then nothing happens. All this isn't something recent.

LOVE
Love's not attachment. Love does not yield sorrow. Love

has no despair or hope. Love cannot be made respectable, part of the social scheme. When it is not there, every form of travail begins.

To possess and to be possessed is considered a form of love. This urge to possess, a person or a piece of property, is not merely the demands of society and circumstances but springs from a far deeper source. It comes from the depths of loneliness. Each one tries to fill this loneliness in different ways, drink, organized religion, belief, some form of activity and so on. All these are escapes but it's still there.

To commit oneself to some organization, to some belief or action is to be possessed by them, negatively; and positively is to possess. The negative and positive possessiveness is doing good, changing the world and the so-called love. To control another, to shape another in the name of love is the urge to possess; the urge to find security, safety in another and the comfort. Self-forgetfulness through another, through some activity makes for attachment. From this attachment, there's sorrow and despair and from this there is the reaction, to be detached. And from this contradiction of attachment and detachment arises conflict and frustration.

There's no escape from loneliness: it is a fact and escape from facts breeds confusion and sorrow.

But not to possess anything is an extraordinary state, not even to possess an idea, let alone a person or a thing. When idea, thought, takes root, it has already become a possession and then the war to be free begins. And this freedom is not freedom at all; it's only a reaction. Reactions take root and our life is the ground in which roots have grown. To cut all the roots, one by one, is a psychological absurdity. It cannot be done. Only the fact, loneliness, must be seen and then all other things fade away.

30th
Yesterday afternoon it was pretty bad, almost unbearable; it went on for several hours.

Walking, surrounded by these violet, bare, rocky mountains, suddenly there was solitude. Complete solitude. Everywhere, there was solitude; it had great, unfathomable richness; it had that beauty which is beyond thought and feeling.
It was not still; it was living, moving, filling every nook and
corner. The high rocky mountain top was aglow with the
setting sun and that very light and colour filled the heavens
with solitude.

It was uniquely alone, not isolated but alone, like a drop
of rain which holds all the waters of the earth. It was neither
joyous nor sad but alone. It had no quality, shape or colour;
these would make it something recognizable, measurable. It
came like a flash and took seed. It did not germinate but it
was there in its entirety. There was no time to mature; time
has roots in the past. This was a rootless, causeless state. So
it is totally "new", a state that has not been and never will
be, for it is living.

Isolation is known and so is loneliness; they are recognizable for they have often been experienced, actually or in
imagination. The very familiarity of these breeds certain
self-righteous contempt and fear from which arises cynicism
and gods. But self-isolation and loneliness do not lead to
aloneness; they must be finished with, not in order to gain
something, but they must die as naturally as the withering
away of a gentle flower. Resistance breeds fear but also
acceptance. The brain must wash itself clean of all these
cunning devices.

Unrelated to all these twists and turns of self-contaminated
consciousness, wholly different is this immense solitude. In it
all creation takes place. Creation destroys and so it is ever the
unknown.

All the evening of yesterday, this solitude was and is there,
and on waking in the middle of the night it sustained itself.

The pressure and the strain continue, increasing and

decreasing in continuous waves. It's pretty bad today, during the afternoon.

July 1st
It's as though everything stood still. There's no movement, no stirring, complete emptiness of all thought, of all seeing. There's no interpreter to translate, to observe, to censor. An immeasurable vastness that is utterly still and silent. There is no space, nor time to cover that space. The beginning and the ending are here, of all things. There is really nothing that can be said about it.

The pressure and the strain have been going on quietly all day; only now they have increased.

2nd
The thing which happened yesterday, that immeasurable still vastness, went on all the evening, even though there were people and general talk. It went on all night; it was there in the morning. Though there was rather exaggerated, emotionally agitated talk, suddenly in the middle of it, it was there. And it's here, there's a beauty and a glory and there's a sense of wordless ecstasy.

The pressure and the strain began rather early.

3rd
Been out all day. All the same, in a crowded town in the afternoon, for two or three hours the pressure and the strain of it was on.

4th
Been busy, but in spite of it, the pressure and the strain of it was there in the afternoon.

Whatever actions one has to do in daily life, the shocks and the various incidents should not leave their scars. These scars become the ego, the self, and as one lives, it becomes strong and its walls almost become impenetrable.

5th

Been too busy but whenever there's some quiet, the pressure and the strain was on.

6th

Last night woke up with that sense of complete stillness and silence; the brain was fully alert and intensely alive; the body was very quiet. This state lasted for about half an hour. This in spite of an exhausting day.

The height of intensity and sensitivity is the experiencing of essence. It's this that is beauty beyond word and feeling. Proportion and depth, light and shade are limited to time-space, caught in beauty-ugliness. But that which is beyond line and shape, beyond learning and knowledge, is the beauty of essence.

7th

Woke up several times shouting. Again there was that intense stillness of the brain and a feeling of vastness. There has been pressure and strain.

Success is brutality. Success is every form, political and religious, art and business. To be successful implies ruthlessness.

8th

Before going to sleep or just going off to sleep, several times there were groans and shouts. The body is too disturbed on account of travelling, as one leaves tonight for London [via Los Angeles]. There is a certain amount of pressure and strain.

9th

As one sat in the aeroplane amidst all the noise, smoking

and loud talking, most unexpectedly, the sense of immensity and that extraordinary benediction which was felt at *il L.*, that imminent feeling of sacredness, began to take place. The body was nervously tense because of the crowd, noise, etc. but in spite of all this, it was there. The pressure and the strain were intense and there was acute pain at the back of the head. There was only this state and there was no observer. The whole body was wholly in it and the feeling of sacredness was so intense that a groan escaped from the body and passengers were sitting in the next seats. It went on for several hours, late into the night. It was as though one was looking, not with eyes only but with a thousand centuries; it was altogether a strange occurrence. The brain was completely empty, all reaction had stopped; during all those hours, one was not aware of this emptiness but only in writing it is the thing known, but this knowledge is only descriptive and not real. That the brain could empty itself is an odd phenomenon. As the eyes were closed, the body, the brain seemed to plunge into unfathomable depths, into states of incredible sensitivity and beauty. The passenger in the next seat began to ask something and having replied, this intensity was there; there was no continuity but only being. And dawn was coming leisurely and the clear sky was filling with light. As this is being written late in the day, with sleepless fatigue, that sacredness is there. The pressure and the strain too.

10th

Little sleep but wake up to be aware that there is a great sense of driving energy which is focused in the head. The body was groaning and yet it was very still, stretched out flat and very peaceful. The room seemed to be full and it was very late and the front door of the next house was shut with a bang.—There was not an idea, not a feeling and yet the brain was alert and sensitive. The pressure and the strain were there causing pain. An odd thing about this pain is that it does not in any way exhaust the body. There seems to be so much happening within the brain but yet it is impossible to put into words what exactly is taking place. There was a sense of measureless expansion.

11th

The pressure and strain have been rather heavy and there is pain. The odd part of all this is that the body in no way protests or puts up resistance in any way. There is an unknown energy involved in all this. Too busy to write much.

12th

It was bad last night, shouting and groaning. The head was painful. Though little sleep, woke up twice and each time there was a sense of expanding intensity and intense inward attention and the brain had emptied itself of all feeling and thought.

Destruction, the complete emptying of the brain, the reaction and memory must without any effort wither away; withering away implies time but it is time that ceases and not the ending of memory.

This timeless expanding that was taking place and the quality and degree of intensity are wholly different from passion and feeling. It was this intensity totally unrelated to any desire, wish or experience, as remembrance, that was rushing through the brain. The brain was only an instrument and it's the mind that is this timeless expanding, exploding intensity of creation. And creation is destruction.

In the aeroplane it's going on.*

13th

I think it's the quietness of the place, of the green slopes of the mountains, the beauty of the trees and the cleanliness, that and other things, has made the pressure and the strain

* Flying to Geneva from where he drove to a friend's chalet at Gstaad.

far greater; the head has been bad all day; it becomes worse when one is by oneself. All last night it seems to have been going on and woke up several times shouting and groaning; even during rest, in the afternoon, it was bad, accompanied by shouting. The body is completely relaxed and at rest here. Last night, after the long and lovely drive through mountainous country, on entering the room, that strange sacred blessing was there. The other also felt it.* The other also felt the quiet, that penetrating atmosphere. There is a feeling of great beauty and love and of mature fullness.

Power is derived from asceticism, from action, from position, from virtue, from domination and so on. All such forms of power are evil. It corrupts and perverts. The use of money, talent, cleverness to gain power or deriving power from any use of these is evil.

But there is a power which is in no way related to that power which is evil. This power is not to be bought through sacrifice, virtue, good works and beliefs, nor is it to be bought through worship, prayers and self-denying or self-destructive meditations. All effort to become or to be must wholly, naturally, cease. Only then that power which is not evil, can be.

14th

The whole process has been going on all day—the pressure, the strain and the pain at the back of the head; woke up shouting several times, and even during the day there was involuntary groaning and shouting. Last night that sacred feeling filled the room and the other felt it also.

How easy it is to deceive oneself about almost everything, especially about deeper and more subtle demands and wishes. To be utterly free of all such urges and demands is arduous. But yet it is essential to be free from them or else the brain breeds every form of illusion. The urge for the repetition of

* The friend he was staying with at Gstaad.

an experience however pleasant, beautiful, fruitful, is the soil in which sorrow grows. The passion of sorrow is as limiting as the passion of power. The brain must cease to make its own ways and be utterly passive.

15th

The whole process was bad last night; it has left one rather tired and sleepless.

Woke up in the middle of the night, with a sense of immense and measureless strength. It was not the strength that will or desire has put together but the strength that is there in a river, in a mountain, in a tree. It is in man when every form of desire and will have completely ceased. It has no value, has no profit to a human being, but without it the human being is not, nor the tree.

The action of man is choice and will and in such action there is contradiction and conflict and so sorrow. All such action has a cause, a motive and hence it is reaction. Action of this strength has no cause, no motive and therefore is immeasurable and the essence.

16th

The whole process went on most of the night; it was rather intense. How much can the body stand! The whole body was quivering and, this morning, woke up with the head shaking.

There was, this morning that peculiar sacredness, filling the room. It had great penetrating power, entering into every corner of one's being, filling, cleansing, making everything of itself. The other felt it too. It's the thing that every human being craves for and because they crave for it, it eludes them. The monk, the priest, the sanyasi torture their bodies and their character in their longing for this but it evades them. For it cannot be bought; neither sacrifice, virtue nor prayer can bring this love. This life, this love cannot be if death is the means. All seeking, all asking must wholly cease.

Truth cannot be exact. What can be measured is not truth.

That which is not living can be measured and its height be found.

17th
We were going up the path of a steep wooded side of a mountain and presently sat on a bench. Suddenly, most unexpectedly that sacred benediction came upon us, the other felt it too, without our saying anything. As it several times filled a room, this time it seemed to cover the mountainside across the wide, extending valley and beyond the mountains. It was everywhere. All space seemed to disappear; what was far, the wide gap, the distant snow-covered peaks and the person sitting on the bench faded away. There was not one or two or many but only this immensity. The brain had lost all its responses; it was only an instrument of observation, it was seeing, not as the brain belonging to a particular person, but as a brain which is not conditioned by time-space, as the essence of all brains.

It was a quiet night and the whole process was not so intense. On waking this morning, there was an experiencing whose duration was perhaps a minute, an hour or timeless. An experiencing that is informed with time ceases to be experiencing; what has continuity ceases to be the experiencing. On waking there was in the very depths, in the measureless depth of the total mind, an intense flame alive and burning furiously, of attention, of awareness, of creation. The word is not the thing; the symbol is not the real. The fires that burn on the surface of life pass, die away, leaving sorrow and ashes and remembrance. These fires are called life but it's not life. It's decay. The fire of creation that is destruction is life. In it there is no beginning, no ending, neither tomorrow or yesterday. It's there and no surface activity will ever uncover it. The brain must die for this life to be.

18th
The process has been very acute, preventing sleep; even in

the morning and in the afternoon shouting and groaning. The pain has been rather bad.

Woke up this morning with a great deal of pain but at the same time there was a flash of a seeing that was revealing. Our eyes and brain register the outward things, trees, mountains, swift running streams; accumulate knowledge, technique and so on. With that same eyes and brain, trained to observe, to choose, to condemn and justify, we turn inward, look inward, recognize objects, build up ideas, which are organized into reason. This inward look does not go very far, for it's still within the limitation of its own observation and reason. This inward gaze is still the outward look and so there's not much difference between the two. What may appear to be different may be similar.

But there's an inward observation which is not the outward observation turned inward. The brain and the eye which observe only partially do not comprehend the total seeing. They must be alive completely but still; they must cease to choose and judge but be passively aware. Then the inward seeing is without the border of time-space. In this flash a new perception is born.

19th

It had been rather bad all the afternoon of yesterday and it seems more painful. Towards the evening that sacredness came and filled the room and the other felt it too. All night it was fairly quiet, though the pressure and strain were there, like the sun behind the clouds; early this morning the process began again.

It appears one's awakened merely to register a certain experience; this has happened quite often, for the past year. One was awakened this morning with a living feeling of joy; it was taking place as one woke up; it wasn't a thing in the past. It was actually taking place. It was coming, this ecstasy, from "outside", not self-induced; it was being pushed through the system, flowing through the organism, with great energy and volume. The brain was not taking part in it but only registering it, not as a remembrance but as an actual fact which was taking place. There was, it seemed, immense strength and vitality behind this ecstasy; it wasn't sentimental nor a feeling, an emotion but as solid and real as that stream crashing down the mountain-side or that solitary pine on the green mountain slope. All feeling and emotion are related to the brain and as love is not, so was this ecstasy. It is with the greatest difficulty, the brain can recall it.

Early this morning there was a benediction that seemed to cover the earth and fill the room. With it comes an all consuming quietness, a stillness that seems to have within it all movement.

20th

The process was particularly intense yesterday afternoon. In the car, waiting, one was almost oblivious of what was going on around one. The intensity increased and it was almost unbearable so that one was forced to lie down. Fortunately there was someone in the room.

The room became full with that benediction. Now what followed is almost impossible to put down in words; words are such dead things, with definite set meaning and what took place was beyond all words and description. It was the centre of all creation; it was a purifying seriousness that cleansed the brain of every thought and feeling; its seriousness was as lightning which destroys and burns up; the profundity of it was not measurable, it was there immovable, impenetrable, a solidity that was as light as the heavens. It was in the eyes, in the breath. It was in the eyes and the eyes could see. The eyes that saw, that looked were wholly different from the eyes of the organ and yet they were the same eyes. There was only seeing, the eyes that saw beyond time-space. There was impenetrable dignity and a peace that was the essence of all movement, action. No virtue touched it for it was beyond all virtue and sanctions of man. There was love that was utterly perishable and so it had the delicacy of all new things, vulnerable, destructible and yet it was beyond all this. It was there imperishable, unnameable, the unknowing. No thought could ever penetrate it; no action could ever touch it. It was "pure", untouched and so ever dyingly beautiful.

All this seemed to affect the brain; it was not as it was before. (Thought is such a trivial thing, necessary but trivial.) Because of it, relationship seems to have changed. As a terrific storm, a destructive earthquake gives a new course to the rivers, changes the landscape, digs deep into the earth, so it has levelled the contours of thought, changed the shape of the heart.

21st

The whole process is going on as usual, in spite of cold and feverish state. It has become more acute and more insistent. One wonders how long the body can carry on.

Yesterday, as we were walking up a beautiful narrow valley, its steep sides dark with pines and green fields full of wild flowers, suddenly, most unexpectedly, for we were talking of other things, a benediction descended upon us, like gentle rain. We became the centre of it. It was gentle, pressing, infinitely tender and peaceful, enfolding us in a power that was beyond all fault and reason.

Early this morning, on waking, changing, changeless purifying seriousness and an ecstasy that had no cause. It simply was there. And during the day, whatever one did it was there in the background and it came directly and immediately to the fore when one was quiet. There is an urgency and beauty in it.

No imagination or desire could ever formulate such profound seriousness.

22nd

Waiting in the doctor's dark, airless office, that benediction, which no desire can construct, came and filled the small room. It was there till we left. If it was felt by the doctor it's impossible to say.

Why is it that there is deterioration? Inwardly as well as outwardly. Why? Time brings destruction to all mechanical organizations; it wears out by use and disease every form of organism. Why should there be deterioration inwardly, psychologically? Beyond all explanations which a good brain can give why do we choose the worse and not the better, why hate rather than love, why greed and not generosity, why self-centred activity and not open total action? Why be mean when there are soaring mountains and flashing streams? Why jealousy and not love? Why? Seeing the fact leads to one thing, and opinions, explanations, to another. Seeing the fact that we decline, deteriorate is all important and not the why and wherefore of it. Explanation has very little significance in face of a fact, but to be satisfied with explanations, with words is one of the major factors of deterioration. Why war and not peace? The fact is we are violent; conflict, inside and outside the skin, is part of our daily life—ambition and success. Seeing this fact and not the cunning explanation and the subtle word, puts an end to deterioration. Choice, one of the major causes of decline, must wholly cease if it's to come to an end. The desire to fulfil and the satisfaction and sorrow that exist in its shadow, is also one of the factors of deterioration.

Woke up early this morning, to experience that benediction. One was "forced" to sit up to be in that clarity and beauty. Later in the morning sitting on a roadside bench under a tree one felt the immensity of it. It gave shelter, protection like the tree overhead whose leaves gave shelter against the strong mountain sun and yet allowed light to come through. All relationship is such protection in which there's freedom, and because there's freedom, there is shelter.

23rd

Woke up early this morning with an enormous sense of power, beauty and incorruptibility. It was not something that had happened, an experience that was past and one woke up to remember it as in a dream, but something that was actually taking place. One was aware of something utterly incorruptible, in which nothing could possibly exist that could become corrupt, deteriorate. It was too immense for the brain to grasp, to remember; it could only register, mechanically, that there is such a "state" of incorruption. Experiencing such a state is vastly important; it was there, limitless, untouchable, impenetrable.

Because of its incorruptibility, there was in it beauty. Not the beauty that fades nor something put together by the hand of man, nor the evil with its beauty. One felt that in its presence all essence exists and so it was sacred. It was a life in which nothing could perish. Death is incorruptible but man makes of it a corruption as, for him, life is.

With it all, there was that sense of power, strength as solid as that mountain which nothing could shatter, which no sacrifice, prayer, virtue could ever touch.

It was there, immense, which no wave of thought could corrupt, a thing remembered. It was there and the eyes, the breath were of it.

Time, laziness, corrupts. It must have gone on for a certain period. Dawn was just coming and there was dew on the car outside and on the grass. The sun wasn't up yet but the sharp snow peak was clear in the grey-blue sky; it was an enchanting morning, with not a cloud. But it wouldn't last, it was too lovely.

Why should all this happen to us? No explanation is good enough, though one can invent a dozen. But certain things are fairly clear. 1. One must be wholly "indifferent" to it coming and going. 2. There must be no desire to continue the experience or to store it away in memory. 3. There must be a certain physical sensitivity, a certain indifference to comfort. 4. There must be self-critical humorous approach. But even if one had all these, by chance, not through deliberate cultivation and humility, even then, they are not enough. Something totally different is necessary or nothing is necessary. It must come and you can never go after it, do what you will. You can also add love to the list but it is beyond love. One thing is certain, the brain can never comprehend it nor can it contain it. Blessed is he to whom it is given. And you can add also a still, quiet brain.

24th

The process has not been so intense, as the body for some days has not been well, but though it is weak, now and then one can feel the intensity of it. It's strange how this process adjusts itself to circumstance.

Yesterday, driving through the narrow valley, a mountain stream noisily making its way beside the wet road, there was this benediction. It was very strong and everything was bathed in it. The noise of the stream was part of it and the high waterfall which became the stream were in it. It was like the gentle rain that was coming down and one became utterly vulnerable; the body seemed to have become light as a leaf, exposed and trembling. This went on through the long, cool drive; talk became monosyllabic; the beauty of it seemed incredible. All the evening it remained and though there was laughter, the solid, the impenetrable seriousness remained.

On waking this morning, early when the sun was still below the horizon, there was the ecstasy of this seriousness. It filled the heart and the brain and there was a sense of immovability.

To look is important. We look to immediate things and out of immediate necessities to the future, coloured by the past. Our seeing is very limited and our eyes are accustomed to near things. Our look is as bound by time-space as our brain. We never look, we never see beyond this limitation; we do not know how to look through and beyond these fragmentary frontiers. But the eyes have to see beyond them, penetrating deeply and widely, without choosing, without shelter; they have to wander beyond man-made frontiers of ideas and values and to feel beyond love.

Then there is a benediction which no god can give.

25th

In spite of a meeting,* the process is going on, rather gently but going on.

Woke up this morning, rather early, with a sense of a mind that had penetrated into unknown depths. It was as though the mind itself was going into itself, deeply and widely and the journey seemed to have been without movement. And there was this experience of immensity in abundance and a richness that was incorruptible.

It's strange that though every experience, state, is utterly different, it is still the same movement; though it seems to change, it is still the changeless.

26th

All yesterday afternoon the process was on and it was pretty bad. Walking in the deep shadow of a mountain, beside a chattering stream, in the intensity of the process, one felt utterly vulnerable, naked and very open; one hardly seemed to exist. And the beauty of the snow-covered mountain, held in the cup of two dark pine slopes of curving hills, was greatly moving.

Early in the morning when the sun was not yet up and the dew on the grass, still in bed, lying quietly, without any thought or movement, there was a seeing, not the superficial seeing with the eyes but seeing through the eyes from behind the head. The eyes and from behind the head were only the instrument through which the immeasurable past was seeing

* The first of nine talks given at Saanen, the village next to Gstaad.

into the immeasurable space that had no time. And later, still in bed, there was a seeing in which all life seemed to be contained.

How easy it is to deceive oneself, to project desirable states which are actually experienced, especially when they are pleasure. There's no illusion, no deception, when there's no desire, conscious or unconscious, for any experience of any kind, when one's wholly indifferent to the coming and going of all experience, when one's not asking for anything.

27th

It was a beautiful drive through two different valleys, up to a pass; the sweeping mountainous rocks, fantastic shapes and curves, their solitude and grandeur, and far away the green, sloping mountain, made an impression on the brain that was still. As we were driving, the strange intensity and the beauty of these many days came more and more pressing upon one. And the other felt it too.

Woke up very early in the morning; that which is a benediction and that which is strength were there and the brain was aware of them as it is aware of a perfume but it was not a sensation, an emotion; they were simply there. Do what one will, they will always be there; there was nothing one could do about it.

There was a talk this morning and during the talk, the brain which reacts, thinks, constructs was absent. The brain was not working, except, probably, for the memory of words.

28th

Yesterday we were walking along the favourite road beside the noisy stream, in the narrow valley of dark pine trees, fields with flowers and in the distance the massive snow-covered mountain and a waterfall. It was enchanting, peaceful and cool. There, walking, that sacred blessing came, a thing that one could almost touch, and deep within one there were movements of change. It was an evening of enchantment and of beauty that was not of this world. The immeasurable was there and then there was stillness.

This morning woke up early to register that the process was intense, and through the back of the head, rushing forward as an arrow with that peculiar sound as it flies through the air, was a force, a movement that came from nowhere and was going nowhere. And there was a sense of vast stability and a "dignity" that could not be approached. And an austerity that no thought could formulate but with it a purity of infinite gentleness. All these are merely words and so they can never represent the real; the symbol is never the real and the symbol is without value.

All the morning the process was on and a cup that had no height and no depth seemed to be full to the overflowing.

29th

Had been seeing people and after they left, one felt as though one was suspended between two worlds. And presently the world of the process and that unquenchable intensity came back. Why this separation? The people one saw were not serious, at least they thought they were serious but they were serious only in a superficial way. One could not give oneself completely and hence this feeling of not being at home again, but all the same, it was an odd experience.

We were talking and a little bit of the stream between the trees was pointed out. It was an ordinary sight, an everyday incident, but as one looked, several things took place, not any outward incidents but clear perception. It's absolutely necessary for maturity that there should be—1. Complete simplicity which goes with humility, not in things or possessions but in the quality of being. 2. Passion with that intensity which is not merely physical. 3. Beauty; not only the sensitivity to outward reality but being sensitive to that beauty which is beyond and above thought and feeling. 4. Love; the totality of it, not the thing that knows jealousy, attachment, dependence; not that as divided into carnal and divine. The whole immensity of it. 5. And the mind that can pursue, that can penetrate without motive, without purpose, into its own immeasurable depths; that has no barrier, that is free to wander without time-space.

Suddenly one was aware of all this and all the implications involved in it; just the mere sight of a stream between decaying branches and leaves on a rainy, dismal day.

As we were talking, for no reason, for what we were talking about was not too serious, out of some unapproachable depths suddenly one felt this immense flame of power, destructive in its creation. It was the power that existed before all things came into being; it was unapproachable and by its very strength one could not come near it. Nothing exists but that one thing. Immensity and awe.

Part of this experience must have "continued" while asleep for on waking early this morning it was there and the intensity of the process had awakened one. It is beyond all thought and words to describe what's going on, the strangeness of it and the love, the beauty of it. No imagination could ever build all this up nor is it an illusion; the strength and the purity of it is not for a make-believe mind-brain. It's beyond and above all faculties of man.

30th

It was a cloudy day, heavy with dark clouds; it had rained in the morning and it had turned cold. After a walk we were talking but more looking at the beauty of the earth, the houses and the dark trees.

Unexpectedly, there was a flash of that unapproachable power and strength that was physically shattering. The body became frozen into immobility and one had to shut one's eyes not to go off into a faint. It was completely shattering and everything that *was* didn't seem to exist. And the immobility of that strength and the destructive energy that came with it, burned out the limitations of sight and sound. It was something indescribably great whose height and depth are unknowable.

Early this morning, just as dawn was breaking, with not a cloud in the sky and the snow-covered mountains just visible, woke up with that feeling of impenetrable strength in one's eyes and throat; it seemed to be a palpable state, something that could never not be there. For nearly an hour it was there and the brain remained empty. It was not a thing to be caught by thought and stored up in memory to be recalled. It was there and all thought was dead. Thought is functional, is only useful in that realm; thought could not think about it for thought is time and it was beyond all time and measure. Thought, desire could not seek for its continuation or for its repetition, for thought, desire, was totally absent. Then what is it that remembers to write this down? Merely a mechanical record but the record, the word is not the thing.

The process goes on, more gently, probably because of the talks and there is also a limit beyond which the body will crack. But it's there, persistent and insistent.

31st

Walking along the path that followed the fast-running stream, cool and pleasant, with many people about, there was that benediction, as gentle as the leaves and there was in it a dancing joy. But there was beyond and through it that immense, solid strength and power that was unapproachable. One felt that there was immeasurable depth behind it, unfathomable. It was there, with every step, with an urgency and yet with infinite "indifference". As a big, high dam holds back the river, forming a vast lake of many miles, so was this immensity.

But every moment there was destruction; not the destruction to bring about a new change—change is never new—but total destruction of what has been so that it can never be. There was no violence in this destruction; there is violence in change, in revolution, in submission, in discipline, in control and domination but here all violence, in any form with a different name, has totally ceased. It is this destruction that is creation.

But creation is not peace. Peace and conflict belong to the world of change and time, to the outward and inward movement of existence, but this was not of time or of any movement in space. It is pure and absolute destruction and only then can the "new" be.

This morning on awaking this essence was there; it must have been there all night, and on waking it seemed to fill the whole head and body. And the process is going on gently. One has to be alone and quiet, then it is there.

As one writes that benediction is there, as the soft breeze among the leaves.

August 1st
It was a beautiful day and driving in the beautiful valley there was that which was not to be denied; it was there as the air, the sky and those mountains.

Woke up early, shouting, for the process was intense but during the day, in spite of the talk,* it has been going on with mildness.

2nd
Woke up early this morning; unwashed one was forced to sit up and one has generally sat up in bed for some time before getting out of bed. But this morning it was beyond the usual procedure, it was an urgent and imperative necessity. As one sat up, in a little while there came that immense benediction and presently one felt that this whole power, this whole impenetrable, stern strength was in one, about one and in the head, and in the very middle of all this immensity, there was complete stillness. It was a stillness which no mind can

---

* The fourth talk at Saanen.

imagine, formulate; no violence can produce this stillness; it had no cause; it was not a result; it was the stillness in the very centre of a tremendous hurricane. It was the stillness of all motion, the essence of all action; it was the explosion of creation and it's only in such stillness that creation can take place.

Again the brain could not capture it; it could not record it in its memories, in the past, for this thing is out of time; it had no future, it had no past or present. If it was of time, the brain could capture it and shape it according to its conditioning. As this stillness is the totality of all motion, the essence of all action, a living that was without shadow, the thing of shadow could not, by any means, measure it. It is too immense for time to hold it and no space could contain it.

All this may have lasted a minute or an hour.

Before sleeping the process was acute and it has continued in a mild way all day long.

3rd

Woke up early with that strong feeling of otherness, of another world that is beyond all thought; it was very intense and as clear and pure as the early morning, cloudless sky. Imagination and illusion are purged from the mind for there is no continuance. Everything is and it has never been before. Where there is a possibility of continuance, there is delusion.

It was a clear morning though soon clouds would be gathering. As one looked out of the window, the trees, the fields were very clear. A curious thing is happening; there is a heightening of sensitivity. Sensitivity, not only to beauty but also to all other things. The blade of grass was astonishingly green; that one blade of grass contained the whole spectrum of colour; it was intense, dazzling and such a small thing, so easy to destroy. Those trees were all of life, their height and their depth; the lines of those sweeping hills and the solitary trees were the expression of all time and space; and the mountains against the pale sky were beyond all the gods of man. It was incredible to see, feel, all this by just looking out of the window. One's eyes were cleansed.

It is strange how during one or two interviews that strength, that power filled the room. It seemed to be in one's eyes and breath. It comes into being, suddenly and most unexpectedly, with a force and intensity that is quite overpowering and at other times it's there, quietly and serenely. But it's there, whether one wants it or not. There is no possibility of getting used to it for it has never been nor will it ever be. But it's there.

The process has been mild, these talks and seeing people probably make it so.

4th

Woke up very early in the morning; it was still dark but dawn would soon come; towards the east there was in the distance a pale light. The sky was very clear and the shape of the mountains and the hills were just visible. It was very quiet.

Out of this vast silence suddenly, as one sat up in bed, when thought was quiet and far away, when there wasn't even a whisper of a feeling, there came that which was now the solid, inexhaustible being. It was solid, without weight, without measure; it was there and besides it, there existed nothing. It was there without another. The words solid, immovable, imperishable do not in any way convey that quality of timeless stability. None of these or any other word could communicate that which was there. It was totally itself and nothing else; it was the totality of all things, the essence.

The purity of it remained, leaving one without thought, without action. It's not possible to be one with it; it is not possible to be one with a swiftly flowing river. You can never be one with that which has no form, no measure, no quality. It is; that is all.

How deeply mature and tender everything has become and strangely all life is in it; like a new leaf, utterly defenceless.

5th

There was, as one woke up this morning early, a flash of "seeing", "looking", that seems to be going on and on for ever. It started nowhere and went nowhere but in that seeing all sight was included and all things. It was a sight that went beyond the streams, the hills, the mountains, past the earth and the horizon and the people. In this seeing, there was penetrating light and incredible swiftness. The brain could not follow it nor could the mind contain it. It was pure light and a swiftness that knew no resistance.

On the walk yesterday, the beauty of light among the trees and on the grass was so intense, that it left one actually breathless and the body frail.

Later this morning, as one was just going to have breakfast, like a knife thrust into a soft earth, there was that benediction, with its power and strength. It came as does lightning and was gone as quickly.

The process was rather intense yesterday afternoon and somewhat less this morning. There's a frailty about the body.

6th

Though one had slept, not too well, on waking one was aware that all night the process was going but, much more, that there was a blossoming of that benediction. One felt as though it was operating upon one.

On waking, there was an outgoing, outpouring of this power and strength. It was as a stream rushing out of the rocks, out of the earth. There was a strange and unimaginable bliss in this, an ecstasy that had nothing to do with thought and feeling.

There is an aspen tree and its leaves are trembling in the breeze and without that dance life is not.

7th

One was done up after the talk* and seeing people and

* The talk had been the day before.

towards the evening we went for a short walk. After a brilliant day, clouds were gathering and it would rain during the night. Clouds were closing in on the mountains and the stream was making a great deal of noise. The road was dusty with cars and across the stream was a narrow, wooden bridge. We crossed it and went up a grassy path and the green slope was full of flowers of so many colours.

The path went up gently past a cow shed but it was empty; the cattle had been taken to pastures much higher up. It was quiet up there, without people but with the noise of the rushing stream. Quietly, it came, so gently that one was not aware of it, so close to the earth, among the flowers. It was spreading, covering the earth and one was in it, not as an observer but of it. There was no thought or feeling, the brain utterly quiet. Suddenly, there was innocence so simple, so clear and delicate. It was a meadow of innocence past all pleasure and ache, beyond all torture of hope and despair. It was there and it made the mind, one's whole being innocent; one was of it, past measure, past word, the mind transparent and the brain young without time.

It went on for some time and it was late and we had to return.

This morning, on waking it took a little time for that immensity to come but it was there and thought and feeling were made still. As one was cleaning one's teeth, the intensity of it was sharp and clear. It comes as suddenly as it goes, nothing can restrain it and nothing can call it.

The process has been rather acute and the pain has been sharp.

8th

On waking, everything was quiet as the previous day had been tiring. It was surprisingly quiet and one sat up to carry on with the usual meditation. Unexpectedly, as one hears a distant sound, it began, quietly, gently, and all of a sudden, it was there in full force. It must have lasted for some minutes. It was gone but it left its perfume deep in one's consciousness and the seeing of it in one's eyes.

During the talk this morning that immensity with its benediction was there.* Each one must have interpreted it in his way and thereby destroying its indescribable nature. All interpretation distorts.

The process has been acute and the body has become rather frail. But beyond all this, there is the purity of incredible beauty, the beauty not of things, which thought or feeling has put together, or the gift of some craftsman, but as a river that wanders, nourishing and indifferent, polluted and made use of; it's there, complete and rich in itself. And a strength that has no value in man's social structure and behaviour. But it is there, unconcerned, immense, untouchable. Because of this, all things are.

9th

Again this morning, on waking one felt it was an empty night; it had been too much, for the body, with the talk [the day before] and seeing people, was tired. Sitting up in bed as usual, it was quiet; the country was asleep, there was no sound and the morning was heavy with clouds. Wherever it has its being, it came suddenly and fully, this benediction with its strength and power. It remained filling the room and beyond, and presently it went, leaving behind a feeling of vastness, whose height was beyond the word.

Yesterday, walking amidst hills, meadows and streams, among pleasant quietness and beauty one was again aware of that strange and deeply moving innocence. It was quietly, without any resistance, penetrating, entering into every corner and twist of one's mind, cleansing it of all thought

* This was the seventh talk. It was principally about meditation.

and feeling. It left one empty and complete. Suddenly all time had stopped. Each one was aware of its passage.*

The process is going on but more gently and deeply.

10th

It had rained sharply and very heavily, washing off the white dust on the big round leaves by the unpaved road that went deep into the mountains. The air was soft and gentle and at that altitude not heavy; the air was clean and pleasant and there was the smell of rain-washed earth. Walking up the road, one was aware of the beauty of the earth and the delicate line of the steep hills against the evening sky; of the massive, rocky mountain with its glacier and wide field of snow; of the many flowers in the meadows. It was an evening of great beauty and quietness. The stream so boisterous, was made muddy by the recent, heavy rain; it had lost that peculiar bright clarity of mountain water but in a few hours it would again become clear.

As one looked at the massive rocks, with their curves and shapes and the sparkling snow, half-dreamily with no thought in mind, suddenly there was an immense, massive dignity of strength and benediction. It filled the valley on the instant and the mind had no measurement; it was deep beyond the word. Again there was innocence.

On waking early this morning, it was there and meditation was a little thing and all thought died and all feeling had ceased; the brain was utterly quiet. Its record is not the real. It was there, untouchable and unknowable. It would never be what has been : it is of never ending beauty.

It was an extraordinary morning. This has been going on for four solid months, whatever the environment, whatever the condition of the body. It's never the same and yet the same; it is destruction and never ending creation. Its power and strength are beyond all comparison and word. And it's never continuous; it is death and life.

* Presumably he had been walking with several friends.

The process has been rather acute and it all seems rather unimportant.

August 11th, 1961*

Sitting in the car, beside a boisterous mountain stream and in the middle of green, rich meadows and a darkening sky, that incorruptible innocence was there, whose austerity was beauty. The brain was utterly quiet and it was touched by it.

The brain is nourished by reaction and experience; it lives on experience. But experience is always limiting and conditioning; memory is the machinery of action. Without experience, knowledge and memory, action is not possible but such action is fragmentary, limited. Reason, organized thought, is always incomplete; idea, response of thought, is barren and belief is the refuge of thought. All experience only strengthens thought negatively or positively.

Experiencing is conditioned by experience, the past. Freedom is the emptying of the mind of experience. When the brain ceases to nourish itself through experience, memory and thought, when it dies to experiencing, then its activity is not self-centered. It then has its nourishment from elsewhere. It is this nourishment that makes the mind religious.

On waking this morning, beyond all meditation and thought and the delusions that feelings create, there was an intense bright light at the very centre of the brain and beyond the brain at the very centre of consciousness, of one's being. It was a light that had no shadow nor was it set in any dimension. It was there without movement. With that light there was present that incalculable strength and beauty beyond thought and feeling.

The process was rather acute in the afternoon.

12th

Yesterday, walking up the valley, the mountains covered

* The larger notebook begins here, giving the year for the first time.

with clouds and the stream seemingly more noisy than ever, there was a sense of astonishing beauty, not that the meadows and hills and the dark pines had changed. Only the light was different, more soft, with a clarity that seemed to penetrate everything, leaving no shadow. As the road climbed, we were able to look down on a farm, with green pasture land around it. It was a green meadow, a rich green that is seen nowhere, but that little farmhouse and that green pasture contained all the earth and all mankind. There was an absolute finality about it; it was the finality of beauty that is not tortured by thought and feeling. The beauty of a picture, a song, a building is put together by man, to be compared, to be criticized, to be added up but this beauty was not the handwork of man. All the handwork of man must be denied with a finality before this beauty can be. For it needs total innocence, total austerity; not the innocence that thought had contrived nor the austerity of sacrifice. Only when the brain is free of time, and its responses utterly still, is there that austere innocency.

Woke up long before dawn when the air is very still and the earth waiting for the sun. Woke up with a clarity that was peculiar and an urgency that demanded full attention. The body was completely motionless, an immobility that was without strain, without tension. And inside the head a peculiar phenomenon was going on. A great wide river was flowing with the pressure of immense weight of water, flowing between high, polished granite rock. On each side of this great wide river was polished, sparkling granite, on which nothing grew, not even a blade of grass; there was nothing but sheer polished rock, soaring up beyond measurable eyesight. The river was making its way, silently, without a whisper, indifferent, majestic. It was actually taking place, it wasn't a dream, a vision nor a symbol to be interpreted. It was there taking place, beyond any doubt; it was not a thing of imagination. No thought could possibly invent it; it was too immense and real for thought to formulate it.

The immobility of the body and this great flowing river

between the polished granite walls of the brain, went on for an hour and a half by the watch. Through the open window the eyes could see the coming dawn. There was no mistaking the reality of what was taking place. For an hour and a half the whole being was attentive, without effort, without wandering off. And all of a sudden it stopped and the day began.

This morning, that benediction filled the room. It was raining hard but there would be blue sky later.

The process, with its pressure and ache, continues gently.

13th

As the path that goes up the mountain can never contain all of the mountain, so this immensity is not the word. And yet walking up the side of the mountain, with the small stream running at the foot of the slope, this incredible, unnameable immensity was there; the mind and heart was filled with it and every drop of water on the leaf and on the grass was sparkling with it.

It had been raining all night and all the morning and it had been heavy with clouds, and now the sun was coming out over the high hills and there were shadows on the green, spotless meadows that were rich with flowers. The grass was very wet and the sun was on the mountains. Up that path there was enchantment and talking now and then seemed in no way to [word left out] the beauty of that light nor the simple peace that lay in the field. The benediction of that immensity was there and there was joy.

On waking this morning, there was again that impenetrable strength whose power is the benediction. One was awakened to it and the brain was aware of it without any of its responses. It made the clear sky and the Pleiades incredibly beautiful. And the early sun on the mountain, with its snow, was the light of the world.

During the talk* it was there, untouchable and pure, and

* This was the last talk. It was chiefly concerned with the religious mind.

in the afternoon in the room it came with a speed of lightning and was gone. But it's always here in some measure, with its strange innocency whose eyes have never been touched.

The process was rather acute last night and as this is being written.

14th

Though the body was done up this morning after the talk [of yesterday] and seeing people, sitting in the car under a spreading tree there was a deep strange activity going on. It was not an activity which the brain, with its customary responses, could comprehend and formulate; it was beyond its scope. But there was an activity, deep within, which was wearing out all obstruction. But the nature of that activity is impossible to tell. Like deep subterranean waters making their way to the surface, so there was an activity far deeper than beyond all consciousness.

One is aware of the increase of sensitivity of the brain; colour, shape, line, the total form of things have become more intense and extraordinarily alive. Shadows seem to have a life of their own, of greater depth and purity. It was a beautiful, quiet evening; there was a breeze among the leaves and the aspen leaves were trembling and dancing. A tall straight stem of a plant, with a crown of white flowers, touched by faint pink, stood as a watcher by the mountain stream. The stream was golden in the setting sun and the woods were deep in silence; even the passing cars didn't seem to disturb them. The snow-covered mountains were deep in dark, heavy clouds and the meadows knew innocence.

The whole mind was far beyond all experience. And the meditator was silent.

15th

Walking beside the stream and with the mountains in clouds, there were moments of intense silence, like the brilliant patches of blue sky among the parting clouds. It was a cold, sharp evening, with a breeze that was coming from the north. Creation is not for the talented, for the gifted; they only know creativeness but never creation. Creation is beyond thought and image, beyond the word and expression. It is not to be communicated for it cannot be formulated, it cannot be wrapped up in words. It can be felt in complete awareness. It cannot be used and put on the market, to be haggled and sold.

It cannot be understood by the brain, with its complicated varieties of responses. The brain has no means to get into touch with it; it's utterly incapable. Knowledge is an impediment and without self-knowing, creation cannot be. Intellect, the sharp instrument of the brain, can in no way approach it. The total brain, with its hidden secret demands and pursuits and the many varieties of cunning virtues, must be utterly quiet, speechless but yet alert and still. Creation is not baking bread or writing a poem. All activity of the brain must cease, voluntarily and easily, without conflict and pain. There must be no shadow of conflict and imitation.

Then there is the astonishing movement called creation. It can only be in total negation; it cannot be in the passage of time, nor can space cover it. There must be complete death, total destruction, for it to be.

On waking this morning, there was complete silence outwardly and inwardly. The body and the measuring and weighing brain were still, in a state of immobility, though both were alive and highly sensitive. And quietly, as the dawn comes, it came from somewhere deep within, that strength with its energy and purity. It seemed to have no roots, no cause but yet it was there, intense and solid, with a depth and a height that are not measurable. It remained for some time by the watch and went away, as the cloud goes behind a mountain.

Every time there is something "new" in this benediction, a "new" quality, a "new" perfume but yet it is changeless. It is utterly unknowable.

The process was acute for a while but it's there in a gentle manner. It is all very strange and unpredictable.

16th

There was a patch of blue sky between two vast, endless clouds; it was a clear, startling blue, so soft and penetrating. It would be swallowed up in a few minutes and it would disappear for ever. No sky of that blue would ever be seen again. It had been raining most of the night and the morning and there was fresh snow on the mountains and on the higher hills. And the meadows were greener and richer than ever but that little patch of limpid blue sky would never be seen again. In that little patch was the light of all heaven and the blue of all the skies. As one watched it, its form began to change and the clouds were rushing to cover it lest too much of it be seen. It was gone never to appear again. But it had been seen and the wonder of it remains.

At that moment, resting on the sofa, as the clouds were conquering the blue, there came, quite unexpectedly, that benediction, with its purity and innocence. It came in abundance and filled the room till the room and the heart could hold no more; its intensity was peculiarly overpowering and penetrating and its beauty was on the land. The sun was shining on a patch of brilliant green and the dark pines were quiet and indifferent.

This morning, it was very early, the dawn wouldn't come for a couple of hours, on waking, with eyes that have lost their sleep, one was aware of an unfathomable cheerfulness; there was no cause to it, no sentimentality or that emotional extravagance, enthusiasm, behind it; it was clear, simple cheer, uncontaminated and rich, untouched and pure. There was no thought or reason behind it and neither could one ever understand it for there was no cause to it. This cheerfulness was pouring out of one's whole being and the being was utterly empty. As a stream of water gushes out from the side of a mountain, naturally and under pressure, this cheer was pouring out in great abundance, coming from nowhere and going nowhere, but the heart and mind would never be the same again.

One was not aware of the quality of this cheer as it was bursting forth; it was taking place and its nature would show itself, probably, to time and time would have no measure for it. Time is petty and it cannot weigh abundance.

The body has been rather frail and empty but last night and this morning the process has been acute, not lasting for long.

17th

It had been a cloudy, rainy day with north-west wind, hard and cold. Up the road that led to the waterfall which became the noisy stream, we were walking; there were few on the roads and few cars went by and the stream rushed on, faster than ever. We walked up the road with the wind behind us and the narrow valley widened and there were patches of sun on the sparkling, green pasture. They were widening the road and as we passed they greeted us, with friendly smiles and a few words in Italian. They had been labouring all day digging and carrying rocks so that it seemed incredible that they should smile at all. But they did and up further on under a large shed, modern machinery was cutting wood, drilling holes and cutting patterns on heavy lumber. And the valley opened more and more and there was a village further on and still further on was the waterfall from the glacier high up in the rocky mountain.

One felt more than one saw the beauty of the land and the weary people, the fast running stream and the quiet meadows. On the way back, near the chalet, all the sky was covered with heavy clouds and suddenly the setting sun was on some rocks, high up in the mountain. That patch of sunlight on the face of those rocks revealed a depth of beauty and feeling that no graven image can hold. It was as though they were alight from within, a light of their own, serene and never fading. It was the end of the day.

Only on waking early next morning, one was aware of the previous evening's splendour and the love that went by. Consciousness cannot contain the immensity of innocence; it can receive it, it cannot pursue it nor cultivate it. The entire consciousness must be still, not wanting, not seeking and never pursuing. The totality of consciousness must be still and only then, that which has no beginning and no end can come into being. Meditation is the emptying of consciousness, not to receive, but to be empty of all endeavour. There must be space for stillness, not the space created by thought and its activities but that space that comes through denial and destruction, when there is nothing left of thought and its projection. In emptiness alone can there be creation.

On waking early this morning the beauty of that strength, with its innocency, was there, deep within and coming to the surface of the mind. It had the quality of infinite flexibility but nothing could shape it; it could not be made to adjust, to conform to the mould of man. It could not be caught in symbols or words. But it was there, immense and untouchable. All meditation seemed trivial and foolish. *It* only stayed and the mind was still.

Several times during the day, at odd moments, that benediction would come and pass away. Desiring and asking have no significance whatsoever.

The process goes on mildly.

18th

It had been raining most of the night and it had turned quite cold; there was quite a lot of fresh snow on the higher hills and mountains. And there was a sharp wind too. The green meadows were extraordinarily bright and the green was startling. And it had been raining most of the day too and only towards the late afternoon it began to clear up and sun was among the mountains. We were walking along a path that went from one village to another, a path that wound around farmhouses, among rich green meadows. The pylons that carried heavy electric cables, stood startlingly against the evening skies; looking up at these towering steel structures against scudding clouds, there was beauty and power. Crossing over a wooden bridge, the stream was full, swollen by all this rain; it was running fast, with an energy and force that only mountain streams have. Looking up and down the stream, held in by tightly packed banks of rocks and trees, one was aware of the movement of time, the past, the present and future; the bridge was the present and all life moved and lived through the present.

But beyond all this, there was along that rain-washed and slushy lane, an otherness, a world which could never be touched by human thought, its activities and its unending sorrows. This world was not the product of hope nor of belief. One was not fully aware of it at that moment, there were too many things to observe, feel and smell; the clouds, the pale blue sky beyond the mountains and the sun among them and the evening light on the sparkling meadows; the smell of cow-sheds and red flowers around the farmhouses. This otherness was there covering all this, never a little thing being missed, and as one lay awake in bed, it came pouring in, filling the mind and the heart. Then one was aware of its subtle beauty, its passion and love. It's not the love that is enshrined in images, evoked by symbols, pictures and words, nor that which is cloaked in envy and jealousy, but that which is there freed from thought and feeling, a curving movement, everlasting. Its beauty is there with the self-abandonment of passion. There's no passion of that beauty if there is no austerity. Austerity is not a thing of the mind, carefully gathered through sacrifice, suppression and discipline. All these must cease, naturally, for they have no meaning for that otherness. It came pouring in with its measureless abundance. This love had no centre nor periphery and it was so complete, so invulnerable that there was no shadow in it and so ever destructible.

We always look from outside within; from knowledge we proceed to further knowledge, always adding and the very taking away is another addition. And our consciousness is made up of a thousand remembrances and recognitions, conscious of the trembling leaf, of the flower, of that man passing by, that child running across the field; conscious of the rock, the stream, the bright red flower and the bad smell of a pig-sty. From this remembering and recognizing, from the outward responses, we try to become conscious of the inner recesses, of the deeper motives and urges; we probe deeper and deeper into the vast depths of the mind. This whole process of challenges and responses, of the movement of experiencing and recognizing the hidden and the open activities, this whole is consciousness bound to time.

The cup is not only the shape, the colour, the design but also that emptiness inside the cup. The cup is the emptiness held within a form; without that emptiness there would be no cup nor form. We know consciousness by outer signs, by its limitations of height and depth, of thought and feeling. But all this is the outer form of consciousness; from the outer we try to find the inner. Is this possible? Theories and speculations are not significant; they actually prevent all discovery. From the outer we try to find the inner, from the known we probe hoping to find the unknown. Is it possible to probe from the inner to the outer? The instrument that probes from the outer, we know but is there such an instrument that probes from the unknown to the known? Is there? And how can there be? There cannot be. If there is one, it's recognizable and if it's recognizable, it's within the area of the known.

That strange benediction comes when it will, but with each visitation, deep within, there is a transformation; it is never the same.

The process goes on, sometimes mild and sometimes acute.

19th

It was a beautiful day, a cloudless day, a day of shadows and light; after the heavy rains the sun shone in a clear, limpid blue sky. The mountains, with their snow, were very close, one could almost touch them; they stood out sharply against the sky. The bright brilliant meadows were sparkling in the sun, every blade of grass did a dance of its own and the leaves were heavier in their movement. The valley was radiant and there was laughter; it was a magnificent day and there were a thousand shadows.

Shadows are more alive than the reality; shadows are longer, deeper, richer; they seem to have a life of their own, independent and protecting; there is a peculiar satisfaction in their invitation. The symbol becomes more important than reality. The symbol gives a shelter; it is easy to take comfort in its shelter. You can do what you will with it, it will never contradict, it will never change; it can be covered with garlands or ashes. There's an extraordinary satisfaction in a dead thing, in a picture, in a conclusion, in a word. They are dead, past all recalling and there is pleasure in the many smells of yesterday. The brain is always the yesterday, and today is the shadow of yesterday, and tomorrow is the continuation of that shadow, somewhat changed but it still smells of yesterday. So the brain lives and has its being in shadows; it is safer, more comforting.

Consciousness is always receiving, accumulating, and from what it has gathered, interpreting; receiving through all its pores; storing up, experiencing from what it has gathered, judging, compiling, modifying. It looks, not only through the eyes, through the brain but through this background. Consciousness goes out to receive and in receiving, it exists. In its hidden depths, it has stored what it has received through centuries, the instincts, the memories, the safeguard, adding, adding, only to take away to add further. When this consciousness looks out, it is to weigh, to balance and to receive. And when it looks within, its look is still the outer

look, to weigh, to balance and to receive; the inward strip-
ping is another form of adding. This time-binding process
goes on and on with an ache, with fleeting joy and sorrow.

But to look, to see, to listen, without this consciousness—
an outgoing in which there is no receiving, is the total movement of freedom. This outgoing has no centre, a point, small
or extensive, from which it moves; thus it moves in all
directions, without the barrier of time-space. Its listening is
total, its look is total. This outgoing is the essence of attention. In attention, all distractions are, for there are no distractions. Only   concentration   knows   the   conflict   of
distraction. All consciousness is thought, expressed or un-
expressed, verbal or seeking the word; thought as feeling,
feeling as thought. Thought is never still; reaction expressing
itself is thought and thought further increases responses.
Beauty is the feeling which thought expresses. Love is still
within the field of thought. Is there love and beauty within
the enclosure of thought? Is there beauty when thought is?
The beauty, the love that thought knows is the opposite of
ugliness and hate. Beauty has no opposite nor has love.

Seeing without thought, without the word, without the
response of memory is wholly different from seeing with
thought and feeling. What you see with thought is superficial;
then seeing is only partial; this is not seeing at all. Seeing
without thought is total seeing. Seeing a cloud over a mountain, without thought and its responses, is the miracle of the
new; it's not "beautiful", it's explosive in its immensity; it is
something that has never been and never will be. To see, to
listen, consciousness in its entirety must be still for the destructive creation to be. It is the totality of life and not the
fragment of all thought. There is no beauty but only a cloud
over the mountain; it is creation.

The setting sun touched the mountain tops, brilliant and
breath-taking and the land was still. There was only colour
and not different colours; there was only listening and not the
many sounds.

This morning, waking late, when the sun was pressing the hills, like a brilliant light that benediction was there; it seems to have a strength and power of its own. Like a distant murmur of waters, there is an activity going on, not of the brain with its volitions and deceptions, but an activity of intensity.

The process goes on with varying intensity; sometimes it is fairly acute.

20th

It was a perfect day; the sky was intensely blue and everything was sparkling in the morning sun. There were a few clouds floating about, leisurely, with nowhere to go. The sun on the fluttering leaves of aspen were brilliant jewels against the green sloping hills. The meadows overnight had changed, more intense, more soft, a green that is utterly unimaginable. There were three cows far up the hill, lazily grazing and their bells could be heard in the clear early morning air; they moved in a line steadily chewing their way from one side of the meadow to the other. And the ski-lift passed over them and they never even bothered to look up or be disturbed. It was a beautiful morning and the snow mountains were sharp against the sky, so clear that one could see the many small waterfalls. It was a morning of long shadows and infinite beauty. Strange, how love has its being in this beauty, there was such gentleness that all things seemed to stand still, lest any movement should awaken a hidden shadow. And there were a few more clouds.

It was a beautiful drive, in a car that seemed to enjoy what it was built for; it took every curve, however sharp, easily and willingly and up the long incline it went never grumbling and there was plenty of power to go up wherever the road went. It was like an animal that knew its own strength. The road curved in and out, through a dark sunlit wood, and every patch of light was alive, dancing with the leaves; every curve of the road showed more light, more dances, more

delight. Every tree, every leaf stood alone, intense and silent.
You saw, through a small opening of the trees, a patch of
startling green of a meadow that was open to the sun. It was
so startling that one forgot that one was on a dangerous
mountain road. But the road became gentle and lazily wound
around to a different valley. The clouds were gathering in
now and it was pleasant not to have a strong sun. The road
became almost flat, if a mountain road can be flat; it went on
past a dark pine-covered hill and there in front were the
enormous, overpowering mountains, rocks and snow, green
fields and waterfalls, small wooden huts and the sweeping,
curving lines of the mountain. One could hardly believe what
the eyes saw, the overpowering dignity of those shaped rocks,
the treeless mountain covered with snow, and crag after crag
of endless rock, and right up to them were the green
meadows, all held together in a vast embrace of a mountain.
It was really quite incredible; there was beauty, love, destruction and the immensity of creation, not those rocks, not those
fields, not those tiny huts; it wasn't in them or part of them.
It was far beyond and above them. It was there with the
majesty, with a roar that no eyes or ears could see or hear;
it was there with such totality and stillness that the brain with
its thoughts became as nothing as those dead leaves in the
woods. It was there with such abundance, such strength that
the world, the trees and the earth came to an end. It was
love, creation and destruction. And there was nothing else.

There was the essence of depth. The essence of thought is
that state when thought is not. However deeply and widely
thought is pursued, thought will always remain shallow,
superficial. The ending of thought is the beginning of that
essence. The ending of thought is negation and what is
negative has no positive way; there is no method, no system
to end thought. The method, the system is a positive approach
to negation and thus thought can never find the essence of
itself. It must cease for the essence to be. The essence of being
is non-being, and to "see" the depth of non-being, there must

be freedom from becoming. There is no freedom if there is
continuity and that which has continuity is time-bound. Every
experience is binding thought to time and a mind that's in
a state of non-experiencing is aware of all essence. This
state in which all experiencing has come to an end is not the
paralysis of the mind; on the contrary, it's the additive mind,
the mind that's accumulating, that is withering away. For
accumulation is mechanical, a repetition; the denial to
acquire and mere acquisition are both repetitive and imitative. The mind that destroys totally this accumulative and
defensive mechanism is free and so experiencing has lost its
significance.

Then there's only the fact and not the experiencing of the
fact; the opinion of the fact, the evaluation of it, the beauty
and non-beauty of it is the experiencing of the fact. The
experiencing of the fact is to deny it, to escape from it. The
experiencing of a fact without thought or feeling is a
profound event.

On waking this morning, there was that strange immobility
of the body and of the brain; with it came a movement of
entering into unfathomable depths of intensity and of great
bliss and there was that otherness.

The process goes on mildly.

21st

Again, it has been a clear, sunny day, with long shadows and
sparkling leaves; the mountains were serene, solid and close;
the sky was of an extraordinary blue, spotless and gentle.
Shadows filled the earth; it was a morning for shadows, the
little ones and the big ones, the long, lean ones and the fat
satisfied ones, the squat homely one and the joyful, spritely
ones. The roof-tops of the farms and the chalets shone like
polished marble, the new and the old. There seemed to be a
great rejoicing and shouting among the trees and meadows;
they existed for each other and above them was heaven, not
the man-made, with its tortures and hopes. And there was

life, vast, splendid, throbbing and stretching in all directions. It was life, always young and always dangerous; life that never stayed, that wandered through the earth, indifferent, never leaving a mark, never asking or calling for anything. It was there in abundance, shadowless and deathless; it didn't care from where it came or where it was going. Wherever it was there was life, beyond time and thought. It was a marvellous thing, free, light and unfathomable. It was not to be closed in; where they closed it, in the places of worship, in the market place, in the home, there was decay and corruption and their perpetual reform. It was there simple, majestic and shattering and the beauty of it is beyond thought and feeling. It is so vast and incomparable that it fills the earth and heavens and the blade of grass that's destroyed so soon. It is there with love and death.

It was cool in the wood, with a shouting stream a few feet below; the pines shot up to the skies, without ever bending to look at the earth. It was splendid there with black squirrels eating tree mushrooms and chasing each other up and down the trees in narrow spirals; there was a robin that bobbed up and down, or what looked like a robin. It was cool and quiet there, except for the stream with its cold mountain waters. And there it was, love, creation and destruction, not as a symbol, not in thought and feeling but an actual reality. You couldn't see it, feel it, but it was there, shatteringly immense, strong as ten thousand and with the power of the most vulnerable. It was there and all things became still, the brain and the body; it was a benediction and the mind was of it.

There is no end to depth; the essence of it is without time and space. It's not to be experienced; experience is such a tawdry thing, so easily got and so easily gone; thought cannot put it together nor can feeling make its way to it. These are silly and immature things. Maturity is not of time, a matter of age, nor does it come through influence and environment. It's not to be bought, neither the books nor the teachers and saviours, the one or the many, can ever create the right climate for this maturity. Maturity is not an end in itself; it comes into being without thought cultivating it, darkly, without meditation, unknowingly. There must be maturity, that ripening in life; not the ripeness that is bred out of disease and turmoil, sorrow and hope. Despair and labour cannot bring this total maturity but it must be there, unsought.

For in this total maturity there is austerity. Not the austerity of ashes and sackcloth but that casual and unpremeditated indifference to the things of the world, its virtues, its gods, its respectability, its hopes and values. These must be totally denied for that austerity which comes with aloneness. No influence of society or of culture can ever touch this aloneness. But it must be there, not conjured up by the brain, which is the child of time and influence. It must come thunderingly out of nowhere. And without it, there's no total maturity. Loneliness—the essence of self-pity and self-defence and life in isolation, in myth, in knowledge and idea—is far away from aloneness; in them there is everlasting attempt to integrate and ever breaking apart. Aloneness is a life in which all influence has come to an end. It's this aloneness that is the essence of austerity.

But this austerity comes when the brain remains clear, undamaged by any psychological wounds that are caused through fear; conflict in any form destroys the sensitivity of the brain; ambition with its ruthlessness, with its ceaseless effort to become, wears down the subtle capacities of the brain; greed and envy make the brain heavy with content and weary with discontent. There must be alertness, without choice, an awareness in which all receiving and adjustment have ceased. Over-eating and indulgence in any form makes the body dull and stupefies the brain.

There is a flower by the wayside, a clear, bright thing open to the skies; the sun, the rains, the darkness of the night, the winds and thunder and the soil have gone into make that

flower. But the flower is none of these things. It is the essence
of all flowers. The freedom from authority, from envy, fear,
from loneliness will not bring about that aloneness, with its
extraordinary austerity. It comes when the brain is not looking for it; it comes when your back is turned upon it. Then
nothing can be added to it or taken away from it. Then it has
a life of its own, a movement which is the essence of all life,
without time and space.

That benediction was there with great peace.

The process goes on mildly.

22nd

The moon was in the clouds but the mountains and the dark
hills were clear and there was a great stillness about them.
There was a large star just hanging over a wooded hill and
the only noise that came out of the valley was the mountain
stream as it rushed over rocks. Everything was asleep save the
distant village but its sound didn't come as high up as this.
The noise of the stream soon faded; it was there but it didn't
fill the valley. There was no breeze and the trees were motionless; there was the light of the pale moon on the scattered
roofs and everything was still, even the pale shadows.

In the air there was that feeling of unbearable immensity,
intense and insistent. It was not a fanciful imagination;
imagination ceases when there's reality; imagination is
dangerous; it has no validity, only fact has. Fancy and
imagination are pleasurable and deceptive and they must be
wholly banished. Every form of myth, fancy and imagination
must be understood and this very understanding deprives
them of their significance. It was there, and what was started
as meditation, ended. Of what significance is meditation when
reality is there! It was not meditation that brought reality
into being, nothing can bring it into being; it was there in
spite of meditation but what was necessary was a very sensitive, alert brain which had stopped entirely, willingly and
easily, its chatter of reason and non-reason. It had become

very quiet, seeing and listening without interpreting, without classifying; it was quiet and there was no entity or necessity to make it quiet. The brain was very still and very alive. That immensity filled the night and there was bliss.

It had no relationship with anything; it was not trying to shape, to change, to assert; it had no influence and therefore was implacable. It was not doing good, not reforming; it was not becoming respectable and so highly destructive. But it was love, not the love which society cultivates, a tortured thing. It was the essence of the movement of life. It was there, implacable, destructive, with a tenderness that the new alone knows, as the new leaf of spring, and it will tell you. And there was strength beyond measure and there was power that only creation has. And all things were quiet. That one star that was going over the hill was now high up and it was bright in its solitude.

In the morning, walking in the woods above the stream, with the sun on every tree, again it was there, that immensity so unexpected, so still that one walked through it, marvelling. A single leaf was dancing rhythmically and the rest of the abundant leaves were still. It was there, that love that's not within the scope of man's longing and measure. It was there and thought could blow it away and a feeling could push it away. It was there, never to be conquered, never to be caught.

The word to feel is misleading; it's more than emotion, than a sentiment, than an experience, than touch or smell. Though that word is apt to be misleading, it must be used to communicate and especially so when we are talking of essence. The feel of essence is not through the brain nor through some fancy; it's not experienceable as a shock; above all it's not the word. You cannot experience it; to experience there must be an experiencer, the observer. Experiencing, without the experiencer, is quite another matter. It is in this "state", in which there is no experiencer, no observer, that there is that "feeling". It is *not* intuition, which the observer interprets or follows, blindly or with reason; it is not the desire, longing, transformed into intuition or the "voice of God" evoked by politicians and religio-social reformers. It's necessary to get away from all this, far away to understand this feeling, this seeing, this listening. To "feel" demands the austerity of clarity, in which there is no confusion and conflict. The "feeling" of essence comes when there is simplicity to pursue to the very end, without any deviation, sorrow, envy, fear, ambition and so on. This simplicity is beyond the capacity of the intellect; intellect is fragmentary. This pursuit is the highest form of simplicity, not the mendicant's robe or one meal a day. The "feeling" of essence is the negation of thought and its mechanical capacities, knowledge and reason. Reason and knowledge are necessary in the operation of mechanical problems, and all the problems of thought and feeling are mechanical. It's this negation of the machinery of memory, whose reaction is thought, that must be denied in the pursuit of the essence. Destroy [in order to] to go to the very end; destruction is not of the outer things but of the psychological refuges and resistances, the gods and their secret shelters. Without this, there's no journey into that depth whose essence is love, creation and death.

On waking early this morning, the body and the brain lay motionless for there was that power and strength which is a benediction.

The process is gentle.

23rd

There were a few wandering clouds in the early morning sky which was so pale, quiet and without time. The sun was waiting for the excellency of the morning to finish. The dew was on the meadows and there were no shadows and the trees were alone, waiting for them. It was very early and even the stream was hesitant to make its boisterous run. It was quiet and the breeze hadn't yet awakened and the leaves were still. There was no smoke yet from any of the farmhouses but the roofs began to glow with the coming light. The stars were yielding reluctantly to dawn and there was that peculiar silent expectation when the sun is about to come; the hills were waiting and so were the trees and meadows open in their joy. Then the sun touched the mountain tops, a gentle soothing touch and the snow became bright with the early morning light; the leaves began to stir from the long night and smoke was going straight up from one of the cottages and the stream was chattering away, without any restraint. And slowly, hesistantly and with delicate shyness the long shadows spread across the land; the mountains cast their shadows on the hills and the hills on the meadows and the trees were waiting for their shadows but soon they were there, the light ones and the deep ones, the feathery and the heavy. And the aspens were dancing, the day had begun.

Meditation is this attention in which there is an awareness, without choice, of the movement of all things, the cawing of the crows, the electric saw ripping through the wood, the trembling of leaves, the noisy stream, a boy calling, the feelings, the motives, the thoughts chasing each other and going deeper, the awareness of total consciousness. And in this attention, time as yesterday pursuing into the space of tomorrow and the twisting and turning of consciousness has become quiet and still. In this stillness there is an immeasurable, not comparable movement; a movement that has no being, that's the essence of bliss and death and life. A movement that cannot be followed for it leaves no path and because it is still, motionless; it is the essence of all motion.

The road went west, curling through rain-soaked meadows, past small villages on the slope of hills, crossing the mountain streams of clear snow waters, past churches with copper steeples; it went on and on into dark, cavernous clouds and rain, with mountains closing in. It began to drizzle, and looking back casually through the back window of the slow-moving car, from where we had come, there were the sunlit clouds, blue sky and the bright, clear mountains. Without saying a word, instinctively, the car stopped, backed and turned and we went on towards light and mountains. It was impossibly beautiful and as the road turned into an open valley, the heart stood still; it was still and as open as the expanding valley, it was completely shattering. We had been through that valley several times; the shape of the hills were fairly familiar; the meadows and the cottages were recognizable and the familiar noise of the stream was there. Everything was there except the brain, though it was driving the car. Everything had become so intense, there was death. Not because the brain was quiet, not because of the beauty of the land, or of the light on the clouds or the immovable dignity of the mountains; it was none of these things, though all these things may have added something towards it. It was literally death; everything suddenly coming to an end; there was no continuity, the brain was directing the body in driving the car and that was all. Literally that was all. The car went on for some time and stopped. There was life and death, so closely, intimately, inseparably together and neither was important. Something shattering had taken place.

There was no deception or imagination; it was much too serious for that kind of silly aberration; it was not something to play about. Death is not a casual affair and it would not go; there's no argument with it. You can have a lifelong discussion with life but it is not possible with death. It's so final and absolute. It wasn't the death of the body; that would be a fairly simple and decisive event. Living with death was quite another matter. There was life and there was death; they were there inexorably united. It wasn't a psychological death; it wasn't a shock that drove out all thought, all feeling; it wasn't a sudden aberration of the brain nor a mental illness. It was none of these things nor a curious decision of a brain that was tired or in despair. It wasn't an unconscious wish for death. It was none of these things; these would be immature and so easily connived at. It was something in a different dimension; it was something that defied time-space description.

It was there, the very essence of death. The essence of self is death but this death was the very essence of life as well. In fact they were not separate, life and death. This was not something conjured up by the brain for its comfort and ideational security. The very living was the dying and dying was living. In that car, with all that beauty and colour, with that "feeling" of ecstasy, death was part of love, part of everything. Death wasn't a symbol, an idea, a thing that one knew. It was there, in reality, in fact, as intense and demanding as the honk of a car that wanted to pass. As life would never leave nor can be set aside, so death now would never leave or be put aside. It was there with an extraordinary intensity and with a finality.

All night one lived with it; it seemed to have taken possession of the brain and the usual activities; not too many of the brain's movements went on but there was a casual indifference about them. There was indifference previously but now it was past and beyond all formulation. Everything had become much more intense, both life and death.

Death was there on waking, without sorrow, but with life. It was a marvellous morning. There was that benediction which was the delight of the mountains and of the trees.

24th

It was a warm day and there were plenty of shadows; the rocks shone with a solid brilliance. The dark pines never seemed to move, unlike those aspens which were ready to tremble at the slightest whisper. There was a strong breeze from the west, sweeping through the valley The rocks were so alive that they seemed to run after the clouds and the clouds clung to them, taking the shape and the curve of the rocks; they flowed around them and it was difficult to separate the rocks from the clouds. And the trees were walking with the clouds. The whole valley seemed to be moving and the small, narrow paths that went up to the woods and beyond, seemed to yield and come alive. And the sparkling meadows were the haunt of shy flowers. But this morning rocks ruled the valley; they were of so many colours that there was only colour; these rocks were gentle this morning and they were of so many shapes and sizes. And they were so indifferent to everything, to the wind, rains and to the explosions for the needs of man. They had been there and they were going to be past all time.

It was a splendid morning and the sun was everywhere and every leaf was stirring; it was a good morning for the drive, not long but enough to see the beauty of the land. It was a morning that was made new by death, not the death of decay, disease or accident but the death that destroys for creation to be. There is no creation if death does not sweep away all the things that the brain has put together to safeguard the self-centred existence. Death, previously, was a new form of continuity; death was associated with continuity. With death came a new existence, a new experience, a new breath and a new life. The old ceased and the new was born and the new then gave place to yet another new. Death was the means to the new state, new invention, to a new way of life, to a new thought. It was a frightening change but that very change brought a fresh hope.

But now death did not bring anything new, a new horizon, a new breath. It is death, absolute and final. And then there's nothing, neither past nor future. Nothing. There's no giving birth to anything. But there's no despair, no seeking; complete death without time; looking out of great depths which are not there. Death is there without the old or the new. It is death without smile and tear. It is not a mask covering up, hiding some reality. The reality is death and there's no need for cover. Death has wiped away everything and left nothing. This nothing is the dance of the leaf, it is the call of that child. It is nothing and there must be nothing. What continues is decay, the machine, the habit, the ambition. There is corruption but not in death. Death is total nothingness. It must be there for out of that, life is, love is. For in this nothingness creation is. Without absolute death, there's no creation.

We were reading something, casually and remarking about the state of the world when suddenly and unexpectedly the room became full with that benediction, which has come so often now. The door was open in the little room and we were just going to eat when through the open door it came. One could literally, physically feel it, like a wave flowing into the room. It became "more" and "more" intense, the more is not comparatively used; it was something that was incredibly strong and immovable, with shattering power. Words are not the thing and the actual thing can never be put into words; it must be seen, heard and lived; then it has quite a different significance.

The process has been acute the last few days; and one need not write about it every day.*

25th
It was very early in the morning; there wouldn't be dawn for another couple of hours or more. Orion was just coming up over the top of that peak that is beyond the curving and wooded hills. There was not a cloud in the sky but from the feel of the air, there would probably be fog. It was an hour of quietness and even the stream was sleeping; there was a fading moonlight and the hills were dark, clear in their shape, against the pale sky. There was no breeze and the trees were still and the stars were bright.

Meditation is not a search; it's not a seeking, a probing, an exploration. It is an explosion and discovery. It's not the taming of the brain to conform nor is it a self-introspective analysis; it is certainly not the training in concentration which includes, chooses and denies. It's something that comes natur-

* The process is not mentioned again, though presumably it continued.

ally, when all positive and negative assertions and accomplishments have been understood and drop away easily. It is the total emptiness of the brain. It's the emptiness that is essential not what's in the emptiness; there is seeing only from emptiness; all virtue, not social morality and respectability, springs from it. It's out of this emptiness love comes, otherwise it's not love. Foundation of righteousness is in this emptiness. It's the end and beginning of all things.

Looking out of the window, as Orion was climbing higher and higher, the brain was intensely alive and sensitive and meditation became something entirely different, something which the brain could not cope with and so fell back upon itself and became silent. The hours till dawn and after seemed to have had no beginning and as the sun came up the mountains and the clouds caught its first rays and there was astonishment in splendour. And day began. Strangely meditation went on.

26th

It had been a beautiful morning, full of sunshine and shadows; the garden in the nearby hotel was full of colours, all colours and they were so bright and the grass so green that they hurt the eye and the heart. And the mountains beyond were glistening with a freshness and a sharpness, washed by the morning dew. It was an enchanting morning and there was beauty everywhere; over the narrow bridge, across the stream, up a path into the wood, where the sunshine was playing with the leaves; they were trembling and their shadows moved; they were common plants but they outdid in their greenness and freshness all the trees that soared up to the blue skies. You could only wonder at all this delight, at the extravagance, at the trembling; you could not but be amazed at the quiet dignity of every tree and plant and at the endless joy of those black squirrels, with long, bushy tails. The waters of the stream were clear and sparkling in the sun that came through the leaves. It was damp in the wood and pleasant. Standing there watching the leaves dancing away suddenly there was the otherness, a timeless occurrence and there was stillness. It was a stillness in which everything moved, danced and shouted; it wasn't a stillness which comes when a machine stops working; mechanical stillness is one thing and the stillness in emptiness is another. The one is repetitive, habitual, corrupting which the conflicting and weary brain seeks as a refuge; the other is exploding, never the same, it cannot be searched out, is never repetitive, and so it does not offer any shelter. Such a stillness came and stayed as we wandered along, and the beauty of the wood intensified and the colours exploded to be caught on the leaves and flowers.

It was not a very old church, about the beginning of the seventeenth century, at least it said so over the arch; it had been renovated and the wood was light-coloured pine and the steel nails looked bright and polished, which was impossible, of course; one was almost sure that those who had gathered there to listen to some music never looked at those nails all over the ceiling. It was not an orthodox church, there was no smell of incense, candles or images. It was there and the sun came in through the windows. There were many children, told not to talk or play which didn't prevent them from being restless, looking terribly solemn and their eyes ready to laugh. One wanted to play, came close but was too shy to come any nearer. They were rehearsing for the concert that evening and everyone was dutifully solemn and there was interest. Outside the grass was bright, the sky clear blue and shadows were numberless.

Why this everlasting struggle to be perfect, to achieve perfection, as the machines are? The idea, the example, the symbol of perfection is something marvellous, ennobling, but is it? Of course there's the attempt to imitate the perfect, the perfect example. Is imitation perfection? Is there perfection or is it merely an idea, given to man by the preacher to keep him respectable? In the idea of perfection there's a great deal of comfort and security and always it is profitable both to the priest and to the one who's trying to become perfect. A mechanical habit, repeated over and over again can eventually be perfected; only habit can be perfected. Thinking, believing the same thing over and over again, without deviation, becomes a mechanical habit and perhaps this is the kind of perfection everyone wants. This cultivates a perfect wall of resistance, which will prevent any disturbance, any discomfort. Besides, perfection is a glorified form of success, and ambition is blessed by respectability and the representatives and heroes of success. There's no perfection, it's an ugly thing, except in a machine. The attempt to be perfect is, really, to break the record, as in golf; competition is saintly. To compete with your neighbour and with God for perfection is called brotherhood and love. But each attempt at perfection leads only to greater confusion and sorrow which only gives greater impetus to be more perfect.

It's curious, we always want to be perfect in or with something; this gives the means for achievement, and the pleasure of achievement, of course, is vanity. Pride in any form is brutal and leads to disaster. The desire for perfection outwardly or inwardly denies love and without love, do what you will, there's always frustration and sorrow. Love is neither perfect nor imperfect; it's only when there's no love that perfection and imperfection arise. Love never strives after something; it does not make itself perfect. It's the flame without the smoke; in striving to be perfect, there's only greater volume of smoke; perfection, then, lies only in striving, which is mechanical, more and more perfect in habit, in imitation, in engendering more fear. Each one is educated to compete, to become successful; then the end becomes all important. Love for the thing itself disappears. Then the instrument is used not for the love of the sound but for what the instrument will bring, fame, money, prestige and so on.

Being is infinitely more significant than becoming. Being is not the opposite of becoming; if it's the opposite or in opposition, then there is no being. When becoming dies completely, then there's being. But this being is not static; it's not acceptance nor is it mere denial; becoming involves time and space. All striving must cease; then only there is being. Being is not within the field of social virtue and morality. It shatters the social formula of life. This being is life, not the pattern of life. Where life is there's no perfection; perfection is an idea, a word; life, the being, is beyond any formula of thought. It is there when the word, the example, and the pattern are destroyed.

It has been there, this benediction, for hours and in flashes. On waking this morning, many hours before sunrise, when there was the eclipse of the moon, it was there with such strength and power, that sleep for a couple of hours was not possible. There is a strange purity and innocency in it.

27th

The stream, joined by other little streams, meandered through the valley, noisily and the chatter was never the same. It had its own moods but never unpleasant, never a dark mood. The little ones had a sharper note, there were more boulders and rocks; they had quiet pools in the shade, shallow with dancing shadows and at night they had quite a different tone, soft, gentle and hesitant. They came down through different valleys from different sources, one much further away than the other; one from a glacier and from a winding waterfall and the other must come from a source too far away to walk to. They both joined the bigger stream which had a deep quiet tone, more dignified, wider and swifter. All the three of them were tree-lined and the long curving line of trees showed where these streams came from and where they went; they were the occupants of the valleys and everyone else was a stranger, including the trees. One could watch them by the hour and listen to their endless chatter; they were very gay and full of fun, even the bigger one, though it had to maintain certain dignity. They were of the mountains, from dizzy heights nearer the heavens and so purer and nobler; they were not snobs but they maintained their way and they were rather distant and chilly. In the dark of the night they had a song of their own, when few were listening. It was a song of many songs.

Crossing the bridge, up in the sun-speckled wood, meditation was quite a different thing. Without any wish and search, without any complaint of the brain, there was unenforced silence; the little birds were chirping away, the squirrels were chasing up the trees, the breeze was playing with the leaves and there was silence. The little stream, the one coming from a long distance, was more cheerful than ever and yet there was silence, not outside but deep, far within. It was total stillness within the totality of the mind, which had no frontiers. It was not the silence within an enclosure, within an area, within the limits of thought and so recognized as stillness. There were no frontiers, no measurements and so the silence was not held within experience, to be recognized and stored away. It may never occur again and if it did, it would be entirely different. Silence cannot repeat itself; only the brain through memory and recollection can repeat what had been, but what had been is not the actual. Meditation was this total absence of consciousness put together through time and space. Thought, the essence of consciousness, cannot, do what it will, bring about this stillness; the brain with all its subtle and complicated activities must quiet down of its own accord, without the promise of any reward or of security. Only then it can be sensitive, alive and quiet. The brain understanding its own activities, hidden and open, is part of meditation; it's the foundation in meditation, without it meditation is only self-deception, self-hypnosis, which has no significance whatsoever. There must be silence for the explosion of creation.

Maturity is not of time and age. There is no interval between now and maturity; there is never "in the meantime". Maturity is that state when all choice has ceased; it's only the immature that choose and know the conflict of choice. In maturity there's no direction but there's a direction which is not a direction of choice. Conflict at any level, at any depth, indicates immaturity. There's no such thing as becoming mature, except organically, the mechanical inevitability of certain things to ripen. The understanding, which is the transcending of conflict, in all its complex varieties, is maturity. However complex it is and however subtle, the depth of conflict, within and without, can be understood. Conflict, frustration, fulfilment is one single movement, within and without. The tide that goes out must come in and for that movement itself, called the tide, there's no out and in. Conflict in all its forms must be understood, not intellectually, but actually, actually coming emotionally into contact with conflict. The emotional contact, the shock, is not possible if it is intellectually, verbally, accepted as necessary or denied sentimentally. Acceptance or denial does not alter a fact nor will reason bring about a necessary impact. What does is "seeing" the fact. There's no "seeing" if there is condemnation or justification or identification with the fact. "Seeing" is only possible when the brain is not actively participating, but observing, abstaining from classification, judgment and evaluation. There must be conflict when there is the urge to fulfil, with its inevitable frustrations; there is conflict when there is ambition, with its subtle and ruthless competition; envy is part of this ceaseless conflict, to become, to achieve, to succeed.

There's no understanding in time. Understanding does not come tomorrow; it will never come tomorrow; it is now or never; there's only now and there's no never. The "seeing" is immediate; when from the brain the significance of "seeing", understanding, eventually is wiped away, then seeing is immediate. "Seeing" is explosive, not reasoned, calculated. It is fear that often prevents "seeing", understanding. Fear, with its defences and its courage, is the origin of conflict. The seeing is not only with the brain but also beyond it. Seeing the fact brings its own action, entirely different from the action of idea, thought; action from idea, thought, breeds conflict; action then is an approximation, comparison with the formula, with the idea, and this brings conflict. There's no end to conflict, small or great, in the field of thought; the essence of conflict is non-conflict which is maturity.

On waking very early in the morning, that strange benediction was meditation and meditation was that benediction. It was there with great intensity, walking in a peaceful wood.

28th
It had been rather a hot sunny day, hot even at this altitude; the snow on the mountains was white and glistening. It had been sunny and hot for several days and the streams were clear and the sky pale blue but there was still that mountain intensity about the blue. The flowers across the way were extraordinarily bright and gay and the meadows were cool; the shadows were dark and there were so many. There's a little path through the meadows going up across the rolling hills, wandering past farm-houses; there was no one on the path except for an old lady carrying a milk can and a small basket of vegetables; she must have been going up and down that path all her life, racing up the hills when she was young and now, all bent and crippled, she was coming up, slowly, painfully, hardly looking up from the ground. She will die and the mountains will go on. There were two goats higher up, white, with those peculiar eyes; they came up to be petted, keeping a safe distance from the electric fence which kept them from wandering off. There was a white and black kitten belonging to the same farm as the goats; it wanted to play; there was another cat higher up still, in a meadow, perfectly still waiting to catch a field rat.

Up there in the shade, it was cool and fresh and beautiful, the mountains and the hills, the valleys and the shadows. The land was boggy in places and there grew reeds, short and golden coloured, and among the gold were white flowers. But this was not all. Going up and coming down, there was during that whole hour and a half that strength which is a benediction. It has the quality of enormous and impenetrable solidity; no matter could have, possibly, that solidity. Matter is penetrable, can be broken down, dissolved, vaporized; thought and feeling have certain weight; they can be measured and they too can be changed, destroyed and nothing left of them. But this strength, which nothing could penetrate, nor dissolve, was not the projection of thought and certainly not matter. This strength was not an illusion, a creation of a brain that was secretly seeking power or that strength that power gives. No brain could formulate such strength, with its strange intensity and solidity. It was there and no thought could invent it or dispel it. There comes an intensity when there is no need for anything. Food, clothes and shelter are necessities and they are not needs. The need is the hidden craving, which makes for attachment. The need for sex, for drinking, for fame, for worship, with their complex causes; the need for self-fulfilment with its ambitions and frustrations; the need for God, for immortality. All these forms of need inevitably breed that attachment which causes sorrow, fear and the ache of loneliness. The need to express oneself through music, through writing or through painting and through some other means, makes for desperate attachment to the means. A musician who uses his instrument to achieve fame, to become the best, ceases to be a musician; he does not love music but the profits of music. We use each other in our needs and call it by sweet-sounding names; out of this grows despair and unending sorrow. We use God as a refuge, as a protection, like some medicine and so the church, the temple, with its priests become very significant, when they have none. We use everything, machines, techniques for our psychological needs and there is no love for the thing itself.

There is love only when there is no need. The essence of the self is this need and the constant change of needs and the everlasting search, from one attachment to another, from one temple to another, from one commitment to another. To commit oneself to an idea, to a formula, to belong to something, to some sect, to some dogma, is the drive of need, the essence of the self, which takes the form of most altruistic activities. It's a cloak, a mask. The freedom from need is maturity. With this freedom comes intensity, which has no cause and no profit.

29th

There is a path beyond the few scattered chalets and farmhouses that goes through the meadows and barbed wire fences; before it goes down, there is a magnificent view of the mountains with their snows and glacier, of the valley and the little town, with so many shops. From there one can see the source of one stream and the dark, pine-covered hills; the lines of these hills against the evening sky were magnificent and they seemed to tell of so many things. It was a lovely evening; there hadn't been a cloud in the sky all day long and now the purity of the sky and of the shadows was startling and the evening light was a delight. The sun was going down behind the hills and they were casting their great shadows across other hills and meadows. Crossing another grassy field, the path went down rather steeply and joined a bigger and wider path, which went through the woods. There was no one on that path, it was deserted, and it was very quiet in the woods except for the stream which seemed to be noisier before it quieted down for the night. There were tall pines there and a perfume in the air. Suddenly as the path turned, through a long tunnel of trees, was a patch of green and a newly cut piece of pine wood with the evening sun on it. It was startling in its intensity and joy. One saw it, and all space and time disappeared; there was only that patch of light and nothing else. It was not that one became that light or one identified oneself with that light; the sharp activities of the brain had stopped and one's whole being was there with that light. The trees, the path, the noise of the stream had completely disappeared and so had the five hundred yards and more between the light and the observer. The observer had ceased and the intensity of that patch of evening sun was the light of all the worlds. That light was all heaven and that light was the mind.

Most deny certain superficial and easy things; there are others who go far in their denial and there are those who deny totally. To deny certain things is comparatively easy, church and its gods, authority and the power of those who have it, the politician and his ways and so on. One can go pretty far in the denial of things that apparently do matter, relationships, the absurdities of society, the conception of beauty as established by the critics and of those who say they know. One can put aside all these and remain alone, alone not in the sense of isolation and frustration but alone because one has seen the significance of all this and has walked away from them casually and without any sense of superiority. They are finished, dead and there's no going back to them. But to go to the very end of denial is quite another matter; the essence of denial is the freedom in aloneness. But few go that far, shattering through every refuge, every formula, every idea, every symbol and be naked, unburnt and clear.

But how necessary it is to deny; deny without reaching out, deny without the bitterness of experience and the hope of knowledge. To deny and stand alone, without tomorrow, without a future. The storm of denial is nakedness. To stand alone, without being committed to any course of action, to any conduct, to any experience, is essential, for this alone frees consciousness from the bondage of time. Every form of influence is understood and denied, giving thought no passage in time. Denying time is the essence of timelessness.

To deny knowledge, experience, the known is to invite the unknown. Denial is explosive; it is not an intellectual ideational affair, something with which the brain can play. In the very act of denial there is energy, the energy of understanding and this energy is not docile, to be tamed by fear and convenience. Denial is destructive; it is unaware of consequences; it is not a reaction and so not the opposite of assertion. To assert that there is or that there is not, is to continue in reaction, and reaction is not denial. Denial has no choice and so is not the outcome of conflict. Choice is conflict and conflict is immaturity. Seeing the truth as truth, the false as false and the truth in the false is the act of denial. It's an act and not an idea. The total denial of thought, the idea and the word brings freedom from the known; with the total denial of feeling, emotion and sentiment there's love. Love is beyond and above thought and feeling.

The total denial of the known is the essence of freedom.

Waking early this morning, the sunrise many hours away, meditation was beyond the responses of thought; it was an arrow into the unknowable and thought could not follow it. And dawn came to brighten the sky and as soon as the sun was touching the highest peaks, there was that immensity whose purity is beyond the sun and the mountains.

30th

It had been a cloudless day, hot, and the earth and the trees were gathering strength for the coming winter; autumn was already turning the few leaves yellow; they were bright yellow against the dark green. They were cutting the meadows and the fields of their rich grass for the cows during the long winter; everyone was working, grown-ups and children. It was serious work and there wasn't much talk or laughter. Machines were taking the place of scythes and here and there scythes were cutting the pasture. And along the stream there's a path, through the fields; it was cool there for the hot sun was already behind the hills. The path went past farmhouses and a sawmill; in the newly cut fields, there were thousands of crocuses, so delicate, with that peculiar perfume of their own. It was a quiet, clear evening and the mountains were closer than ever. The stream was quiet, there were not too many rocks and the water ran fast. You would have to run to keep with it. There was, in the air, the smell of freshly cut grass, in a land that was prosperous and contented. Every farm had electricity and there seemed to be peace and plenty.

How few see the mountains or a cloud. They look, make some remarks and pass on. Words, gestures, emotions prevent seeing. A tree, a flower is given a name, put into a category and that's that. You see a landscape through an archway or from a window, and if you happen to be an artist or are familiar with art, you say almost immediately, it is like those medieval paintings or mention some name of some recent painter. Or if you are a writer, you look in order to describe; if you are a musician, probably you have never seen the curve of a hill or the flowers at your feet; you are caught up in your daily practice, or ambition has you by the throat. If you are a professional of some kind, probably you never see. But to see there must be humility whose essence is innocency. There's that mountain with the evening sun on it; to see it for the first time, to see it, as though it had never been seen before, to see it with innocency, to see it with eyes that have been bathed in emptiness, that have not been hurt with knowledge—to see then is an extraordinary experience. The word experience is ugly, with it goes emotion, knowledge, recognition and a continuity; it is none of these things. It is something totally new. To see this newness there must be humility, that humility which has never been contaminated by pride, by vanity. With this certain happening, that morning, there was this seeing, as with the mountain top, with the evening sun. The totality of one's whole being was there, which was not in a state of need, conflict and choice; the total being was passive, whose passivity was active. There are two kinds of attention, one is active and the other is without movement. What was happening was actually new, a thing that had never happened before. To "see" it happening was the wonder of humility; the brain was completely still, without any response though it was fully awake. To "see" that mountain peak, so splendid with the evening sun, though one had seen it a thousand times, with eyes that had no knowledge, was to see the birth of the new. This is not silly romanticism or sentimentality with its cruelties and moods, or emotion with its waves of enthusiasm and depression. It is something so utterly new, that in this total attention is silence. Out of this emptiness the new is.

Humility is not a virtue; it is not to be cultivated; it's not within the morality of the respectable. The saints do not know it, for they are recognized for their saintliness; the worshipper does not know it for he is asking, seeking; nor the devotee and the follower for he is following. Accumulation denies humility, whether it be property, experience or capacity. Learning is not an additive process; knowledge is. Knowledge is mechanical; learning never is. There can be more and more knowledge but there is never more in learning. Where there is comparison learning ceases. Learning is the immediate seeing which is not in time. All accumulation and knowledge are measurable. Humility is not comparable; there's no more or less of humility; so it cannot be cultivated. Morality and technique can be cultivated, there can be more or less of them. Humility is not within the capacity of the brain, nor is love. Humility is ever the act of death.

Very early this morning, many hours before dawn, on waking there was that piercing intensity of strength with its sternness. There was in this sternness, bliss. By the watch it "lasted" for forty-five minutes with increasing intensity. The stream and the quiet night, with their brilliant stars, were within it.

31st
Meditation without a set formula, without a cause and reason, without end and purpose is an incredible phenomenon. It is not only a great explosion which purifies but also it is death, that has no tomorrow. Its purity devastates, leaving no hidden corner where thought can lurk in its own dark shadows. Its purity is vulnerable; it is not a virtue brought into being through resistance. It is pure because it has

no resistance, like love. There is no tomorrow in meditation, no argument with death. The death of yesterday and of tomorrow does not leave the petty present of time, and time is always petty, but a destruction that is the new. Meditation is this, not the silly calculations of the brain in search of security. Meditation is destruction to security and there is great beauty in meditation, not the beauty of the things that have been put together by man or by nature but of silence. This silence is emptiness in which and from which all things flow and have their being. It is unknowable, neither intellect nor feeling can make their way to it; there is no way to it and a method to it is the invention of a greedy brain. All the ways and means of the calculating self must be destroyed wholly; all going forward or backward, the way of time, must come to an end, without tomorrow. Meditation is destruction; it's a danger to those who wish to lead a superficial life and a life of fancy and myth.

The stars were very bright, brilliant so early in the morning. Dawn was far away; it was surprisingly quiet, even the boisterous stream was quiet and the hills were silent. A whole hour passed in that state when the brain was not asleep but awake, sensitive and only watching; during that state the totality of the mind can go beyond itself, without directions for there is no director. Meditation is a storm, destroying and cleansing. Then, far away, came dawn. In the east there was spreading light, so young and pale, so quiet and timid; it came past those distant hills and it touched the towering mountains and the peaks. In groups and singly, the trees stood still, the aspen began to wake up and the stream shouted with joy. That white wall of a farm-house, facing west, became very white. Slowly, peacefully, almost begging it came and filled the land. Then the snow peaks began to glow, bright rose and the noises of the early morning began. Three crows flew across the sky, silently, all in the same direction;

from far came the sound of a bell on a cow and still there was quiet. Then a car was coming up the hill and day began.

On that path in the wood, a yellow leaf fell; for some of the trees autumn was here. It was a single leaf, with not a blemish on it, unspotted, clean. It was the yellow of autumn, it was still lovely in its death, no disease had touched it. It was still the fullness of spring and summer and still all the leaves of that tree were green. It was death in glory. Death was there, not in the yellow leaf, but actually there, not an inevitable traditionalized death but that death which is always there. It was not a fancy but a reality that could not be covered up. It is always there round every bend of a road, in every house, with every god. It was there with all its strength and beauty.

You can't avoid death; you may forget it, you may rationalize it or believe that you will be reborn or resurrected. Do what you will, go to any temple or book it is always there, in festival and in health. You must live with it to know it; you can't know it if you are frightened of it; fear only darkens it. To know it you must love it. To live with it you must love it. The knowledge of it isn't the ending of it. It's the end of knowledge but not of death. To love it is not to be familiar with it; you can't be familiar with destruction. You can't love something you don't know but you don't know anything, not even your wife or your boss, let alone a total stranger. But yet you must love it, the stranger, the unknown. You only love that of which you are certain, that which gives comfort, security. You do not love the uncertain, the unknown; you may love danger, give your life for another or kill another for your country, but this is not love; these have their own reward and profit; gain and success you love though there's pain in them. There's no profit in knowing death but strangely death and love always go together; they never separate. You can't love without death; you can't embrace without death being there. Where love is there is also death, they are inseparable.

But do we know what love is? You know sensation, emotion, desire, feeling and the mechanism of thought but none of these is love. You love your husband, your children; you hate war but you practice war. Your love knows hate, envy, ambition, fear; the smoke of these is not love. Power and prestige you love but power and prestige are evil, corrupting. Do we know what love is? Never knowing it is the wonder of it, the beauty of it. Never knowing, which does not mean remaining in doubt nor does it mean despair; it's the death of yesterday and so the complete uncertainty of tomorrow. Love has no continuity, nor has death. Only memory and the picture in the frame have continuity but these are mechanical and even machines wear out, yielding place to new pictures, new memories. What has continuity is ever decaying and what decays isn't death. Love and death are inseparable and where they are there's always destruction.

September 1st
The snow was melting fast in the mountains for there have been many unclouded days and hot sun; the stream had become muddy and there was more water and it had become more noisy and impetuous. Crossing the little wooden bridge and looking up the stream, there was the mountain, surprisingly delicate, aloof, with inviting strength; its snow was glistening in the evening sun. It was beautiful, caught between the trees on either side of the stream and the fast-running waters. It was startlingly immense, soaring into the sky, suspended in the air. It wasn't only the mountain that was beautiful but the evening light, the hills, the meadows, the trees and the stream. Suddenly the whole land with its shadows and peace became intense, so alive and absorbing. It pushed its way through the brain as a flame burning away the insensitivity of thought. The sky, the land and the watcher, all were caught up in this intensity and there was only the flame and nothing else. Meditation during that walk, beside the stream on a path which meandered gently

through many green fields, was not there because of silence or because the beauty of the evening absorbed all thought; it went on in spite of some talk. Nothing could interfere with it; meditation went on, not unconsciously somewhere in the recesses of the brain and memory, but it was there, taking place, like the evening light among the trees. Meditation is not a purposeful pursuit which breeds distraction and conflict; it's not the discovery of a toy that will absorb all thought, as a child is absorbed by a toy; it's not the repetition of a word to still the mind. It begins with self-knowing and goes beyond knowing. On the walk, it was going on, stirring deeply and moving in no direction. Meditation was going on beyond thought, conscious or hidden, and a seeing beyond the capacity of thought.

Look beyond the mountain; in that look are the nearby houses, the meadows, the shapely hills and the mountains themselves; when you drive a car, you look well ahead, three hundred yards or more; that look takes in the side roads, that car that is parked, the boy that is crossing and the lorry that's coming towards you, but if you merely watched the car ahead of you, you would have an accident. The distant look includes the near but looking at what is near does not include the distant. Our life is spent in the immediate, in the superficial. Life in totality gives attention to the fragment but the fragment can never understand the totality. Yet this is what we are always attempting to do; hold on to the little and yet try to grasp the whole. The known is always the little, the fragment, and with the small we seek the unknown. We never let the little go; of the little we are certain, in it we are secure, at least we think we are. But actually we can never be certain about anything, except probably, about superficial and mechanical things and even they fail. More or less, we can rely on outward things, like trains, to operate and be certain of them. Psychologically, inwardly, however much we may crave it, there's no certainty, no permanency; neither in our relationships, in our beliefs, in the gods of our brain. The intense longing for certainty, for some kind of permanency and the fact that there is no permanency whatsoever is the essence of conflict, illusion and reality. The power to create illusion is vastly more significant to understand than to understand reality. The power to breed illusion must cease completely, not to gain reality; there's no bargaining with fact. Reality is not a reward; the false must go, not to gain what's true but because it's false.

Nor is there renunciation.

2nd

It was a beautiful evening in the valley, along the stream, the green meadows, so rich in pasturage, the clean farm-houses and the rapturous clouds, so full of colour and clarity. There was one that hung over the mountain with such vivid brilliancy that it seemed to be the favourite of the sun. The valley was cool, pleasant and so intensely alive. There was a quietness about it and a peace. Modern farm machinery was there but they still used the scythe and the pressure and the brutality of civilization hadn't touched it. The heavy electric cables on pylons ran through the valley and they too seemed a part of that unsophisticated world. As we walked along the narrow grassy path through fields, the mountains, with their snow and colour, seemed so close and delicate, so utterly unreal. The goats were bleating to be milked. Quite unexpectedly, all this extravagant beauty, colour, the hills, this rich earth, this intense valley, all this was within one. It wasn't within one, one's own heart and brain were so completely open, without the barrier of time and space, so empty of thought and feeling, that there was only this beauty, without sound or form. It was there and everything else ceased to be. The immensity of this love, with beauty and death, was there filling the valley and one's whole being which was that valley. It was an extraordinary evening.

There's no renunciation. What is given up is ever there and renunciation, giving up, sacrifice do not exist where there is understanding. Understanding is the very essence of non-conflict; renunciation is conflict. To give up is the action of will, which is born of choice and conflict. To give up is to exchange and in exchange there is no freedom but only more confusion and misery.

4th

Coming down from the valleys and high mountains into a big, noisy, dirty town affects the body.* It was a lovely day when we left, through deep valleys, waterfalls and deep woods to a blue lake and wide roads. It was a violent change from the peaceful, isolated place to a town that's noisy night and day, to a hot clammy air. Sitting quietly in the afternoon, looking over the roof-tops, watching the shape of roofs and their chimneys, most unexpectedly, that benediction, that strength, that otherness came with gentle clarity; it filled the room and remained. It is here as this is being written.

5th†

From the top of an eighth-floor window, the trees along the avenue were becoming yellow, russet and red in the midst of a long line of rich green. From this height the tops of the trees were brilliant in their colour and the roar of the traffic came up through them, somewhat softening the noise. There's only colour, not different colours; there's only love and not different expressions of it; the different categories of love are not love. When love is broken up into fragmentation, as divine and carnal, it ceases to be love. Jealousy is the smoke that smothers the fire, and passion becomes stupid without austerity, but there is no austerity if there is no self-abandonment, which is humility in utter simplicity. Looking down on that mass of colour, with different colours, there's

---

* He had flown to Paris where he stayed with friends in an eighth-floor apartment in the Avenue de la Bourdonnais.

† He gave the first of nine talks in Paris on this day. They lasted until September 24th.

only purity, however much it may be broken up; but impurity however much it may be changed, covered over, resisted, will always remain impure, like violence. Purity is not in conflict with impurity. Impurity can never become pure, any more than violence can become non-violence. Violence simply has to cease.

There are two pigeons who have made their home under the slate roof across the courtyard. The female goes in first and then slowly, with great dignity, the male follows and then for the night they remain there; early this morning they came out, the male first and then the other. They stretched their wings, preened and lay down flat on the cold roof. Soon from nowhere other pigeons came, a dozen of them; they settled around these two, preening, cooing, pushing each other in a friendly way. Then, all of a sudden, they all flew away, except the first two. The sky was overcast, there were heavy clouds, full of light on the horizon and a long streak of blue sky.

Meditation has no beginning and no end; in it there's no achievement and no failure, no gathering and no renunciation; it is a movement without finality and so beyond and above time and space. The experiencing of it is the denying of it, for the experiencer is bound to time and space, memory and recognition. The foundation for true meditation is that passive awareness which is the total freedom from authority and ambition, envy and fear. Meditation has no meaning, no significance whatsoever without this freedom, without self-knowing; as long as there's choice there's no self-knowing. Choice implies conflict which prevents the understanding of what is. Wandering off into some fancy, into some romantic beliefs, is not meditation; the brain must strip itself of every myth, illusion and security and face the reality of their falseness. There's no distraction, everything is in the movement of meditation. The flower is the form, the scent, the colour and the beauty that is the whole of it. Tear it to pieces actually or verbally, then there is no flower, only a remembrance of what was, which is never the flower. Meditation is the whole flower in its beauty, withering and living.

6th

The sun was just beginning to show through the clouds, early in the morning and the daily roar of traffic had not yet begun; it was raining and the sky was dull grey. On the little terrace the rain was beating down and the breeze was fresh. Standing in the shelter, watching a stretch of the river and the autumnal leaves, there came that otherness, like a flash and it remained for a while to be gone again. It's strange how very intense and actual it has become. It was as real as these roof-tops with hundreds of chimneys. In it there is a strange driving strength; because of its purity, it is strong, the strength of innocency which nothing can corrupt. And it was a benediction.

Knowledge is destructive to discovery. Knowledge is always in time, in the past; it can never bring freedom. But knowledge is necessary, to act, to think, and without action existence is not possible. But action however wise, righteous and noble will not open the door to truth. There's no path to truth; it cannot be bought through any action nor through any refinement of thought. Virtue is only order in a disordered world and there must be virtue, which is a movement of non-conflict. But none of these will open the door to that immensity. The totality of consciousness must empty itself of all its knowledge, action and virtue; not empty itself for a purpose, to gain, to realize, to become. It must remain empty though functioning in the everyday world of thought and action. Out of this emptiness, thought and action must come. But this emptiness will not open the door. There must be no door nor any attempt to reach. There must be no centre in this emptiness, for this emptiness has no measurement; it's the centre that measures, weighs, calculates. This emptiness is beyond time and space; it's beyond thought and feeling. It comes as quietly, unobtrusively, as love; it has no beginning and end. It's there unalterable and immeasurable.

7th

How important it is for the body to be in one place for a length of time; this constant travelling, change of climate, change of houses does affect the body; it has to adjust itself and during the period of adjustment nothing very "serious" can take place. And then one has to leave again. All this is a trial on the body. But this morning, on waking, early before the sun was up, when dawn had already come, in spite of the body, there was that strength with its intensity. It's curious how the body reacts to it; it has never been lazy, though often tired, but this morning, though the air was cold, it became or rather wanted to be active. Only when the brain is quiet, not asleep or sluggish but sensitive and alert, can the "otherness" come into being. It was altogether unexpected this morning for the body is still adjusting itself to new environment.

The sun came up in a clear sky; you couldn't see it for there were many chimneys in the way but its radiance filled the sky; and the flowers on the little terrace seemed to come to life and their colour became more brilliant and intense. It was a beautiful morning full of light and the sky became a marvellous blue. Meditation included that blue and those flowers; they were part of it; they wound their way through it; they were not a distraction. There's no distraction really, for meditation is not concentration, which is exclusion, a cutting off, a resistance and so a conflict. A meditative mind can concentrate which then is not an exclusion, a resistance, but a concentrated mind cannot meditate. It's curious how all-important meditation becomes; there's no end to it nor is there a beginning to it. It's like a rain-drop; in that drop are all the streams, the great rivers, the seas and the waterfalls; that drop nourishes the earth and man; without it, the earth would be a desert. Without meditation the heart becomes a desert, a wasteland. Meditation has its own movement; you can't direct it, shape it or force it, if you do it ceases to be meditation. This movement ceases if you are merely an observer, if you are the experiencer. Meditation is the movement that destroys the observer, the experiencer; it's a movement that is beyond all symbol, thought and feeling. Its rapidity is not measurable.

But the clouds were covering the sky and there was a battle going on between them and the wind, and the wind was conquering. There was a wide expanse of blue, so blue and the clouds were extravagant, full of light and darkness and those to the north seemed to have forgotten time, but space was theirs. In the park [the Champ de Mars] the ground was covered with autumn leaves and the pavement was full of them. It was a bright, fresh morning and the flowers were splendid in their summer colours. Beyond the huge, tall open tower [the Eiffel Tower], the main attraction, passed a funeral procession, the coffin and the hearse covered with flowers, followed by many cars. Even in death, we want to be important, to our vanity and pretence there is no end. Everyone wants to be somebody or be associated with someone who is somebody. Power and success, little or great, and recognized. Without recognition they have no meaning, recognized by the many or by the one who is dominated. Power is always respected and so is made respectable. Power is always evil, wielded by the politician or by the saint or by the wife over the husband. However evil it is, everyone craves for it, and those who have it want more of it. And that hearse with those gay flowers in the sun seems so far away and even death does not end power for it continues in another. It's the torch of evil that continues from generation to generation. Few can put it aside, widely and freely, without looking back; they have no reward. Reward is success, the halo of recognition. Not to be recognized, failure long forgotten, being nobody when all striving and conflict has ceased, there comes a blessing which is not of the church nor of the gods of man.

Children were calling and playing as the hearse passed by, never even looking at it, absorbed in their game and laughter.

8th

Even the stars can be seen in this well-lighted town and there are other sounds than the roar of traffic—the cooing of pigeons and the chirping of sparrows; there are other smells than the monoxide gases—the smell of autumn leaves and the scent of flowers. There were a few stars in the sky and fleecy clouds early this morning and with them came that intense penetration into the depth of the unknown. The brain was still, so still it could hear the faintest noise and being still and so incapable of interfering, there was a movement which began from nowhere and went on, through the brain, into unknown depth where the word lost its meaning. It swept through the brain and went on beyond time and space. One is not describing a fantasy, a dream, an illusion but an actual fact which took place, but what took place is not the word or the description. There was a burning energy, a bursting immediate vitality and with it came this penetrating movement. It was like a tremendous wind, gathering strength and fury as it rushed along, destroying, purifying, leaving a vast emptiness. There was a complete awareness of the whole thing and there was great strength and beauty; not the strength and beauty that are put together but of something that was completely pure and incorruptible. It lasted by the watch ten minutes but it was something incalculable.

The sun arose amidst a glory of clouds, fantastically alive and deep in colour. The roar of the town had not begun yet and the pigeons and sparrows were out. How curiously shallow the brain is; however subtle and deep thought is, it's nevertheless born of shallowness. Thought is bound by time and time is petty; it's this pettiness that perverts "seeing". Seeing is always instantaneous, as understanding, and the brain which is put together by time, prevents and also perverts seeing. Time and thought are inseparable; put an end to one, you put an end to the other. Thought cannot be destroyed by will for will is thought in action. Thought is one thing and the centre from which thought arises is another. Thought is the word and the word is the accumulation of memory, of experience. Without the word is there thought? There's a movement which is not word and it is not of thought. This movement can be described by thought but it is not of thought. This movement comes into being when the brain is still but active, and thought can never search out this movement.

Thought is memory and memory is accumulated responses and so thought is always conditioned however much it may imagine it is free. Thought is mechanical, tied to the centre of its own knowledge. The distance thought covers depends on knowledge and knowledge is always the remains of yesterday, of the movement that's gone. Thought can project itself into the future but it is tied to yesterday. Thought builds its own prison and lives in it, whether it's in the future or in the past, gilded or plain. Thought can never be still, by its very nature it is restless, ever pushing and withdrawing. The machinery of thought is ever in motion, noisily or quietly, on the surface or hidden. It cannot wear itself out. Thought can refine itself, control its wanderings; can choose its own direction and conform to environment.

Thought can not go beyond itself; it may function in narrow or wide fields but it will always be within the limitations of memory and memory is always limited. Memory must die psychologically, inwardly, but function only outwardly. Inwardly, there must be death and outwardly sensitivity to every challenge and response. The inward concern of thought prevents action.

9th
To have such a beautiful day in town seems such a waste; there isn't a cloud in the sky, the sun is warm and the pigeons are warming themselves on the roof but the roar of the town

goes on without pity. The trees feel the autumnal air and
their leaves are turning, slowly and languidly, without care.
The streets are crowded with people, always looking at shops,
very few at the sky; they see each other as they pass by but
they are concerned with themselves, how they look, what
impression they give; envy and fear is always there in spite
of their make-up, in spite of their polished appearance. The
labourers are too tired, heavy and grumbling. And the massed
trees against the wall of a museum seem so utterly sufficient
to themselves; the river held in by cement and stone seems
so utterly indifferent. The pigeons are plentiful, with a
strutting dignity of their own. And so a day passed by on the
street, in the office. It's a world of monotony and despair,
with laughter that soon passes away. In the evening the
monuments, the streets, are lit up but there's a vast emptiness
and unbearable pain.

There's a yellow leaf on the pavement, just fallen; it's still
full of summer and though in death it's still very beautiful;
not a part of it is withered, it has still the shape and grace of
spring but it's yellow and will wither away by the evening.
Early in the morning, when the sun was just showing itself
in a clear sky, there was a flash of otherness, with its benediction and the beauty of it remains. It's not that thought has
captured it and holds it but it has left its imprint on consciousness. Thought is always fragmentary and what it holds
is always partial, as memory. It cannot observe the whole;
the part cannot see the whole and the imprint of benediction
is non-verbal and non-communicable through words, through
any symbol. Thought will always fail in its attempt to discover, to experience that which is beyond time and space. The
brain, the machinery of thought can be quiet; the very active
brain can be quiet; its machinery can run very slowly. The
quietness of the brain, though intensely sensitive, is essential;
then only can thought disentangle itself and come to an end.
The ending of thought is not death; then only can there be

innocency, freshness; a new quality to thought. It's this quality that puts an end to sorrow and despair.

10th

It's a morning without a cloud; the sun seems to have banished every cloud from sight. It is peaceful except for the roar of traffic, even though it is Sunday. The pigeons are warming themselves on the zinc roofs and are almost the same colour at the roof. There's not a breath of air, though it's cool and fresh.

There's peace beyond thought and feeling. It's not the peace of the politician nor the priest nor of the one who seeks it. It is not to be sought. What is sought must already be known and what's known is never the real. Peace is not to the believer, to the philosopher who specializes in theory. It is not a reaction, a contrary response to violence. It has no opposite; all opposites must cease, the conflict of duality. There's duality, light and darkness, man and woman and so on but the conflict between the opposites is in no way necessary. Conflict between the opposites arises only when there's need, the compulsion to fulfil, the need for sex, the psychological demand for security. Then only is there conflict between the opposites; the escape from the opposites, attachment and detachment, is the search for peace through church and law. Law can and does give superficial order; the peace that church and temple offer is fancy, a myth to which a confused mind can escape. But this is not peace. The symbol, the word must be destroyed, not destroyed in order to have peace but they must be shattered for they are an impediment to understanding. Peace is not for sale, a commodity of exchange. Conflict, in every form, must cease and then perhaps it is there. There must be total negation, the cessation of demand and need; then only does conflict come to an end. In emptiness there is birth. All the inward structure of resistance and security must die away; then only is there emptiness.

Only in this emptiness is there peace whose virtue has no value nor profit.

It was there early in the morning, it came with the sun in a clear, opaque sky; it was a marvellous thing full of beauty, a benediction that asked nothing, no sacrifice, no disciple, no virtue, no midnight hour. It was there in abundance and only an abundant mind and heart could receive it. It was beyond all measure.

11th

In the park it was crowded; everywhere there were people, children, nurses, different races, they were talking, shouting, playing and the fountains were going. The head gardener must have very good taste; there were so many flowers and so many colours all mixed together. It was quite spectacular and they had an air of gay festivity. It was a pleasant afternoon and everyone seemed to be out, in their best clothes. Going through the park, crossing a main thoroughfare, there was a quiet street with trees and old houses, well kept; the sun was just going down, setting fire to the clouds and to the river. It promised to be a nice day again tomorrow, and this morning, the early sun caught a few clouds, turning them bright pink and rose. It was a good hour to be quiet, to be meditative. Lethargy and quietness don't go together; to be quiet, there must be intensity and meditation, then it is not a meandering but very active and forceful. Meditation is not a pursuit of thought or idea; it is the essence of all thought, which is to be beyond all thought and feeling. Then it is a movement into the unknown.

Intelligence is not the mere capacity of design, remembrance and communication; it is more than that. One can be very informed and clever at one level of existence and quite dull at other levels. There knowledge, however deep and wide, does not necessarily indicate intelligence. Capacity is not intelligence. Intelligence is sensitive awareness of the totality of life; life with its problems, contradictions, miseries, joys. To be aware of all this, without choice and without being caught by any one of its issues and to flow with the whole of life is intelligence. This intelligence is not the result of influence and environment; it is not the prisoner of either of them and so can understand them and thus be free of them. Consciousness is limited, open or hidden, and its activity, however alert, is confined within the borders of time; intelligence is not. Sensitive awareness, without choice, of the totality of life is intelligence. This intelligence cannot be used for gain and profit, personal or collective. This intelligence is destruction and so the form has no significance and reform then becomes a retrogression. Without destruction all change is modified continuity. Psychological destruction of all that has been, not mere outward change, that is the essence of intelligence. Without this intelligence every action leads to misery and confusion. Sorrow is the denial of this intelligence.

Ignorance is not the lack of knowledge but of self-knowing; without self-knowing there is no intelligence. Self-knowing is not accumulative as knowledge; learning is from moment to moment. It is not an additive process; in the process of gathering, adding, a centre is formed, a centre of knowledge, of experience. In this process, positive or negative, there is no understanding, for as long as there is an intention of gathering or resisting, the movement of thought and feeling are not understood, there is no self-knowing. Without self-knowing there's no intelligence. Self-knowing is active present, not a judgment; all self-judgment implies an accumulation, evaluation from a centre of experience and knowledge. It is this past that prevents the understanding of the active present. In the pursuit of self-knowing there is intelligence.

12th

A town is not a pleasant place, however beautiful the town is and this is. The clean river, the open spaces, the flowers, the noise, the dirt and the striking tower, the pigeons and the people, all this and the sky make for a pleasant town but it is not the country, the fields, the woods and the clear air; the country is always beautiful, so far away from all the smoke and the roar of traffic, so far away and there is the earth, so plentiful, so rich. Walking along the river, with the ceaseless roar of traffic, the river seemed to contain all the earth; though it was held by rock and cement, it was vast, it was the waters of every river from the mountains to the plains. It became the colour of the sunset, every colour that the eye had ever seen, so splendid and fleeting. The evening breeze was playing with everything and autumn was touching every leaf. The sky was so close, embracing the earth and there was peace past belief. And night came slowly.

On waking this morning early, when the sun was below the horizon and dawn had begun, meditation yielded to that otherness whose benediction is clarity and strength. It was there last night as one was getting into bed, so unexpectedly, so clearly. One had not been with it for some days, the body was adjusting itself to the ways of the town, and so when it came, there was great intensity and beauty and everything became still; it was filling the room and far beyond the room. There was a certain rigidity, no, a certain immobility of the body, though relaxed. All during the night it must have gone on, for on waking it was there actively present, filling the room and beyond. All description of it is of no significance for the word can never cover the immensity nor the beauty of it. Everything ceases when that is, and strangely the brain with all its responses and activities, finds itself suddenly and voluntarily quiet, without a single response, without a single memory nor is there any recording of what is going on. It is very much alive but utterly quiet. It is too immense for any imagination, which is rather immature and silly anyway. What is actually, is so vital and significant that all imagination and illusion have lost their meaning.

The understanding of need is of great significance. There is the outward need, necessary and essential, food, clothes and shelter; but beyond that is there any other need? Though each one is caught up in the turmoil of inward needs, are they essential? The need for sex, the need to fulfil, the compulsive urge of ambition, envy, greed, are they the way of life? Each one has made them the way of life for thousands of years; society and church respects and honours them greatly. Each one has accepted that way of life or, being so conditioned to that life, goes along with it, struggling feebly against the current, discouraged, seeking escapes. And escapes become more significant than the reality. The psychological needs are a defensive mechanism against something much more significant and real. The need to fulfil, to be important springs from the fear of something which is there but not experienced, known. Fulfilment and self importance, in the name of one's country or party or because of some gratifying belief, are escapes from the fact of one's own nothingness, emptiness, loneliness, of one's own self-isolating activities. The inward needs which seem to have no end multiply, change and continue. This is the source of contradictory and burning desire.

Desire is always there; the objects of desire change, diminish or multiply but it is always there. Controlled, tortured, denied, accepted, suppressed, allowed to run freely or cut off, it is always there, feeble or strong. What is wrong with desire? Why this incessant war against it? It is disturbing, painful, leading to confusion and sorrow but yet it is there, always there, weak or rich. To understand it completely, not to suppress it, not to discipline it out of all recognition is to understand need. Need and desire go together, like fulfilment and frustration. There's no noble or ignoble desire but only desire, ever in conflict within itself. The hermit and the party boss are burning with it, call it by different names but it is there, eating away the heart of things. When there is total understanding of need, the outward and the inner, then desire is not a torture. Then it has quite a different meaning, a significance far beyond the content of thought and it goes beyond feeling, with its emotions, myths and illusions. With the total understanding of need, not the mere quantity or the quality of it, desire then is a flame and not a torture. Without this flame life itself is lost. It is this flame that burns away the pettiness of its object, the frontiers, the fences that have been imposed upon it. Then call it by whatever name you will, love, death, beauty. Then it is there without an end.

13th

It was a strange day yesterday. That otherness was there all day yesterday, on the short walk, while resting and very intensely during the talk.* It was persistently there most of the night, and this morning, waking early, after little sleep, it continued. The body is too tired and needs rest. Strangely, the body becomes very quiet, very still, motionless but every inch of it very alive and sensitive.

As far as the eye can see, there are short small chimneys, all without smoke for the weather is very warm; the horizon is far away, uneven, cluttered up; the town seems to stretch far out endlessly. Along the avenue there are trees, waiting for winter, for autumn is slowly beginning already. The sky was silver, polished and bright and the breeze made patterns on the river. Pigeons stirred early in the morning and as the sun made the zinc roofs warm they were there warming themselves. Mind, in which are the brain, thought, feeling and every subtle emotion, fancy and imagination, is an extraordinary thing. All its contents do not make up the mind and yet without them, it is not; it is more than what it contains. Without the mind the contents would not be; they exist because of it. In the total emptiness of the mind, intellect, thought, feeling, all consciousness have their existence. A tree is not the word, nor the leaf, the branch or the roots; the whole of it is the tree and yet it is none of these things.

* This was the third talk, chiefly about conflict and consciousness.

Mind is that emptiness in which the things of the mind can exist but the things are not the mind. Because of this emptiness time and space come into being. But the brain and the things of the brain cover a whole field of existence; it is occupied with its multiple problems. It cannot capture the nature of the mind, as it functions only in fragmentation and the many fragments do not make the whole. And yet it is occupied with putting together the contradictory fragments to make the whole. The whole can never be gathered and put together.

The activity of memory, knowledge in action, the conflict of opposing desire, the search for freedom are still within the confines of the brain; the brain can refine, enlarge, accumulate its desires but sorrow will go on. There's no ending of sorrow as long as thought is merely a response of memory, of experience. There's a "thinking" born out of the total emptiness of the mind; that emptiness has no centre and so is capable of infinite movement. Creation is born out of this emptiness but it is not the creation of man putting things together. That creation of emptiness is love and death.

Again, it has been a strange day. That otherness has been present wherever one has been, whatever the daily activity. It is as though one's brain was living in it; the brain has been very quiet without going to sleep, sensitive and alert. There's a sense of watching from infinite depth. Though the body is tired, there's a peculiar alertness. A flame that is always burning.

14th
It has been raining all night and it is pleasant after many weeks of sun and dust. The earth has been dry, parched and there were cracks; heavy dust covered the leaves and lawns were being watered. In a crowded and dirty city, so many days of sun was unpleasant; the air was heavy and now it has been raining for many hours. Only the pigeons don't like it; they take shelter where they can, depressed and have stopped

cooing. The sparrows used to take their bath wherever there was water with the pigeons and now they are hidden away somewhere; they used to come on the terrace, shy and eager but the driving rain has taken over and the earth is wet.

Again, most of the night, that blessing, that otherness was there; though there was sleep, it was there; one felt it on waking, strong, persistent, urgent; it was there, as though it had continued throughout the night. With it, there is always great beauty, not of images, feeling or thought. Beauty is neither thought nor feeling; it has nothing whatsoever to do with emotion or sentiment.

There is fear. Fear is never an actuality; it is either before or after the active present. When there is fear in the active present, is it fear? It is there and there is no escape from it, no evasion possible. There, at that actual moment, there is total attention at the moment of danger, physical or psychological. When there is complete attention there is no fear. But the actual fact of inattention breeds fear; fear arises when there is an avoidance of the fact, a flight; then the very escape itself is fear.

Fear and its many forms, guilt, anxiety, hope, despair, is there in every movement of relationship; it is there in every search for security; it is there in so-called love and worship; it is there in ambition and success; it is there in life and in death; it is there in physical things and in psychological factors. There is fear in so many forms and at all the levels of our consciousness. Defence, resistance and denial spring from fear. Fear of the dark and fear of light; fear of going and fear of coming. Fear begins and ends with the desire to be secure; inward and outward security, with the desire to be certain, to have permanency. The continuity of permanence is sought in every direction, in virtue, in relationship, in action, in experience, in knowledge, in outward and inward things. To find and be secure is the everlasting cry. It is this insistent demand that breeds fear.

But is there permanency, outwardly or inwardly? Perhaps in a measure, outwardly there might be, and even that is precarious; wars, revolutions, progress, accident and earthquakes. There must be food, clothes and shelter; that is essential and necessary for all. Though it is sought after, blindly and with reason, is there ever inward certainty, inward continuity, permanency? There is not. The flight from this reality is fear. The incapacity to face this reality breeds every form of hope and despair.

Thought itself is the source of fear. Thought is time; thought of tomorrow is pleasure or pain; if it's pleasurable, thought will pursue it, fearing its end; if it's painful, the very avoidance of it is fear. Both pleasure and pain cause fear. Time as thought and time as feeling bring fear. It is the understanding of thought, the mechanism of memory and experience, that is the ending of fear. Thought is the whole process of consciousness, the open and the hidden; thought is not merely the thing thought upon but the origin of itself. Thought is not merely belief, dogma, idea and reason but the centre from which these arise. This centre is the origin of all fear. But is there the experiencing of fear or is there the awareness of the cause of fear from which thought is taking flight? Physical self-protection is sane, normal and healthy but every other form of self-protection, inwardly, is resistance and it always gathers, builds up strength which is fear. But this inward fear makes outward security a problem of class, prestige, power, and so there is competitive ruthlessness.

When this whole process of thought, time and fear is seen, not as an idea, an intellectual formula, then there is total ending of fear, conscious or hidden. Self-understanding is the awakening and ending of fear.

And when fear ceases, then the power to breed illusion, myth, visions, with their hope and despair also ceases, and then only begins a movement of going beyond consciousness, which is thought and feeling. It is the emptying of the innermost recesses and deep hidden wants and desires. Then when there is this total emptiness, when there is absolutely and literally nothing, no influence, no value, no frontier, no word, then in that complete stillness of time-space, there is that which is unnameable.

15th

It was a lovely evening, the sky was clear and in spite of city light, the stars were brilliant; though the tower was flooded with light from all sides, one could see the distant horizon and down below patches of light were on the river; though there was the everlasting roar of traffic, it was a peaceful evening. Meditation crept on one like a wave covering the sands. It was not a meditation which the brain could capture in its net of memory; it was something to which the total brain yielded without any resistance. It was a meditation that went far beyond any formula, method; method and formula and repetition destroy meditation. In its movement it took everything in, the stars, the noise, the quiet and the stretch of water. But there was no meditator; the meditator, the observer must cease for meditation to be. The breaking up of the meditator is also meditation; but when the meditator ceases then there's an altogether different meditation.

It was very early in the morning; Orion was coming up over the horizon and the Pleiades were nearly overhead. The roar of the city had quietened and at that hour there were no lights in any of the windows and there was a pleasant, cool breeze. In complete attention there is no experiencing. In inattention there is; it is this inattention that gathers experience, multiplying memory, building walls of resistance; it is this inattention that builds up the self-centred activities. Inattention is concentration, which is exclusion, a cutting off; concentration knows distraction and the endless conflict of control and discipline. In the state of inattention, every response to any challenge is inadequate; this inadequacy is experience. Experience makes for insensitivity; dulls the mechanism of thought; thickens the walls of memory, and habit, routine, become the norm. Experience, inattention, is not liberating. Inattention is slow decay.

In complete attention there is no experiencing; there's no centre which experiences, nor a periphery within which experience can take place. Attention is not concentration which is narrowing, limiting. Total attention includes, never excludes. Superficiality of attention is inattention; total attention includes the superficial and the hidden, the past and its influence on the present, moving into the future. All consciousness is partial, confined, and total attention includes consciousness, with its limitations and so is able to break down the borders, the limitations. All thought is conditioned and thought cannot uncondition itself. Thought is time and experience; it is essentially the result of non-attention.

What brings about total attention? Not any method nor any system; they bring about a result, promised by them. But total attention is not a result, any more than love is; it cannot be induced, it cannot be brought about by any action. Total attention is the negation of the results of inattention but this negation is not the act of knowing attention. What is false must be denied not because you already know what is true; if you knew what is true the false would not exist. The true is not the opposite of the false; love is not the opposite of hate. Because you know hate, you do not know love. Denial of the false, denial of the things of non-attention is not the outcome of the desire to achieve total attention. Seeing the false as the false and the true as the true and the true in the false is not the result of comparison. To see the false as the false is attention. The false as the false cannot be seen when there is opinion, judgment, evaluation, attachment and so on, which are the result of non-attention. Seeing the whole fabric of non-attention is total attention. An attentive mind is an empty mind.

The purity of the otherness is its immense and impenetrable

strength. And it was there with extraordinary stillness this morning.

16th

It was a clear bright evening; there wasn't a cloud. It was so lovely that it was surprising that such an evening should happen in a town. The moon was between the arches of the tower and the whole setting seemed so artificial and unreal. The air was so soft and pleasant that it might have been a summer's evening. On the balcony it was very quiet and every thought had subsided and meditation seemed a casual movement, without any direction. But there was, though. It began nowhere and went on into vast, unfathomable emptiness where the essence of everything is. In this emptiness there is an expanding, exploding movement whose very explosion is creation and destruction. Love is the essence of this destruction.

Either we seek through fear or being free from it, we seek without any motive. This search does not spring from discontent; not being satisfied with every form of thought and feeling, seeing their significance, is not discontent. Discontent is so easily satisfied when thought and feeling have found some form of shelter, success, a gratifying position, a belief and so on, only to be roused again when that shelter is attacked, shaken or broken down. With this cycle most of us are familiar, hope and despair. Search, whose motive is discontent, can only lead to some form of illusion, a collective or a private illusion, a prison of many attractions. But there is a seeking without any motive whatsoever; then is it a seeking? Seeking implies, does it not, an objective, an end already known or felt or formulated. If it's formulated it's the calculation of thought, putting together all the things it has known or experienced; to find what is sought after methods and systems are devised. This is not seeking at all; it is merely a desire to gain a gratifying end or merely to escape into some fancy or promise of a theory or belief. This is not seeking. When fear, satisfaction, escape have lost their significance, then is there seeking at all?

If the motive of all search has withered away, discontent and the urge to succeed are dead; is there seeking? If there is no seeking, will consciousness decay, become stagnant? On the contrary, it is this seeking, going from one commitment to another, from one church to another, that weakens that essential energy to understand what is. The "what is" is ever new; it has never been and it will never be. The release of this energy is only possible when every form of search ceases.

It was a cloudless morning, so early and time seemed to have stopped. It was four-thirty but time seemed to have lost its entire meaning. It was as though there was no yesterday or tomorrow or the next moment. Time stood still and life without a shadow went on; life without thought and feeling went on. The body was there on the terrace, the high tower with its flashing warning light was there and the countless chimneys; the brain saw all these but it went no further. Time as measure, and time as thought and feeling had stopped. There was no time; every movement had stopped but there was nothing static. On the contrary there was an extraordinary intensity and sensitivity, a fire that was burning, without heat and colour. Overhead were the Pleiades and lower down towards the east was Orion and the morning star was over the top of the roofs. And with this fire there was joy, bliss. It wasn't that one was joyous but there was ecstasy. There was no identification with it, there couldn't be for time had ceased. That fire could not identify itself with anything nor be in relationship with anything. It was there for time had stopped. And dawn was coming and Orion and the Pleiades faded away and presently the morning star too went its way.

17th

It had been a hot, smothering day and even the pigeons were hiding and the air was hot and in a city it was not at all pleasant. It was a cool night and the few stars that were visible were bright, even the city lights couldn't dim them. They were there with amazing intensity.

It was a day of the otherness; it went on quietly all day and at moments it flared up, became very intense and became quiet again, to go on quietly.* It was there with such intensity that all movement became impossible; one was forced to sit down. On waking in the middle of the night it was there with great force and energy. On the terrace, with the roar of the city not so insistent, every form of meditation became inadequate and unnecessary for it was there in full measure. It's a benediction and everything seems rather silly and infantile. On these occasions, the brain is always very quiet but in no way asleep and the whole of the body becomes motionless. It is a strange affair.

How little one changes. Through some form of compulsion, pressure, outward and inner, one changes, which is really an adjustment. Some influence, a word, a gesture, makes one change the pattern of habit but not very much. Propaganda, a newspaper, an incident does alter, to some extent, the course of life. Fear and reward break down the habit of thought only to re-form into another pattern. A new invention, a new ambition, a new belief does bring about certain changes. But all these changes are on the surface, like strong wind on water; they are not fundamental, deep, devastating. All change that comes through motive, is no change at all. Economic, social revolution is a reaction and any change brought about through reaction is not a radical change; it is only a change in pattern. Such change is merely adjustment, a mechanical affair of desire for comfort, security, mere physical survival.

* He gave the fifth talk that morning.

Then what brings about fundamental mutation? Consciousness, the open and the hidden, the whole machinery of thought, feeling, experience, is within the borders of time and space. It is an indivisible whole; the division, conscious and hidden, is there only for the convenience of communication but the division is not factual. The upper level of consciousness can and does modify itself, adjust itself, change itself, reform itself, acquire new knowledge, technique; it can change itself to conform to a new social, economic pattern but such changes are superficial and brittle. The unconscious, the hidden, can and does intimate and hint through dreams its compulsions, its demands, its stored-up desires. Dreams need interpretations but the interpreter is always conditioned. There is no need for dreams if during the waking hours there is a choiceless awareness in which every fleeting thought and feeling is understood; then sleep has altogether a different meaning. Analysis of the hidden implies the observer and the observed, the censor and the thing that is judged. In this there is not only conflict but the observer himself is conditioned and his evaluation, interpretation, can never be true; it will be crooked, perverted. So self-analysis or an analysis by another, however professional, may bring about some superficial changes, an adjustment in relationship and so on but analysis will not bring about a radical transformation of consciousness. Analysis does not transform consciousness.

18th
The late afternoon sun was on the river and among the russet leaves of autumnal trees along the long avenue; the colours were burning intensely and of such variety; the narrow water was aflame. A whole long queue was waiting along the wharf to take the pleasure boat and the cars were making an awful noise. On a hot day the big town was almost unbearable; the sky was clear and the sun was without mercy. But very early this morning when Orion was overhead and only

one or two cars passed along the river, there was on the terrace quietness and meditation with a complete openness of mind and heart, verging on death. To be completely open, to be utterly vulnerable is death. Death then has no corner to take shelter; only in the shade, in the secret recesses of thought and desire there is death. But death is always there to a heart that has withered in fear and hope; it is always there where thought is waiting and watching. In the park an owl was hooting and it was a pleasant sound, so clear and so early; it came and went with varied intervals and it seemed to like its own voice for not another replied.

Meditation breaks down the frontiers of consciousness; it breaks down the mechanism of thought and the feeling which thought arouses. Meditation caught in a method, in a system of rewards and promises, cripples and tames energy. Meditation is the freeing of energy in abundance, and control, discipline and suppression spoil the purity of that energy. Meditation is the flame burning intensely without leaving any ashes. Words, feeling, thought, always leave ashes and to live on ashes is the way of the world. Meditation is danger for it destroys everything, nothing whatsoever is left, not even a whisper of desire, and in this vast, unfathomable emptiness there is creation and love.

To continue—analysis, personal or professional, does not bring about mutation of consciousness. No effort can transform it; effort is conflict and conflict only strengthens the walls of consciousness. No reason, however logical and sane, can liberate consciousness, for reason is idea wrought by influence, experience and knowledge and all these are the children of consciousness. When all this is seen as false, a false approach to mutation, the denial of the false is the emptying of consciousness. Truth has no opposite nor has love; the pursuit of the opposite does not lead to truth, only the denial of the opposite. There is no denial if it is the outcome of hope or of attaining. There is denial only when there is no reward or exchange. There is renunciation only when there is no gain in the act of renouncing. Denial of the false is the freedom from the positive; the positive with its opposite. The positive is authority with its acceptance, conformity, imitation, and experience with its knowledge.

To deny is to be alone; alone from all influence, tradition and from need, with its dependence and attachment. To be alone is to deny the conditioning, the background. The frame in which consciousness exists and has its being is its conditioning; to be choicelessly aware of this conditioning and the total denial of it is to be alone. This aloneness is not isolation, loneliness, self-enclosing occupation. Aloneness is not withdrawal from life; on the contrary it is the total freedom from conflict and sorrow, from fear and death. This aloneness is the mutation of consciousness; complete transformation of what has been. This aloneness is emptiness, it is not the positive state of being, nor the not being. It is emptiness; in this fire of emptiness the mind is made young, fresh and innocent. It is innocency alone that can receive the timeless, the new which is ever destroying itself. Destruction is creation. Without love, there is no destruction.

Beyond the enormous sprawling town were the fields, woods and hills.

19th
Is there a future? There is a tomorrow, already planned; certain things that have to be done; there is also the day after tomorrow, with all the things that are to be done; next week and next year. These cannot be altered, perhaps modified or changed altogether but the many tomorrows are there; they cannot be denied. And there is space, from here to there, near and far; the distance in kilometers; space between entities; the distance which thought covers in a flash; the other side of the river and the distant moon. Time to cover space, distance, and time to cross over the river; from here to there, time is necessary to cover that space, it may take a

minute, a day or a year. This time is by the sun and by the
watch, time is a means to arrive. This is fairly simple and
clear. Is there a future apart from this mechanical, chrono-
logical time? Is there an arriving, is there an end for which
time is necessary?

The pigeons were on the roof, so early in the morning;
they were cooing, preening and pursuing each other. The
sun wasn't up yet and there were a few vapourous clouds,
scattered all over the sky; they had no colour yet and the
roar of traffic had not yet begun. There was plenty of time
yet for the usual noises to begin and beyond all these walls
were the gardens. In the evening yesterday, the grass where
no one is allowed to walk except of course the pigeons and a
few sparrows, was very green, startlingly green and the
flowers were very bright. Everywhere else was man with his
activities and interminable work. There was the tower, so
strongly and delicately put together, and presently it would
be flooded with brilliant light. The grass seemed so perishable and the flowers would fade, for autumn was everywhere.
But long before the pigeons were on the roof, on the terrace
meditation was gladness. There was no reason for this ecstasy
—to have a cause for joy is no longer joy; it was simply there
and thought could not capture it and make it into a
remembrance. It was too strong and active for thought to
play with it and thought and feeling became very quiet and
still. It came wave upon wave, a living thing which nothing
could contain and with this joy there was benediction. It was
all so utterly beyond all thought and demand. Is there
an arriving? To arrive is to be in sorrow and within the
shadow of fear. Is there an arriving inwardly, a goal to be
reached, an end to be gained? Thought has fixed an end,
God, bliss, success, virtue and so on. But thought is only a
reaction, a response of memory and thought breeds time to
cover the space between what is and what should be. The
what should be, the ideal, is verbal, theoretical; it has no

reality. The actual has no time; it has no end to achieve, no distance to travel. The fact is and everything else is not. There is no fact if there's not death to ideal, to achievement, to an end; the ideal, the goal are an escape from the fact. The fact has no time and no space. And then is there death? There is a withering away; the machinery of the physical organism deteriorates, gets worn out which is death. But that is inevitable, as the lead of this pencil will wear out. Is that what causes fear? Or the death of the world of becoming, gaining, achieving? That world has no validity; it's the world of make-believe, of escape. The fact, the what is, and the what should be are two entirely different things. The what should be involves time and distance, sorrow and fear. Death of these leaves only the fact, the what is. There is no future to what is; thought, which breeds time, cannot operate on the fact; thought cannot change the fact, it can only escape from it and when all the urge to escape is dead, then the fact undergoes a tremendous mutation. But there must be death to thought which is time. When time as thought is not, then is there the fact, the what is? When there is destruction of time, as thought, there's no movement in any direction, no space to cover, there's only the stillness of emptiness. This is total destruction of time as yesterday, today and tomorrow, as the memory of continuity, of becoming.

Then being is timeless, only the active present but that present is not of time. It is attention without the frontiers of thought and the borders of feeling. Words are used to communicate and words, symbols, have no significance in themselves whatsoever. Life is always the active present; time always belongs to the past and so to the future. And death to time is life in the present. It is this life that is immortal, not the life in consciousness. Time is thought in consciousness and consciousness is held within its frame. There is always fear and sorrow within the network of thought and feeling. The ending of sorrow is the ending of time.

20th

It had been a very hot day and in that hot hall with a large crowd, it was suffocating.* But in spite of all this and tiredness, woke up in the middle of the night, with the otherness in the room. It was there with great intensity, not only filling the room and beyond but it was there deep down within the brain, so profoundly that it seemed to go through and beyond all thought, space and time. It was incredibly strong, with such energy that it was impossible to be in bed, and on the terrace, with fresh, cool wind blowing, the intensity of it continued. It went on for nearly an hour, with great force and drive; all the morning it had been there. It is not a make-believe, it's not desire taking this form of sensation, excitement; thought has not built it up from past incidents; no imagination could formulate such otherness. Strangely every time this takes place, it's something totally new, unexpected and sudden. Thought, having tried, realizes that it cannot recall what had taken place at other times nor can it awaken the memory of what had taken place this morning. It is beyond all thought, desire and imagination. It is too vast for thought or desire to conjure it up; it is too immense for the brain to bring it about. It's not an illusion.

The strange part of all this is that one's not even concerned about all this; if it comes, it is there, without invitation, and if it doesn't, there is an indifference. The beauty and the strength of it is not to be played with; there's no invitation or denial of it. It comes and goes, as it will.

Early this morning, somewhat before sunrise, meditation, in which every kind of effort has long ago ceased, became a silence, a silence in which there was no centre and so no periphery. It was just silence. It had no quality, no movement, neither depth nor height. It was completely still. It is

* At his talk the day before. It was the seventh talk and had been concerned mostly with death. At the beginning he politely suggested to his audience that they should refrain from taking notes.

this stillness that had movement expanding endlessly and the measurement of it was not in time and space. This stillness was exploding, ever moving away. But it had no centre; if there was a centre, it would not be stillness, it would be stagnant decay; it had nothing whatsover to do with the intricacies of the brain. The quality of the stillness which the brain can bring about, is entirely different, in every way, from the stillness that was there this morning. It was a stillness that nothing could disturb, for it had no resistance; everything was in it and it was beyond everything. The early morning traffic of lorries bringing foodstuff and other things to the town, in no way disturbed that stillness nor the revolving beams of light from the high tower. It was there, without time.

As the sun rose, a magnificent cloud caught it, sending streaks of blue light across the sky. It was light playing with darkness and the play went on till the fantastic cloud went down behind the thousand chimneys. How curiously petty the brain is, however intelligently educated and learned. It will always remain petty, do what it will; it can go to the moon and beyond or go down into the deepest parts of the earth; it can invent, put together the most complicated machines, computers that will invent computers; it can destroy itself and recreate itself but do what it will, it will ever remain petty. For it can only function in time and space; its philosophies are bound by its own conditioning; its theories, its speculations, are spun out of its own cunningness. It cannot escape from itself, do what it will. Its gods and its saviours, its masters and leaders are as small and petty as itself. If it's stupid, it tries to become clever and its cleverness is measured in terms of success. It is always pursuing or being chased. Its shadow is its own sorrow. Do what it will, it will ever remain petty.

Its action is the inaction of pursuing itself; its reform is action that ever needs further reform. It is held by its own action and inaction. It never sleeps and its dreams are the awakening of thought. However active, however noble or ignoble, it is petty. There is no end to its pettiness. It cannot run away from itself; its virtue is mean and its morality mean. There is only one thing it can do—be utterly and completely quiet. This quietness is not sleep or laziness. The brain is sensitive and to remain sensitive, without its familiar self-protective responses, without its customary judgments, condemnation and approval, the only thing it can do is to be utterly quiet, which is to remain in a state of negation, complete denial of itself and its activities. In this state of negation, it's no longer petty; then it is no longer gathering to achieve, to fulfil, to become. It is then what it is, mechanical, inventive, self-protective, calculating. A perfect machine is never petty and when it functions at that level it is a wonderful thing. Like all machines, it wears out and dies. It becomes petty when it proceeds to investigate the unknown, that which is not measurable. Its function is in the known and it cannot function in the unknown. Its creations are in the field of the known but the creation of the unknowable it can never capture, neither in paint nor in word; its beauty it can never know. Only when it is utterly quiet, silent without a word and still without a gesture, without movement, there is that immensity.

21st

The evening light was on the river and the traffic across the bridge was furious and fast. The pavement was crowded with people returning home after a day's work in offices. The river was sparkling; there were ripples, small ones pursuing each other, with such delight. You could almost hear them but the fury of the traffic was too much. Further down the river the light on the water was changing, becoming more deep and it would soon be dark. The moon was on the other side of the huge tower, looking so out of place, so artificial; it had no reality but the high steel tower had; there were people on it;

the restaurant up there was lit up and you could see crowds of people going into it. And as the night was hazy, the beams of the revolving lights were far stronger than the moon. Everything seemed so far away except the tower. How little we know about ourselves. We seem to know so much about other things, the distance to the moon, the atmosphere of Venus, how to put together the most extraordinary and complicated electronic brains, to break up the atoms and the minutest particle of matter. But we know so little about ourselves. To go to the moon is far more exciting than to go into ourselves; perhaps one's lazy or frightened, or it's not profitable, in the sense of money and success, to go into ourselves. It's a much longer journey than to go to the moon; no machines are available to take this journey and no one can help, no book, no theories, no guide. You have to do it yourself. You have to have much more energy than in inventing and putting together parts of a vast machine. You cannot get this energy through any drug, through any interaction of relationship nor through control, denial. No gods, rituals, beliefs, prayers can give it to you. On the contrary, in the very act of putting these aside, in being aware of their significance, that energy comes to penetrate into consciousness and beyond.

You can't buy that energy through accumulating knowledge about yourself. Every form of accumulation and the attachment to it, diminishes and perverts that energy. Knowledge about yourself binds, weighs, ties you down; there's no freedom to move, and you act and move within the limits of that knowledge. Learning about yourself is never the same as accumulating knowledge about yourself. Learning is active present and knowledge is the past; if you are learning in order to accumulate, it ceases to be learning; knowledge is static, more can be added to it or taken away from it, but learning is active, nothing can be added or taken away from it for there is no accumulation at any time. Knowing, learning about yourself has no beginning and no end, whereas knowledge has. Knowledge is finite, and learning, knowing, is infinite.

You are the accumulated result of the many thousand centuries of man, his hopes and desires, his guilts and anxieties, his beliefs and gods, his fulfilments and frustrations; you are all that and more additions made to it in recent times. Learning about all this, deep down and on the surface, is not mere verbal or intellectual statements of the obvious, the conclusions. Learning is the experiencing of these facts, emotionally and directly; to come into contact with them not theoretically, verbally, but actually, like a hungry man.

Learning is not possible if there's a learner; the learner is the accumulated, the past, the knowledge. There is a division between the learner and the thing he is learning about and so there is conflict between them. This conflict destroys, diminishes energy to learn, to pursue to the very end the total make-up of consciousness. Choice is conflict and choice prevents seeing; condemnation, judgment also prevent seeing. When this fact is seen, understood, not verbally, theoretically, but actually seen as fact, then learning is a moment to moment affair. And there is no end to learning; learning is all important, not the failures, successes and mistakes. There is only seeing and not the seer and the thing seen. Consciousness is limited; its very nature is restriction; it functions within the frame of its own existence, which is experience, knowledge, memory. Learning about this conditioning breaks down the frame; then thought and feeling have their limited function; they then cannot interfere with the wider and deeper issues of life. Where the self ends, with all its secret and open intrigues, its compulsive urges and demands, its joys and sorrows, there begins a movement of life that is beyond time and its bondage.

22nd

There is a little bridge across the river only meant for people; it is fairly quiet there. The river was full of light and a big

barge was going up, full of sand brought from the beaches;
it was fine, clean sand. There was a heap of it in the park,
purposely put there for children to play with. There were
several and they were making deep tunnels, a big castle with
a moat around it; they were having great fun. It was a
pleasant day, fairly cool, the sun not too strong and there
was dampness in the air; more trees were turning brown and
yellow and there was the smell of autumn. The trees were
getting ready for the winter; many branches were already
naked, black against the pale sky; every tree had its own
pattern of colour, in varying strength, from the russet brown
to pale yellow. Even in dying they were beautiful. It was a
pleasant evening full of light and peace, in spite of the roar
of the traffic.

There are a few flowers on the terrace, and this morning,
the yellow ones were more bright and eager than ever; in the
early morning light they seemed more awake and had more
colour, much more so than their neighbours. The east was
beginning to get brighter and there was that otherness in the
room; it had been there for some hours. On waking in the
middle of the night, it was there, something wholly objective
which no thought or imagination could possibly bring about.
Again, on waking the body was perfectly still, without any
movement as was also the brain. The brain was not dormant
but very much awake, watching without any interpretation.
It was the strength of unapproachable purity, with an energy
that was startling. It was there, ever new, ever penetrating.
It wasn't just outside there in the room or on the terrace, it
was inside and outside but there was no division. It was
something in which the whole mind and heart were caught
up and the mind and heart ceased to be.

There is no virtue, only humility; where it is, there is all
virtue. Social morality is not virtue; it is merely an adjustment to a pattern and that pattern varies and changes
according to time and climate. It is made respectable by
society and organized religion, but it is not virtue. Morality,

as recognized by church, society, is not virtue; morality is put together, it conforms; it can be taught and practised; it can be brought about through reward and punishment, through compulsion. Influence shapes morality as does propaganda. In the structure of society there are varying degrees of morality, of different shades. But it is not virtue. Virtue is not of time and influence; it cannot be cultivated; it is not the result of control and discipline; it is not a result at all as it has no cause. It cannot be made respectable. Virtue is not divisible as goodness, charity, brotherly love and so on. It is not the product of an environment, of social affluence or poverty nor of the monastery nor of any dogma. It is not born out of a cunning brain; it is not the outcome of thought and emotion; nor is it a revolt against social morality, with its respectability; a revolt is a reaction and a reaction is a modified continuity of what has been.

Humility cannot be cultivated; when it is, it is pride taking on the cloak of humility which has become respectable. Vanity can never become humility, any more than love can become hate. Violence cannot become non-violence; violence has to cease. Humility is not an ideal to be pursued; ideals have no reality; only what is has reality. Humility is not the opposite of pride; it has no opposite. All opposites are interrelated and humility has no relationship with pride. Pride has to end, not by any decision or discipline or for some profit; it ceases only in the flame of attention, not in the contradiction and confusion of concentration. To see pride, outwardly and inwardly, in its many forms, is the ending of it. To see it is to be attentive to every movement of pride; in attention there is no choice. There is attention only in the active present; it cannot be trained; if it is, then it becomes another cunning faculty of the brain and humility is not its product. There is attention when the brain is utterly still, alive and sensitive, but still. There is no centre from which to attend whereas concentration has a centre, with its exclusions. Attention, the complete and instant seeing of the whole significance of pride, ends pride. This awakened "state" is humility. Attention is virtue, for in it flowers goodness and charity. Without humility there is no virtue.

23rd
It was hot and rather oppressive, even in the gardens; it had been so hot for so long which was unusual. A good rain and cool weather will be pleasant. In the gardens they were watering the grass and in spite of the heat and lack of rain the grass was bright and sparkling and the flowers were splendid; there were some trees in flower, out of season, for winter will be here soon. Pigeons were all over the place, shyly avoiding the children and some of the children were chasing them for fun and the pigeons knew it. The sun was red in a dull, heavy sky; there was no colour except in the flowers and in the grass. The river was opaque and indolent.

Meditation at that hour was freedom and it was like entering into an unknown world of beauty and quietness; it is a world without image, symbol or word, without waves of memory. Love was the death of every minute and each death was the renewing of love. It was not attachment, it had no roots; it flowered without cause and it was a flame that burned away the borders, the carefully built fences of consciousness. It was beauty beyond thought and feeling; it was not put together on canvas, in words or in marble. Meditation was joy and with it came a benediction.

It's very odd how each one craves power, the power of money, position, capacity, knowledge. In gaining power, there's conflict, confusion and sorrow. The hermit and the politician, the housewife and the scientist are seeking it. They will kill and destroy each other to get it. The ascetics through self-denial, control, suppression gain that power; the politician by his word, capacity, cleverness derives that power; the domination of the wife over the husband and he over her feel this power; the priest who has assumed, who has taken upon himself the responsibility of his god, knows this power. Everyone seeks this power or wants to be associated with divine or worldly power. Power breeds authority and with it comes conflict, confusion and sorrow. Authority corrupts him that has it and those that are near it or seeking it. The power of the priest and the housewife, of the leader and the efficient organizer, of the saint and the local politician is evil; the more power the greater the evil. It is a disease that every man catches and cherishes and worships. But with it comes always endless conflict, confusion and sorrow. But no one will deny it, put it aside.

With it goes ambition and success and a ruthlessness that has been made respectable and so acceptable. Every society, temple and church gives it its blessing and so love is perverted and destroyed. And envy is worshipped and competition is moral. But with it all comes fear, war and sorrow, but yet no man will put these aside. To deny power, in every form, is the beginning of virtue; virtue is clarity; it wipes away conflict and sorrow. This corrupting energy, with its endless cunning activities, always brings its inevitable mischief and misery; there is no end to it; however much it is reformed and fenced in, by law or by moral convention, it will find its way out, darkly and unbidden. For it is there, hidden in the secret corners of one's thoughts and desires. It is these that must be examined and understood if there is to be no conflict, confusion and sorrow. Each one has to do this, not through another, not through any system of reward or punishment. Each one has to be aware of the fabric of his own make-up. To see what is, is the ending of that which is.

With the complete ending of this power, with its confusion, conflict and sorrow, each one faces what he is, a bundle of memories and deepening loneliness. The desire for power and success are an escape from this loneliness and the ashes which are memories. To go beyond, one has to see them, face them, not avoid them in any way, by condemning or through fear of what is. Fear arises only in the very act of running away from the fact, the what is. One must completely and utterly, voluntarily and easily put aside power and success and then in facing, seeing, being passively aware, without choice, the ashes and loneliness have a wholly different significance. To live with something is to love it, not to be attached. To live with the ashes of loneliness there must be great energy and this energy comes when there is no longer fear.

When you have gone through this loneliness, as you would go through a physical door, then you will realise that you and the loneliness are one, you are not the observer watching that feeling which is beyond the word. You are that. And you cannot get away from it as you did before in many subtle ways. You are that loneliness; there is no way to avoid it and nothing can cover it or fill it. Then only are you living with it; it is part of you, it is the whole of you. Neither despair nor hope can banish it nor any cynicism nor any intellectual cunning. You are that loneliness, the ashes that had once been fire. This is complete loneliness, irremediable, beyond all action. The brain can no longer devise ways and means of escape; it is the creator of this loneliness, through its incessant activities of self-isolation, of defence and aggression. When it is aware of this, negatively, without any choice, then it is willing to die, to be utterly still.

Out of this loneliness, out of these ashes, a new movement is born. It is the movement of the alone. It is that state when all influences, all compulsion, every form of search and achievement have naturally and completely stopped. It is death of the known. Then only is there the never-ending journey of the unknowable. Then is there power whose purity is creation.

24th*

There was a beautifully kept lawn, not too large and it was incredibly green; it was behind an iron grill, well watered,

* He gave his last talk in Paris on this day.

carefully looked after, rolled and splendidly alive, sparkling in its beauty. It must have been many hundred years old; not even a chair was on it, isolated and guarded by a high and narrow railing. At the end of the lawn, was a single rose bush, with a single red rose in full bloom. It was a miracle, the soft lawn and the single rose; they were there apart from the whole world of noise, chaos and misery; though man had put them there, they were the most beautiful things, far beyond the museums, towers and the graceful line of bridges. They were splendid in their splendid aloofness. They were what they were, grass and flower and nothing else. There was great beauty and quietness about them and the dignity of purity. It was a hot afternoon, with no breeze and the smell of exhaust of so many cars was in the air but there the grass had a smell of its own and one could almost smell the perfume of the solitary rose.

On waking so early, with the full moon coming into the room, the quality of the brain was different. It wasn't asleep nor heavy with sleep; it was fully awake, watching; it wasn't watching itself but something beyond itself. It was aware, aware of itself as a part of a whole movement of the mind. The brain functions in fragmentation; it functions in part, in division. It specializes. It's never the whole; it tries to capture the whole, to understand it but it cannot. By its very nature, thought is always incomplete, as is feeling; thought, the response of memory, can function only in the known things or interpret from what it has known, knowledge. The brain is the product of specialization; it cannot go beyond itself. It divides and specializes—the scientist, the artist, the priest, the lawyer, the technician, the farmer. In functioning, it projects its own status, the privileges, the power, the prestige. Function and status go together for the brain is a self-protective organism. From the demand for status begins the opposing and contradictory elements in society. The specialist cannot see the whole.

25th

Meditation is the flowering of understanding. Understanding is not within the borders of time, time never brings understanding. Understanding is not a gradual process to be gathered little by little, with care and patience. Understanding is now or never; it is a destructive flash, not a tame affair; it is this shattering that one is afraid of and so one avoids it, knowingly or unknowingly. Understanding may alter the course of one's life, the way of thought and action; it may be pleasant or not but understanding is a danger to all relationship. But without understanding, sorrow will continue. Sorrow ends only through self-knowing, the awareness of every thought and feeling, every movement of the conscious and that which is hidden. Meditation is the understanding of consciousness, the hidden and the open, and of the movement that lies beyond all thought and feeling.

The specialist cannot perceive the whole; his heaven is what he specializes in but his heaven is a petty affair of the brain, the heaven of religion or of the technician. Capacity, gift, is obviously detrimental, for it strengthens self-centredness; it is fragmentary and so breeds conflict. Capacity has significance only in the total perception of life which is in the field of the mind and not of the brain. Capacity and its function is within the limits of the brain and so becomes ruthless, indifferent to the total process of life. Capacity breeds pride, envy, and its fulfilment becomes all important and so it brings about confusion, enmity and sorrow; it has its meaning only in the total awareness of life. Life is not merely at one fragmentary level, bread, sex, prosperity, ambition; life is not fragmentary; when it's made to be, it becomes utterly a matter of despair and endless misery. Brain functions in specialization of the fragment, in self-isolating activities and within the limited field of time. It is incapable of seeing the whole of life; the brain is a part, however educated it be; it is not the whole. Mind alone sees the whole and within the field of the mind is the brain; the brain cannot contain the mind, do what it will.

To see wholly, the brain has to be in a state of negation. Negation is not the opposite of the positive; all opposites are related within the fold of each other. Negation has no opposite. The brain has to be in a state of negation for total seeing; it must not interfere, with its evaluations and justifications, with its condemnations and defences. It has to be still, not made still by compulsion of any kind, for then it is a dead brain, merely imitating and conforming. When it is in a state of negation, it is choicelessly still. Only then is there total seeing. In this total seeing which is the quality of the mind, there is no seer, no observer, no experiencer; there's only seeing. The mind then is completely awake. In this fully wakened state, there is no observer and the observed; there is only light, clarity. The contradiction and conflict between the thinker and thought ceases.

27th*

Walking along the pavement overlooking the biggest basilica and down the famous steps to a fountain and many picked flowers of so many colours, crossing the crowded square, we went along a narrow one-way street [via Margutta], quiet, with not too many cars; there in that dimly lit street, with few unfashionable shops, suddenly and most unexpectedly, that otherness came with such intense tenderness and beauty that one's body and brain became motionless. For some days now, it had not made its immense presence felt; it was there vaguely, in the distance, a whisper but there the immense was manifesting itself, sharply and with waiting patience. Thought and speech were gone and there was peculiar joy and clarity. It followed down the long, narrow street till the roar of traffic and the over-crowded pavement swallowed us all. It was a benediction that was beyond all image and thoughts.

* He was now in Rome. He had flown there on the 25th.

28th

At odd and unexpected moments, the otherness has come, suddenly and unexpectedly and went its way, without invitation and without need. All need and demand must wholly cease for it to be.

Meditation, in the still hours of early morning, with no car rattling by, was the unfolding of beauty. It was not thought exploring with its limited capacity nor the sensitivity of feeling; it was not any outward or inward substance which was expressing itself; it was not the movement of time, for the brain was still. It was total negation of everything known, not a reaction but a denial that had no cause; it was a movement in complete freedom, a movement that had no direction and dimension; in that movement there was boundless energy whose very essence was stillness. Its action was total inaction and the essence of that inaction is freedom. There was great bliss, a great ecstasy that perished at the touch of thought.

30th

The sun was setting in great clouds of colour behind the Roman hills; they were brilliant, splashed across the sky and the whole earth was made splendid, even the telegraph poles and the endless rows of building. It was soon becoming dark and the car was going fast.* The hills faded and the country became flat. To look with thought and to look without thought are two different things. To look at those trees by the roadside and the buildings across the dry fields with thought, keeps the brain tied to its own moorings of time, experience, memory; the machinery of thought is working endlessly, without rest, without freshness; the brain is made dull, insensitive, without the power of recuperation. It is everlastingly responding to challenge and its response is inadequate and not fresh. To look with thought keeps the

* On the way to Circeo, near the sea, between Rome and Naples.

brain in the groove of habit and recognition; it becomes tired and sluggish; it lives within the narrow limitations of its own making. It is never free. This freedom takes place when thought is not looking; to look without thought does not mean a blank observation, absence in distraction. When thought does not look, then there is only observation, without the mechanical process of recognition and comparison, justification and condemnation; this seeing does not fatigue the brain for all mechanical processes of time have stopped. Through complete rest the brain is made fresh, to respond without reaction, to live without deterioration, to die without the torture of problems. To look without thought is to see without the interference of time, knowledge and conflict. This freedom to see is not a reaction; all reactions have causes; to look without reaction is not indifference, aloofness, a cold-blooded withdrawal. To see without the mechanism of thought is total seeing, without particularization and division, which does not mean that there is not separation and dissimilarity. The tree does not become a house or the house a tree. Seeing without thought does not put the brain to sleep; on the contrary, it is fully awake, attentive, without friction and pain. Attention without the borders of time is the flowering of meditation.

October 3rd
The clouds were magnificent; the horizon was filled with them, except in the west where the sky was clear. Some were black, heavy with thunder and rain; others were pure white, full of light and splendour. They were of every shape and size, delicate, threatening, billowy; they were piled up one against the other, with immense power and beauty. They seemed motionless but there was violent movement within them and nothing could stop their shattering immensity. A gentle wind was blowing from the west, driving these vast, mountainous clouds against the hills; the hills were giving shape to the clouds and they were moving with these clouds

of darkness and light. The hills with their scattered villages, were waiting for the rains that were so long in coming; they would soon be green again and the trees would soon lose their leaves with the coming winter. The road was straight with shapely trees on either side and the car was holding the road at great speed, even at the curves; the car was made to go fast and to hold the road and it was performing very well that morning.* It was shaped for speed, low, hugging the road. We were too soon leaving the country and entering into the town [Rome] but those clouds were there, immense, furious and waiting.

In the middle of the night [at Circeo], when it was utterly quiet, save for an occasional hoot of an owl which was calling without a reply, in a little house in the woods,† meditation was pure delight, without a flutter of thought, with its endless subtleties; it was a movement that had no end and every movement of the brain was still, watching from emptiness. It was an emptiness that had known no knowing; it was emptiness that had known no space; it was empty of time. It was empty, past all seeing, knowing and being. In this emptiness there was fury; the fury of a storm, the fury of exploding universe, the fury of creation which could never have any expression. It was the fury of all life, death and love. But yet it was empty, a vast, boundless emptiness which nothing could ever fill, transform or cover up. Meditation was the ecstasy of this emptiness.

The subtle inter-relationship of the mind, the brain and the body is the complicated play of life. There is misery when one predominates over the other and the mind cannot dominate the brain or the physical organism; when there is harmony between the two, then the mind can consent to

* On the way back to Rome from Circeo where he had spent three nights in the hotel la Baya d'argento.

† One of the little cottages belonging to the hotel at Circeo, situated in a wood-garden. It was very quiet there. Each cottage contained two bedrooms, a bathroom and sitting-room.

abide with them; it is not a plaything of either. The whole can contain the particular but the little, the part, can never formulate the whole. It is incredibly subtle for the two to live together in complete harmony, without one or the other forcing, choosing, dominating. The intellect can and does destroy the body and the body with its dullness, insensitivity can pervert, bring about the deterioration of the intellect. The neglect of the body with its indulgence and demanding tastes, with its appetites can make the body heavy and insensitive and so make dull thought. And thought becoming more refined, more cunning can and does neglect the demands of the body which then sets about to pervert thought. A fat, gross body does interfere with the subtleties of thought, and thought, escaping from the conflicts and problems it has bred, does make the body a perverse thing. The body and the brain have to be sensitive and in harmony to be with the incredible subtleness of the mind which is ever explosive and destructive. The mind is not a plaything of the brain, whose function is mechanical.

When the absolute necessity of complete harmony of the brain and body is seen, then the brain will watch over the body, not dominating it and this very watching sharpens the brain and makes the body sensitive. The seeing is the fact and with the fact there is no bargaining; it can be put aside, denied, avoided but it still remains a fact. The understanding of the fact is essential and not the evaluation of the fact. When the fact is seen, then the brain is watchful of the habits, the degenerating factors of the body. Then thought does not impose a discipline on the body nor control it; for discipline, control makes for insensitivity and any form of insensitivity is deterioration, a withering away.

Again on waking, when there were no cars roaring up the hill and the smell of a small wood near by was in the air* and

* He was staying in Rome in the via dei colli della Farnesina, a new road with very little traffic on it; the small wood was across the way.

rain was tapping on the window, there was that otherness again filling the room; it was intense and there was a sense of fury; it was the fury of a storm, of a full, roaring river, the fury of innocency. It was there in the room with such abundance that every form of meditation came to an end and the brain was looking, feeling out of its own emptiness. It lasted for considerable time and in spite of the fury of its intensity or because of it. The brain remained empty, full of that otherness. It shattered everything that one thought of, that one felt or saw; it was an emptiness in which nothing existed. It was complete destruction.

4th
The train [to Florence] was going very fast, over ninety miles an hour; the towns on the hills were familiar and the lake [Trasimenus] seemed a friend. It was a familiar country, the olive and the cypress and the road that followed the railway. It was raining and the earth was glad of it, for months had passed without rain and now there were new shoots of green and the rivers were running brown, fast and full. The train was following the valleys, shouting at the crossroads, and the workmen labouring along the metalled way stopped and waved as the train slowed down. It was a pleasant cool morning and autumn was turning many leaves brown and yellow; they were ploughing deep for the winter sowing and the hills seemed so friendly, never too high, gentle and old. The train was again running very fast and the drivers of this electric train welcomed us and asked us to come into their cab for we had met several times in several years; before the train started they said we must come and see them; they were as friendly as the rivers and the hills. From their window the country was open and the hills with their towns and the river that we were following seemed to be waiting for the familiar roar of their train. The sun was touching a few of the hills and there was a smile upon the face of the land. As we raced north, the sky was becoming clear and the cypress

and the olive against the blue sky were delicate in their splendour. The earth, as ever, was beautiful.

It was deep in the night when meditation was filling the spaces of the brain and beyond. Meditation is not a conflict, a war between what is and what should be; there was no control and so no distraction. There was no contradiction between the thinker and the thought for neither existed. There was only seeing without the observer; this seeing came out of emptiness and that emptiness had no cause. All causation breeds inaction, which is called action.

How strange love is and how respectable it has become, the love of God, the love of the neighbour, the love of the family. How neatly it has been divided, the profane and the sacred; duty and responsibility; obedience and the willingness to die and to deal out death. The priests talk of it and so do the generals, planning wars; the politicians and the housewife everlastingly complain about it. Jealousy and envy nourish love, and relationship is held in its prison. They have it on the screen and in the magazine and every radio and television blares it out. When death takes away love there is the photo in the frame or the image which memory keeps on revising or it is tightly held in belief. Generation after generation is bred upon this and sorrow goes on without an end.

Continuity of love is pleasure and with it comes always pain but we try to avoid the one and cling to the other. This continuity is the stability and security in relationship, and in relationship there must be no change for relationship is habit and in habit there is security and sorrow. To this unending machinery of pleasure and pain we cling and this thing is called love. To escape from its weariness, there is religion and romanticism. The word changes and becomes modified with each one but romanticism offers a marvellous escape from the fact of pleasure and sorrow. And, of course, the ultimate refuge and hope is God who has become so very respectable and profitable.

But all this isn't love. Love has no continuity; it cannot

be carried over to tomorrow; it has no future. What has is memory, and memories are ashes of everything dead and buried. Love has no tomorrow; it cannot be caught in time and made respectable. It is there when time is not. It has no promise, no hope; hope breeds despair. It belongs to no god and so to no thought and feeling. It is not conjured up by the brain. It lives and dies each minute. Is a terrible thing, for love is destruction. It is destruction without tomorrow. Love is destruction.

5th
There is a huge, tall tree in the garden,* it has an enormous trunk and during the night its dry leaves were noisy in the autumnal wind; every tree in the garden was alive, rustling, and winter was still far away; they were all whispering, shouting and the wind was restless. But the tree dominated the garden; it towered over the four-storey house and the river [the Mugnone] fed it. It was not one of those large rivers, sweeping and dangerous; its life had been made famous and it curves in and out of the valleys and enters the sea, some distance away. There is always water in it and there are fishermen hanging over the bridges and along its banks. In the night the small waterfall complains a great deal and its noise fills the air; the rustle of leaves, the waterfall and the restless wind seem to be talking to each other a great deal. It was a lovely morning with a blue sky and a few clouds scattered about; there are two cypresses beyond all others that stand clear against the sky.

Again, well after midnight, when the wind was noisy among the trees, meditation became a fierce explosion, destroying all the things of the brain; every thought shapes every response and limits action. Action born of idea is non-action; such non-action breeds conflict and sorrow. It was in the still moment of meditation that there was strength.

* An ilex. He was staying in a villa, Il Leccio, north of Florence, above Fiesole.

Strength is not the many threads of will; will is resistance and the action of will breeds confusion and sorrow, within and without. Strength is not the opposite of weakness; all opposites contain their own contradiction.

7th

It had begun to rain and the sky was heavy with clouds; before the sky was covered over entirely immense clouds filled the horizon and it was a marvellous thing to see them. They were so immense and peaceful; it was the peace of enormous power and strength. And the Tuscan hills were so close to them, waiting for their fury. It came during the night, shattering thunder and lightning that showed every leaf aquiver with wind and life. It was a splendid night full of storm, life and immensity. All the afternoon the otherness had been coming, in the car and in the street. It was there most of the night and early this morning, long before dawn, when meditation was making its way into the unknown depths and heights; it was there with insistent fury. Meditation yielded to the otherness. It was there in the room, with the branches of that huge tree in the garden; it was there with such incredible power and life that the very bones felt it; it seemed to press right through one and made the body and brain completely motionless. It had been there all night in a mild and gentle way and sleep became a very light affair, but as dawn was coming near, it became a crushing, penetrating power. The body and the brain were very alert, listening to the rustle of leaves and seeing the dawn coming through the dark branches of a tall, straight pine. It had great tenderness and beauty that was past and beyond all thought and emotion. It was there and with it was benediction.

Strength is not the opposite of weakness; all opposites breed further opposites. Strength is not an event of will and will is action in contradiction. There is a strength that has no cause, that is not put together through multiple decisions. It is that strength that exists in negation and denial; it is that strength that comes into being out of total aloneness. It is that strength which comes when all conflict and effort have completely ceased. It is there when all thought and feeling have come to an end and there is only seeing. It is there when ambition, greed, envy have come to an end without any compulsion; they wither away with understanding. There is that strength when love is death and death life. The essence of strength is humility.

How strong is the new-born leaf in spring, so vulnerable, so easily destroyed. Vulnerability is the essence of virtue. Virtue is never strong; it cannot stand the glare of respectability and the vanity of the intellect. Virtue is not a mechanical continuity of an idea, of thought in habit. The strength of virtue is that it is easily destroyed to be reborn again anew. Strength and virtue go together for neither can exist without the other. They can only survive in emptiness.

8th

It had been raining all day; the roads were slushy and there was more brown water in the river and the slight fall of the river was making more noise. It was a still night, an invitation to the rains which never stopped till early this morning. And the sun suddenly came out and towards the west the sky was blue, rain washed and clean, with those enormous clouds full of light and splendour. It was a beautiful morning and looking to the west, with the sky so intensely blue, all thought and emotion disappeared and the seeing was from emptiness.

Before dawn, meditation was the immense opening into the unknown. Nothing can open the door save the complete destruction of the known. Meditation is explosion in understanding. There is no understanding without self-knowing; learning about the self is not accumulating knowledge about it; gathering of knowledge prevents learning; learning is not an additive process; learning is from moment to moment, as is understanding. This total process of learning is explosion in meditation.

9th

Early this morning, the sky was without a cloud; the sun was coming up behind the Tuscan hills, grey with olive, with dark cypress. There were no shadows on the river and the aspen leaves were still. A few birds that had not yet migrated were chattering and the river seemed motionless; as the sun came up behind the river it cast long shadows on the quiet water.* But a gentle breeze was coming over the hills and through the valleys; it was among the leaves, setting them trembling and dancing with the morning sun on them. There were long and short shadows, fat ones and little ones on the brown sparkling waters; a solitary chimney began to smoke, grey fumes carrying across the trees. It was a lovely morning, full of enchantment and beauty, there were so many shadows and so many leaves trembling. There was perfume in the air and though it was an autumnal sun there was the breath of spring. A small car was going up the hill, making an awful noise but a thousand shadows remained motionless. It was a lovely morning.

In the afternoon yesterday, it began suddenly, in a room overlooking a noisy street;† the strength and the beauty of the otherness was spreading from the room outward over the traffic, past the gardens and beyond the hills. It was there immense and impenetrable; it was there in the afternoon, and just as one was getting into bed it was there with furious intensity, a benediction of great holiness. There is no getting used to it for it is always different, there's something always new, a new quality, a subtle significance, a new light, something that had not been seen before. It was not a thing to be stored up, remembered and examined, at leisure; it was there and no thought could approach for the brain was still and there was no time, to experience, to store up. It was there and all thought became still.

The intense energy of life is always there, night and day.

* A little pond formed by the stream in a wood.
† An apartment in Florence where he was paying a visit.

It is without friction, without direction, without choice and effort. It is there with such intensity that thought and feeling cannot capture it to mould it according to their fancies, beliefs, experiences and demands. It is there with such abundance that nothing can diminish it. But we try to use it, to give it direction, to capture it within the mould of our existence and thereby twist it to conform to our pattern, experience and knowledge. It is ambition, envy, greed that narrow down its energy and so there is conflict and sorrow; the cruelty of ambition, personal or collective, distorts its intensity, causing hatred, antagonism, conflict. Every action of envy perverts this energy, causing discontent, misery, fear; with fear there is guilt and anxiety and the never ending misery of comparison and imitation. It is this perverted energy that makes the priest and the general, the politician and the thief. This boundless energy made incomplete by our desire for permanency and security is the soil in which grow barren ideas, competition, cruelty and war; it is the cause of everlasting conflict between man and man.

When all this is put aside, with ease and without effort, then only is there that intense energy which can only exist and flower in freedom. In freedom alone, it causes no conflict and sorrow; then alone it increases and has no end. It is life that has no beginning and no end; it is creation which is love, destruction.

Energy used in one direction leads to one thing, conflict and sorrow; energy that is the expression of total life is bliss beyond measure.

12th
The sky was yellow in the setting sun and the dark cypress and the grey olive were startlingly beautiful, and down below the winding river was golden. It was a splendid evening, full of light and silence. From that height* you could see the city

* From S. Miniato al Monte on the south side of the Arno.

in the valley, the dome and the beautiful campanile and the river curving through the town. Going down the incline and down the steps, one felt the great beauty of the evening; there were few people and the odd, restless tourists had passed by there earlier, always chattering, taking photos and hardly ever seeing. There was perfume in the air and as the sun went down, the silence became intense, rich and unfathomable. Out of this silence only, there is seeing, listening really, and out of this came meditation, though the little car went down the curving road noisily, with a great many bumps. There were two Roman pines against the yellowing sky and though one had seen them often before it was as if they were never seen; the gentle sloping hill was silver-grey with the olive and the darkly solitary cypress was everywhere. Meditation was explosion, not carefully planned, contrived and joined together with determined pursuit. It was an explosion without leaving any remnant of the past. It exploded time, and time never need again stop. In this explosion everything was without shadow and to see without shadow is to see beyond time. It was a marvellous evening so full of humour and space. The noisy town with its lights and the smooth running train were in this vast silence and its beauty was everywhere.

The train, going south [back to Rome] was crowded with many tourists and businessmen; they were endlessly smoking, eating heavily when the meal was served. The country was beautiful, rain washed, fresh and there was not a cloud in the sky. There were old walled towns on the hills and the lake of many memories was blue, without a ripple; the rich land yielded to poor and arid soil and the farms seemed less prosperous, the chickens were thinner, there were no cattle about and there were few sheep. The train was going fast trying to make up the time that it had lost. It was a marvellous day and there in that smoky compartment, with passengers that hardly looked out of the window, there was that otherness. All that night, it was there with such intensity that the brain felt its pressure. It was as though at the very centre of all existence, it was operating in its purity and immensity. The brain watched, as it was watching the scene racing by, and in this very act, it went beyond its own limitations. And during the night at odd moments, meditation was a fire of explosion.

13th

The skies are clear, the small wood across the way is full of light and shadows. Early in the morning before the sun showed over the hill, when dawn was still on the land and there were no cars going up the hill, meditation was inexhaustible. Thought is always limited, it cannot go very far, for it is rooted in memory, and when it does go far, it becomes merely speculative, imaginative, without validity. Thought cannot find what is and what is not beyond its own borders of time; thought is time-binding. Thought unravelling itself, untangling itself from the net of its own making is not the total movement of meditation. Thought in conflict with itself is not meditation; the ending of thought and the beginning of the new is meditation. The sun was making patterns on the wall, cars were coming up the hill and presently the workmen were whistling and singing on the new building across the way.

The brain is restless, an astonishingly sensitive instrument. It's always receiving impressions, interpreting them, storing them away; it is never still, waking or sleeping. Its concern is survival and security, the inherited animal responses; on the basis of these, its cunning devices are built, within and without; its gods, its virtues, its moralities are its defences; its ambitions, desires, compulsions and conformities are the urges of survival and security. Being highly sensitive, the brain with its machinery of thought, begins the cultivation of time, the yesterdays, the today and the many tomorrows; this gives it an opportunity of postponement and fulfilment; the postponement, the ideal and the fulfilment are the continuity of itself. But in this there is always sorrow; from this there is the flight into belief, dogma, action and into multiple forms of entertainment, including the religious rituals. But there is always death and its fear; thought then seeks comfort and escape in rational and irrational beliefs, hopes, conclusions. Words and theories become amazingly important, living on these and building its whole structure of existence on these feelings which words and conclusions arouse. The brain and its thought function at a very superficial level, however deeply thought may have hoped it has journeyed. For thought, however experienced, however clever and erudite, is superficial. The brain and its activities are a fragment of the whole totality of life; the fragment has become completely important to itself and its relationship to other fragments. This fragmentation and the contradiction it breeds is its very existence; it cannot understand the whole and when it attempts to formulate the totality of life, it can only think in terms of opposites and reactions which only breed conflict, confusion and misery.

Thought can never understand or formulate the whole of life. Only when the brain and its thought are completely still, not asleep or drugged by discipline, compulsion, or hypnotized, then only is there the awarenes of the whole. The brain which is so astonishingly sensitive can be still, still in its sensitivity, widely and deeply attentive but entirely quiet. When time and its measure cease then only is there the whole, the unknowable.

14th

In the gardens [of the Villa Borghese], right in the middle of the noisy and smelly town, with its flat pines and many trees, turning yellow and brown and the smell of damp ground, there, walking with certain seriousness, was the awareness of the otherness. It was there with great beauty and tenderness; it was not that one was thinking about it—it avoids all thought—but it was there so abundantly that it caused surprise and great delight. Seriousness of thought is so *frag-*

mentary and immature but there must be seriousness which is not the product of desire. There is a seriousness that has the quality of light whose very nature is to penetrate, a light that has no shadow; this seriousness is infinitely pliable and therefore joyous. It was there and every tree and leaf, every blade of grass and flower became intensely alive and splendid; colour intense and the sky immeasurable. The earth, moist and leaf-strewn, was life.

15th

The morning sun is on the little wood on the other side of the road; it is a quiet, peaceful morning, soft, the sun not too hot and the air is fresh and cool. Every tree is so fascinatingly alive, with so many colours and there are so many shadows; they are all calling and waiting. Long before the sun was up, when it was quiet with no car going up the hill, meditation was a movement in benediction. This movement flowed into the otherness, for it was there in the room, filling it and over-flowing it, outward and beyond, without end. There was in it a depth that was unfathomable, of such immensity and there was peace. This peace never knew conflict, was un-contaminated by thought and time. It was not the peace of ultimate finality; it was something that was tremendously and dangerously alive. And it was without defence. Every form of resistance is violence, so also is concession. It was not the peace that conflict engenders; it was beyond all conflict and its opposites. It was not the fruit of satisfaction and discontent, in which are the seeds of deterioration.

16th

It was before dawn, when there was no noise and the city was still asleep, that the waking brain became quiet for the otherness was there. It came in so quietly and with hesitant care for there was sleep still in the eyes but there was great delight, the delight of great simplicity and purity.

18th

On the plane.* There was thunder and a great downpour of
rain; it woke one up in the middle of the night [in Rome]
and the rain was beating on the window and among the trees
across the road. The day had been hot and the air was now
pleasantly cool; the town was asleep and the storm had taken
over. The roads were wet and there was hardly any traffic
so early in the morning; the sky was still heavy with clouds
and dawn was over the land. The church [S. Giovanni in
Laterano] with its golden mosaic was bright with artificial
light. The airport was far away† and the powerful car was
running beautifully; it was trying to race the clouds. It passed
the few cars that were on the road and hugged the road
round every corner at high speed. It had been held too long
in the city and now it was on the open road. And there was
the airport too soon. The smell of the sea and the damp earth
was in the air; the freshly ploughed fields were dark and the
green of the trees so bright, though autumn had touched a
few leaves; the wind was blowing from the west and there
would be no sun during all that day on the land. Every leaf
was washed clean and there was beauty and peace on the
land.

In the middle of the night, when it was quiet after thunder
and lightning, the brain was utterly still and meditation was
an opening into immeasurable emptiness. The very sensitivity
of the brain made it still; it was still for no cause; the action
of stillness with cause is disintegration. It was so still that the
limited space of a room had disappeared and time had
stopped. There was only an awakened attention, with a centre
which was attentive; it was the attention in which the origin
of thought had ceased, without any violence, naturally, easily.
It could hear the rain and movement in the next room; it was
listening without any interpretation and watching without

* Flying to Bombay where he arrived on the 20th. There is
no entry for the 19th.

† Ciampino. The airport at Fiumincino had not yet been built.

knowledge. The body was also motionless. Meditation yielded
to the otherness; it was of shattering purity. Its purity left no
residue; it was there, that is all and nothing existed. As there
was nothing, it was. It was the purity of all essence. This
peace is a vast, boundless space, of immeasurable emptiness.

20th

The sea, far below, nearly forty thousand feet below, seemed
to be without a wave, so calm, so vast, so empty of any movement; the desert, the burning red hills, treeless, beautiful and
pitiless; more sea and the distant lights of the town where all
the passengers were getting down; the clamour, the mountain
of bags, inspection and the long drive through ill-lit streets
and the pavement crowded with ever increasing population;
the many penetrating odours, the shrill voices, the decorated
temples, cars festooned with flowers, for it was a day of
festival, the rich houses, the dark slums and down a steep
incline, the car stopped and the door was opened.

There is a tree full of green bright leaves, very quiet in its
purity and dignity, surrounded by houses that are ill pro-
portioned with people that have never looked at it or one
single leaf of it. But they make money, go to offices, drink,
beget children and eat enormously. There was a moon over
it last night and all the splendid darkness was alive. And
waking towards dawn, meditation was the splendour of light
for the otherness was there, in an unfamiliar room. Again it
was an imminent and urgent peace, not the peace of politicians or of the priests nor of the contented; it was too vast to
be contained in space and time, to be formulated by thought
or feeling. It was the weight of the earth and the things upon
it; it was the heavens and beyond it. Man has to cease for it
to be.

Time is always repeating its challenge and its problems; the
responses and answers are concerned with the immediate. We
are taken up with the immediate challenge and with the immediate reply to it. This immediate answer to the immediate

call is worldliness, with all its indissoluble problems and agonies; the intellectual answers with action born of ideas which have their roots in time, in the immediate, and the thoughtless, amazed, follow him; the priest of the well-organized religion of propaganda and belief responds to the challenge according to what he has been taught; the rest follow the pattern of like and dislike, of prejudice and malice. And every argument and gesture is the continuity of despair, sorrow and confusion. There is no end to it. To turn your back on it all, calling this activity by different names, is not to end it. It is there whether you deny it or not; whether you have critically analysed it or whether you say the whole thing is an illusion, maya. It is there and you are always measuring it. It is these immediate answers to a series of immediate calls that has to come to an end. Then you will answer from the emptiness of no time to the immediate demand of time or you may not answer at all which may be the true response. All reply of thought and emotion will only prolong the despair and the agony of problems that have no answers; the final answer is beyond the immediate.

In the immediate is all your hope, vanity and ambition, whether that immediacy is projected into the future of many tomorrows or in the now. This is the way of sorrow. The ending of sorrow is never in the immediate response to the many challenges. The ending lies in seeing this fact.

21st

The palms were swaying with great dignity, bending with pleasure in the westerly breeze from the sea; they seemed so far away from the noisy crowded street. Against the evening sky, they were dark, their tall trunks were shapely, made slender with many years of patient work; they dominated the evening of stars and the warm sea. They almost stretched their palms to receive you, to snatch you away from the sordid street but the evening breeze took them away to fill the sky with their movement. The street was crowded; it would never be clean, too many people had spat on it; its walls were made filthy with the announcements of latest films; they were plastered with names to whom you must give your vote, the party symbols; it was a sordid street though it was one of the main thoroughfares; unwashed buses roared by; taxis honked at you and many dogs seemed to have passed by. A little further on was the sea and the setting sun. It was a round red ball of fire, it had been a scorching day; it made the sea and the few clouds red. The sea was without a ripple but it was restless and dreamy. It was too hot to be a pleasant evening and the breeze seemed to have forgotten its delight. Along that sordid street, with people pushing into you, meditation was the very essence of life. The brain so delicate and observant was completely still, watching the stars, aware of the people, the smells, the barking of the dogs. A single yellow leaf was falling on the dirty road and the passing car destroyed it; it was so full of colour and beauty and destroyed so easily.

As one walked along the street of few palms, the otherness came like a wave that purified and strengthened; it was there like a perfume, a breath of immensity. There was no senti- ment, the romance of illusion or the brittleness of thought; it was there, sharp and clear, without any vague possibility, unhesitating, definite. It was there, a holy thing and nothing could touch it, nothing could break its finality. The brain was aware of the closeness of the passing buses, the wet street and the squealing brakes; it was aware of all these things and, beyond, the sea, but the brain had no relation to any of these things; it was completely empty, without any roots, watching, observing out of this emptiness. The otherness was pressing in with sharp urgency. It was not a feeling, a sensation but as factual as the man who was calling. It was not an emotion that changes, varies and continues, and thought could not touch it. It was there with the finality of death which no reason could dissuade. As it had no roots and relation, nothing could contaminate it; it was indestructible.

23rd

The complete stillness of the brain is an extraordinary thing; it is highly sensitive, vigorous, fully alive, aware of every outward movement but utterly still. It is still as it is completely open, without any hindrance, without any secret wants and pursuits; it is still as there is no conflict which is essentially a state of contradiction. It is utterly still in emptiness; this emptiness is not a state of vacuum, a blankness; it is energy without a centre, without a border. Walking down the crowded street, smelly and sordid, with the buses roaring by, the brain was aware of the things about it and the body was walking along, sensitive, alive to the smells, to the dirt, to the sweating labourers but there was no centre from which watching, directing, censoring took place. During the whole of that mile and back the brain was without a movement, as thought and feeling; the body was getting tired, unaccustomed to the frightful heat and humidity though the sun had set some time ago. It was a strange phenomenon though it had happened several times before. One can never get used to any of these things for it is not a thing of habit and desire. It is always surprising, after it is over.

The crowded plane [to Madras] was hot and even at that height, about eight thousand feet up, it never seemed to get cool. In that morning plane, suddenly and most unexpectedly the otherness came. It is never the same, always new, always unexpected; the odd thing about it is that thought cannot go back over it, reconsider it, examine it leisurely. Memory has no part in it, for every time it happens it is so totally new and unexpected that it does not leave any memory behind it. For it is a total and complete happening, an event that leaves no record, as memory. So it it always new, young, unexpected. It came with extraordinary beauty, not because of the fantastic shape of clouds and the light in them nor of the blue sky, so infinitely blue and tender; there was no reason, no cause for its incredible beauty and that is why it was beautiful. It was the essence not of all the things put together and boiled down to be felt and seen but of all life that has been and that is and that will be, life without time. It was there and it was the fury of beauty.

The little car was going home to its valley,* far from cities and civilizations; it was going over bumpy roads, over potholes, round sharp corners, groaning, creaking but it went; it was not old but it had been assembled carelessly; it smelled of petrol and oil but it was racing home as fast as it could over the paved and unpaved roads. The country was beautiful; it had rained recently, the night before. The trees were alive with bright, green leaves—the tamarind and the banyan and other innumerable trees; they were so vital, fresh and young though some of them must have been quite old. There were hills and the red earth; they were not thundering hills but gentle and old, some of the oldest on earth, and in the evening light they were serene, with that ancient blue which only certain hills have. Some were rocky and barren, others had scrubby bushes and a few had some trees but they were friendly as though they had seen all sorrow. And the earth at their feet was red; the rains had made it more red; it was not the red of blood or of the sun or of any man-made dye; it was the red, the colour of all reds; there was a clarity and purity about it and the green was the more startling against it. It was a lovely evening and it was getting cooler for the valley was at some height.

In the midst of the evening light and the hills becoming more blue and the red earth richer, the otherness came silently with benediction. It is marvellously new each time but yet it is the same. It was immense with strength, the strength of destruction and vulnerability. It came with such fullness and was gone in a flash; the moment was beyond all time. It was a tiring day but the brain was strangely alert, seeing without the watcher; seeing not with experience but out of emptiness.

* Rishi Valley, some 170 miles north of Madras and 2,500 feet above sea level. There is a Krishnamurti school there where he stayed.

24th

The moon was just coming over the hills, caught in a long serpentine cloud, giving her a fantastic shape. She was huge, dwarfing the hills, the earth and the green pastures; where she was coming up was more clear, fewer clouds, but she soon disappeared in dark rain-bearing clouds. It began to drizzle and the earth was glad; it doesn't rain much here and every drop counts; the big banyan and the tamarind and the mango would struggle through but the little plants and the rice crop were rejoicing at even a little rain. Unfortunately even the few drops stopped and presently the moon shone in a clear sky. It was raining furiously on the coast but here where the rain was needed, the rain-bearing clouds passed away. It was a beautiful evening, and there were deep dark shadows of many patterns. The moon was very bright and the shadows were very still and the leaves, washed clean, were sparkling. Walking and talking, meditation was going on below the words and the beauty of the night. It was going on at a great depth, flowing outwardly and inwardly; it was exploding and expanding. One was aware of it; it was happening; one wasn't experiencing it, experiencing is limiting; it was taking place. There was no participation in it; thought could not share it for thought is such a futile and mechanical thing anyhow, nor could emotion get entangled with it; it was too disturbingly active for either. It was happening at such an unknown depth for which there was no measurement. But there was great stillness. It was quite surprising and not at all ordinary.

The dark leaves were shining and the moon had climbed quite high; she was on the westerly course and flooding the room. Dawn was many hours away and there was not a sound; even the village dogs, with their shrill yapping, were quiet. Waking, it was there, with clarity and precision; the otherness was there and waking up was necessary, not sleep; it was deliberate, to be aware of what was happening, to be aware with full consciousness of what was taking place.

Asleep, it might have been a dream, a hint of the unconscious, a trick of the brain, but fully awake, this strange and
unknowable otherness was a palpable reality, a fact and not
an illusion, a dream. It had a quality, if such a word can be
applied to it, of weightlessness and impenetrable strength.
Again these words have certain significance, definite and
communicable, but these words lose all their meaning when
the otherness has to be conveyed in words; words are symbols
but no symbol can ever convey the reality. It was there with
such incorruptible strength that nothing could destroy it for
it was unapproachable. You can approach something with
which you are familiar, you must have the same language to
commune, some kind of thought process, verbal or non-
verbal; above all there must be mutual recognition. There
was none. On your side you may say it is this or that, this or
that quality, but at the moment of the happening there was
no verbalization for the brain was utterly still, without any
movement of thought. But the otherness is without relationship to anything and all thought and being is a cause-effect
process and so there was no understanding of it or relationship with it. It was an unapproachable flame and you could
only look at it and keep your distance. And on waking
suddenly, it was there. And with it came unexpected ecstasy,
an unreasonable joy; there was no cause for it for it has never
been sought or pursued. There was this ecstasy on waking
again at the usual hour; it was there and continued for a
lengthy period of time.

25th
There is a long-stemmed weed, grass of some kind, which
grows wildly in the garden and it has a feathery flowering,
burnt gold, flashing in the breeze, swaying till it almost breaks
but never breaking, except in a strong wind. There is a clump
of these weeds of golden beige and when the breeze blows it
sets them dancing; each stem has its own rhythm, its own
splendour and they are like a wave when they all move

together; the colour then, with the evening light, is indescribable; it is the colour of the sunset, of the earth and of the golden hills and clouds. The flowers beside them were too definite, too crude, demanding that you look at them. These weeds had a strange delicacy; they had a faint smell of wheat and of ancient times; they were sturdy and pure, full of abundant life. An evening cloud was passing by, full of light as the sun went down behind the dark hill. The rain had given to the earth a goodly smell and the air was pleasantly cool. The rains were coming and there was hope in the land.

Of a sudden it happened, coming back to the room; it was there with an embracing welcome, so unexpected. One had come in only to go out again; we had been talking about several things, nothing too serious. It was a shock and a surprise to find this welcoming otherness in the room; it was waiting there with such open invitation that an apology seemed futile. Several times, on the Common,* far away from here under some trees, along a path that was used by so many, it would be waiting just as the path turned; with astonishment one stood there, near those trees, completely open, vulnerable, speechless, without a movement. It was not a fancy, a self-projected delusion; the other, who happened to be there, felt it too; on several occasions it was there, with an all-embracing welcome of love and it was quite incredible; every time, it had a new quality, a new beauty, a new austerity. And it was like that in this room, something totally new and wholly unexpected. It was beauty that made the entire mind still and the body without a movement; it made the mind, the brain and the body intensely alert and sensitive; it made the body tremble and in a few minutes that welcoming otherness was gone, as swiftly as it must have come. No thought or fanciful emotion could ever conjure up such a happening; thought is petty, do what it will, and feeling is so fragile and deceitful; neither of them, in their wildest en-

* Wimbledon Common. He was remembering London where he had stayed in May in a house at Wimbledon.

deavour could build up these happenings. They are too immeasurably great, too immense in their strength and purity for thought or feeling; these have roots and they have none. They are not to be invited or held; thought-feeling can play every kind of clever and fanciful trick but they cannot invent or contain the otherness. It is by itself and nothing can touch it.

Sensitivity is wholly different from refinement; sensitivity is an integral state, refinement is always partial. There is no partial sensitivity, either it is the state of one's whole being, total consciousness or it is not there at all. It is not to be gathered bit by bit; it cannot be cultivated; it is not the result of experience and thought, it is not a state of emotionalism. It has the quality of precision, no overtones of romanticism and fancy. Only the sensitive can face the actual, without escaping into all kinds of conclusions, opinions and evaluations. Only the sensitive can be alone and this aloneness is destructive. This sensitivity is stripped of all pleasure and so it has the austerity, not of desire and will but of seeing and understanding. There is pleasure in refinement; it has to do with education, culture, environment. The way of refinement is endless; it is the outcome of choice, conflict and pain and there is always the chooser, the one who refines, the censor. And so there is always conflict and contradiction and pain. Refinement leads to isolation, self-enclosing aloofness, the separation which intellect and knowledge breed. Refinement is self-centred activity, however enlightened aesthetically and morally. There is great satisfaction in the refining process but no joy of depth; it is superficial and petty, without great significance. Sensitivity and refinement are two different things; one leads to isolating death and the other to life that has no end.

26th
There is a tree, just across the verandah with large leaves and

with many large red flowers; they are spectacular and the green, after the recent rains, is vivid and strong. The flowers are orange-red and against the green and the rocky hill, they seem to have taken the earth to themselves and they cover the whole space of the early morning. It was a beautiful morning, cloudy and there was that light which made every colour clear and strong. Not a leaf was stirring and they were all waiting, hoping for more rain; the sun would be hot and the earth needed far more rain. The river beds had been silent for many years; bushes were growing in them and water was needed everywhere; the wells were very low and the villagers would suffer if there was not more water. The clouds were black over the hills, heavy with the promise of rain. There was thunder and distant lightning and presently there was a downpour. It didn't last long but enough for the time being and there was a promise of more.

Where the road goes down and over the bridge of a dry river bed of red sand, the westerly hills were dark, heavy with brooding; and in the evening light, the luscious green fields of rice were incredibly beautiful. Across them were dark green trees and the hills to the north were violet; the valley lay open to the heavens. There was every colour, seen or unseen, in that valley that evening; every colour had its overtones, hidden and open, and every leaf and every blade of rice was exploding in the delight of colour. Colour was god, not mild and gentle. The clouds were gathering black and heavy, especially over the hills and there were flashes of lightning, far away over the hills and silent. There were already a few drops; it was raining among the hills and it would soon be here. A blessing to a starving land.

We were all talking after a light dinner about things pertaining to the school, how this and that was necessary, how difficult it was to find good teachers, how the rains were needed and so on. They went on talking and there, sudden and unexpectedly, the otherness appeared; it was there with such immensity and with such sweeping force that one became utterly quiet; the eyes saw it, the body felt it and the brain was alert without thought. The conversation was not too serious and in the midst of this casual atmosphere, something tremendous was taking place. One went to bed with it and it went on as a whisper during the night. There is no experiencing of it; it is simply there with a fury and benediction. To experience there must be an experiencer but when there is neither, it is an altogether different phenomenon. There is neither accepting it or denying it; it is simply there, as a fact. This fact had no relation to anything, neither in the past nor in the future and thought could not establish any communication with it. It had no value in terms of utility and profit, nothing could be got out of it. But it was there and by its very existence there was love, beauty, immensity. Without it, there is nothing. Without rain the earth would perish.

Time is illusion. There is tomorrow and there have been many yesterdays; this time is not an illusion. Thought which uses time as a means to bring about an inward change, a psychological change is pursuing a non-change, for such a change is only a modified continuity of what has been; such thought is sluggish, postpones, takes shelter in the illusion of gradualness, in ideals, in time. Through time mutation is not possible. The very denial of time is mutation; mutation takes place where the things which time has brought into being, habit, tradition, reform, the ideals, are denied. Deny time and mutation has taken place, a total mutation, not the alteration in patterns nor the substitution of one pattern by another. But acquiring knowledge, learning a technique, require time which cannot and must not be denied; they are essential for existence. Time to go from here to there is not an illusion but every other form of time is illusion. In this mutation, there is attention and from this attention there is a totally different kind of action. Such action does not become a habit, a repetition of a sensation, of an experience, of knowledge which dulls the brain, insensitive to a mutation. Virtue then is not the better habit, the better conduct; it has

no pattern, no limitation; it has not the stamp of respectability; it is not then an ideal to be pursued, put together by
time. Virtue then is a danger not a tame thing of society. To
love then is destruction; a revolution, not economic and social
but of total consciousness.

27th

Several of us were chanting and singing; learning new chants
and songs; the room overlooked the garden that was with
great difficulty maintained as there was little water; the
flowers and the bushes were watered by small buckets, really
kerosene tins. It was quite a nice garden with many flowers
but the trees dominated the garden; they were shapely, wide-
spreading and at certain seasons, full of flowers; now only
one tree was flowering, orange-red flowers with large petals,
a profusion of them. There were several trees with fine, small
delicate leaves, mimosa-like trees but with greater abundance
of foliage. So many birds came and now after two long heavy
showers they looked bedraggled, soaked to the skin, their
feathers drenched. There was a yellow bird with black wings,
larger than a starling, nearly as big as a blackbird; the yellow
was so bright against the dark-green foliage and its bright
elongated eyes were watching everything, the slightest movement among the leaves and the coming and going of other
birds. There were two black birds, smaller than crows, their
feathers soaked, sitting close to the yellow one on the same
tree; they had spread out their tail feathers and were fluttering their wings to get them dry; several other birds of different sizes came to that tree, all at peace with each other, all
alertly watching. The valley needed the rain very badly and
every drop was welcome; the wells were very low and the
big urban tanks were empty and these rains would help to fill
them. They had been empty for many years and there was
hope now. The valley had become very beautiful, rain-
washed, fresh, filled with varying rich green. The rocks had
been washed clean and had lost their heat and the stunted

bushes that grew among the rocks in the hills looked pleased and the dry river beds were singing again. The land was smiling again.

The chant and the song went on in that rather bare room, without furniture, and to sit on the floor seemed normal and comfortable. In the midst of a song quite suddenly and unexpected the other appeared; others went on with the song but they too became silent, not being aware of their silence. It was there with a benediction and it filled the space between the earth and the heavens. About ordinary things, up to a certain point, communication is possible through words; words have significance but words lose altogether their limited significance when we are trying to commune about events that cannot be verbalized. Love is not the word and it is something entirely different when all verbalization and the silly division of what is and what is not ceases. This event is not an experience, not a thing of thought, the recognition of a happening of yesterday, not the product of consciousness at whatever depth. It is not contaminated by time. It is something beyond and above all this; it was there and that is enough for heaven and earth.

Every prayer is a supplication and there is no asking when there is clarity and the heart unburdened. Instinctively, in time of trouble, a supplication of some kind comes to the lips, to avert the trouble, the ache or to gain some advantage. There is hope that some earthly god or the gods of the mind will answer satisfactorily, and sometimes by chance or through some strange coincidence of events, a prayer is answered. Then god has answered and faith has been justified. The gods of men, the only true gods, are there to comfort, to shelter, to answer all the petty and noble demands of man. Such gods are plentiful, every church, every temple and mosque has them. The earthly gods are even more powerful and more immediate; every state has them. But man goes on suffering in spite of every form of prayer and supplication. With the fury of understanding only can sorrow end but the other is easier, respectable and less demanding. And sorrow wears away the brain and the body, makes it dull, insensitive and weary. Understanding demands self-knowing, which is not an affair of the moment; learning about oneself is endless and the beauty and the greatness of it is that it is endless. But self-knowing is from moment to moment; this self-knowing is only in the active present; it has no continuity as knowledge. But what has continuity is habit, the mechanical process of thought. Understanding has no continuity.

28th

There is a red flower among the dark green leaves and from the verandah you only see that. There are the hills, the red sand of the river-beds, the big high banyan tree and the many tamarinds, but you only see that flower, it is so gay, so full of colour; there is no other colour; the patches of blue sky, the burning clouds of light, the violet hills, the rich green of the rice field, all these fade away and only this wondrous colour of that flower remains. It fills the whole sky and the valley; it will fade and fall away; it will cease and the hills will endure. But this morning it was eternity, beyond all time and thought; it held all love and joy; there was no sentiment and romantic absurdities in it; nor was it a symbol of something else. It was itself, to die in the evening but it contained all life. It was not something you reasoned out nor was it a thing of unreason, some romantic fancy; it was as actual as those hills and those voices calling to each other. It was the complete meditation of life, and illusion exists only when the impact of fact ceases. That cloud so full of light is a reality whose beauty has no furious impact on a mind that is made dull and insensitive by influence, habit and the everlasting search for security. Security in fame, in relationship, in knowledge destroys sensitivity and deterioration sets in. That flower, those hills and the blue restless sea are the challenges, as nuclear bombs, of life, and only the sensitive mind can respond to them totally; only a total response leaves no marks of conflict, and conflict indicates partial response.

The so-called saints and sanyasis have contributed to the dullness of mind and to the destruction of sensitivity. Every habit, repetition, rituals strengthened by belief and dogma, sensory responses, can be and are refined, but the alert awareness, sensitivity, is quite another matter. Sensitivity is absolutely essential to look deeply within; this movement of going within is not a reaction to the outer; the outer and the inner are the same movement, they are not separate. The division of this movement as the outer and as the inner breeds insensitivity. Going within is the natural flow of the outer; the movement of the inner has its own action, expressed outwardly but it is not a reaction of the outer. Awareness of this whole movement is sensitivity.

29th
It was really quite an extraordinarily beautiful evening. It had been drizzling off and on all day; one had been cooped up indoors all day; there was a talk-discussion, seeing people and so on. It had stopped raining for some hours and it was good to get out. To the west the clouds were dark, almost black, heavy with rain and thunder; they were hanging over the hills making them dark purple and unusually heavy and threatening. The sun was setting in a tumultuous fury of clouds. To the east, clouds shot up full of evening light; each one was a different shape with a light of its own, towering over the hills, immense, shatteringly alive, soaring up into high heavens. There were patches of blue sky, so intensely blue, green of such a delicacy that it faded into the white light of bursting clouds. The hills were sculptured with the dignity of endless time; there was one that was alight from within, transparent and strangely delicate, so utterly artificial; another one was chiselled out of granite, darkly alone, with a shape of all the temples of the world. Every hill was alive, full

of movement and aloof with the depth of time. It was a marvellous evening, full of beauty, silence and light.

We had started all of us walking together but now we had fallen silent, separate, a little distance from each other. The road was rough crossing the valley, over the dry, red sandy river-beds which had thin trickles of rain water. The road turned and went east. Down the valley there is a white farmhouse surrounded by trees and one huge tree covering them all. It was a peaceful sight and the land seemed enchanted. The house was a mile or so away among the green, luscious rice fields and silent. One had often seen it, as the road went on to the mouth of the valley and beyond it; it was the only road in and out of the valley by car and foot. The white house among few trees had been there for some years and it had always been a pleasant sight, but seeing it, that evening, as the road turned, there was an altogether different beauty and feeling about it. For the otherness was there, and coming up the valley; it was like a curtain of rain but only there was no rain; it was coming as a breeze comes, soft and gently and it was there inside and outside. It was not thought, it was not feeling nor was it a fancy, a thing of the brain. Each time it is so new and amazing, the pure strength and vastness of it that there is astonishment and joy. It is something totally unknown and the known has no contact with it. The known must wholly die for it to be. Experience is still within the field of the known, and so it was not an experience. All experience is a state of immaturity. You can only experience and recognize as experience something which you have already known. But this was not experienceable, knowable; every form of thought must cease and every feeling; for they are all known and knowable; the brain and the totality of consciousness must be free of the known and be empty without any form of effort. It was there, inside and outside; one was walking in it and with it. The hills, the land, the earth were with it.

It was quite early in the morning and it was still dark. The night was thunderous and rainy; windows banged and rain was pouring into the room. Not a star was visible, the sky and the hills were covered with clouds and it was raining with fury and noise. On waking, the rain had stopped and it was still dark. Meditation is not a practice, following a system, a method; these only lead to the darkening of the mind and it is ever a movement within the boundaries of the known; there is despair and illusion within their activity. It was very quiet so early in the morning and not a bird or leaf was stirring. Meditation which began at unknown depths and went on with increasing intensity and sweep, carved the brain into total silence, scooping out the depths of thought, up rooting feeling, emptying the brain of the known and its shadow. It was an operation and there was no operator, no surgeon; it was going on, as a surgeon operates for cancer, cutting out every tissue which has been contaminated, lest the contamination should again spread. It was going on, this meditation for an hour by the watch. And it was meditation without the meditator. The meditator interferes with his stupidities and vanities, ambitions and greed. The meditator is thought, nurtured in these conflicts and injuries, and thought in meditation must totally cease. This is the foundation for meditation.

30th

Everywhere there was silence; the hills were motionless, the trees were still and the river-beds empty; the birds had found shelter for the night and everything was still, even the village dogs. It had rained and the clouds were motionless. Silence grew and became intense, wider and deeper. What was out-side was now inside; the brain which had listened to the silence of the hills, fields and groves was itself now silent; it no longer listened to itself; it had gone through that and had become quiet, naturally, without any enforcement. It was still ready to stir itself on the instant. It was still, deep within itself; like a bird that folds its wings, it had folded upon itself; it was not asleep nor lazy, but in folding upon itself, it had entered into depths which were beyond itself. The brain is essentially superficial; its activities are superficial, almost mechanical; its activities and responses are immediate, though this immediacy is translated in terms of the future. Its thoughts and feelings are on the surface, though it may think and feel far into the future and way back into the past. All experience and memory are deep only to the extent of their own limited capacity but the brain being still and turning upon itself, it was no longer experiencing outwardly or inwardly. Consciousness, the fragments of so many experiences, compulsions, fears, hopes and despairs of the past and the future, the contradictions of the race and its own self-centred activities, was absent; it was not there. The entire being was utterly still and as it became intense, it was not more or less; it was intense, there was an entering into a depth or a depth which came into being which thought, feeling, consciousness could not enter into. It was a dimension which the brain could not capture or understand. And there was no observer, witnessing this depth. Every part of one's whole being was alert, sensitive but intensely still. This new, this depth was expanding, exploding, going away, developing in its own explosions but out of time and beyond time and space.

31st

It was a beautiful evening; the air was clean, the hills were blue, violet and dark purple; the rice fields had plenty of water and were a varying rich green from light to metallic to dark flashing green; some trees had already withdrawn for the night, dark and silent and others were still open and held the light of day. The clouds were black over the western hills, and to the north and east the clouds were full of the [reflection of the] evening sun which had set behind the heavy purple hills. There was no one on the road, the few that passed were silent and there wasn't a patch of blue sky, clouds were gathering in for the night. Yet everything seemed to be awake, the rocks, the dry river-bed, the bushes in the fading light. Meditation, along that quiet and deserted road came like a soft rain over the hills; it came as easily and naturally as the coming night. There was no effort of any kind and no control with its concentrations and distractions; there was no order and pursuit; no denial or acceptance nor any continuity of memory in meditation. The brain was aware of its environment but quiet without response, uninfluenced but recognizing without responding. It was very quiet and words had faded with thought. There was that strange energy, call it by any other name, it has no importance whatsoever, deeply active, without object and purpose; it was creation, without the canvas and the marble, and destructive; it was not the thing of human brain, of expression and decay. It was not approachable, to be classified and analysed, and thought and feeling are not the instruments of its comprehension. It was completely unrelated to everything and totally alone in its vastness and immensity. And walking along that darkening road, there was the ecstasy of the impossible, not of achievement, arriving, success and all those immature demands and responses, but the aloneness of the impossible. The possible is mechanical and the impossible can be envisaged, tried and perhaps achieved which in turn becomes mechanical. But the ecstasy had no cause, no reason. It was simply there, not as an experience but as a fact, not to be accepted or denied, to be argued over and dissected. It was not a thing to be sought after for there is no path to it. Everything has to die for it to be, death, destruction which is love.

A poor, worn-out labourer, in torn dirty clothes, was returning home with his bone-thin cow.

November 1st
The sky was burning with fantastic colour, great splashes of incredible fire; the southern sky was aflame with clouds of exploding colour and each cloud was more intensely furious than the other. The sun had set behind the sphinx-shaped hill

but there was no colour there, it was dull, without the serenity of a beautiful evening. But the east and the south held all the grandeur of a fading day. To the east it was blue, the blue of a morning-glory, a flower so delicate that to touch it is to break the delicate, transparent petals; it was the intense blue with incredible light of pale green, violet and the sharpness of white; it was sending out, from east to west, rays of this fantastic blue right across the sky. And the south was now the home of vast fires that could never be put out. Across the rich green of rice fields was a stretch of sugar cane in flower; it was feathery, pale violet, the tender light beige of a mourning dove; it stretched over and across the luscious green rice fields with the evening light through it to the hills, which were almost the same colour as the sugar-cane flower. The hills were in league with the flower, the red earth and the darkening sky, and that evening the hills were shouting with joy for it was an evening of their delight. The stars were coming out and presently there was not a cloud and every star shone with astonishing brilliance in a rain-washed sky. And early this morning, with dawn far away, Orion held the sky and the hills were silent. Only across the valley, the hoot of a deep-throated owl was answered by a light-throated one, at a higher pitch; in the clear still air their voices carried far and they were coming nearer until they seemed quiet among a clump of trees; then they rhythmically kept calling to each other, one at a lower note than the other till a man called and a dog barked.

It was meditation in emptiness, a void that had no border. Thought could not follow; it had been left where time begins, nor was there feeling to distort love. This was emptiness without space. The brain was in no way participating in this meditation; it was completely still and in that stillness going within itself and out of itself but in no way sharing with this vast emptiness. The totality of the mind was receiving or perceiving or being aware of what was taking place and yet it was not outside of itself, something extraneous, something foreign. Thought is an impediment to meditation but only through meditation can this impediment be dissolved. For thought dissipates energy and the essence of energy is freedom from thought and feeling.

2nd

It had become very cloudy, all the hills were heavy with them and clouds were piling up in every direction. It was spitting with rain and there wasn't a blue patch anywhere; the sun had set in darkness and the trees were aloof and distant. There is an old palm tree that stood out against the darkening sky and whatever light there was was held by it; the river-beds were silent, their red sand moist but there was no song; the birds had become silent taking shelter among the thick leaves. A breeze was blowing from north-east and with it came more dark clouds and a spattering of rain but it hadn't begun in earnest; that would come later in gathering fury. And the road in front was empty; it was red, rough, and sandy and the dark hills looked down on it; it was a pleasant road with hardly any cars and the villagers with their ox-drawn carts going from one village to another; they were dirty, skeleton-thin, in rags, and their stomachs drawn in but they were wiry and enduring; they had lived like that for centuries and no government is going to change all this over-night. But these people had a smile, though their eyes were weary. They could dance after a heavy day's labour and they had fire in them, they were not hopelessly beaten down. The land had not had good rains for many years and this may be one of those fortunate years which may bring more food for them and fodder for their thin cattle. And the road went on and joined at the mouth of the valley the big road with few buses and cars. And on this road, far away were the cities with their filth, industries, rich houses, temples and dull minds. But here on this open road, there was solitude and the many hills, full of age and indifference.

Meditation is the emptying the mind of all thought, for

thought and feeling dissipate energy; they are repetitive, producing mechanical activities which are a necessary part of existence. But they are only part, and thought and feeling cannot possibly enter into the immensity of life. Quite a different approach is necessary, not the path of habit, association and the known; there must be freedom from these. Meditation is the emptying of the mind of the known. It cannot be done by thought or by the hidden prompting of thought, nor by desire in the form of prayer, nor through the self-effacing hypnotism of words, images, hopes and vanities. All these have to come to an end, easily, without effort and choice, in the flame of awareness.

And there walking on that road, there was complete emptines of the brain, and the mind was free of all experience, the knowing of yesterday, though a thousand yesterdays have been. Time, the thing of thought, had stopped; literally there was no movement before and after; there was no going or arriving or standing still. Space as distance was not; there were the hills and bushes but not as high and low. There was no relationship with anything but there was an awareness of the bridge and the passer-by. The totality of the mind, in which is the brain with its thoughts and feelings, was empty; and because it was empty, there was energy, a deepening and widening energy without measure. All comparison, measurement belong to thought and so to time. The otherness was the mind without time; it was the breath of innocence and immensity. Words are not reality; they are only means of communication but they are not the innocence and the immeasurable. The emptiness was alone.

3rd
It had been a dull, heavy day; the clouds were pressing in and it had rained violently. The red river-beds had some water in them but the land needed lots more rain for the big catchments, tanks, and the wells to get filled up; there would be no rains for several months and the hot sun would

burn the land. Water was needed urgently for this part of the country and every drop was welcome. One had been indoors all day and it was good to get out. The roads were running with water, there was a heavy shower and under every tree there was a puddle and the trees were dripping with water. It was getting dark; the hills were visible, they were just dark against the sky, the colour of the clouds; the trees were silent and motionless, lost in their brooding; they had withdrawn and refused to communicate. One was aware, suddenly, of that strange otherness; it was there and it had been there, only there had been talks, seeing people and so on and the body had not had enough rest to be aware of the strangeness but on going out it was there and only then was there a realization that it had been there. Still it was unexpected and sudden, with that intensity which is the essence of beauty. One went with it down the road not as something separate, not as an experience, something to be observed and examined, to be remembered. These were the ways of thought but thought had ceased and so there was no experiencing of it. All experiencing is separative and deteriorating, it is part of the machinery of thought and all mechanical processes deteriorate. It was something, each time, totally new and that which is new has no relation whatsoever with the known, with the past. And there was beauty, beyond all thought and feeling.

There was no call of the owl across the silent valley; it was very early; the sun would not be over the hill for several hours yet. It was cloudy and no stars were visible; if the sky were clear, Orion would be this side of the house, facing west, but everywhere there was darkness and silence. Habit and meditation can never abide together; meditation can never become a habit; meditation can never follow the pattern laid down by thought which forms habit. Meditation is the destruction of thought and not thought caught in its own intricacies, visions and its own vain pursuits. Thought shattering itself against its own nothingness is the explosion of meditation. This meditation has its own movement, direction-less and so is causeless. And in that room, in that peculiar silence when the clouds are low, almost touching the tree-tops, meditation was a movement in which the brain emptied itself and remained still. It was a movement of the totality of the mind in emptiness and there was timelessness. Thought is matter held within the bonds of time; thought is never free, never new; every experience only strengthens the bond-age and so there is sorrow. Experience can never free thought; it makes it more cunning, and refinement is not the ending of sorrow. Thought, however astute, however experienced, can never end sorrow; it can escape from it but it can never end it. The ending of sorrow is the ending of thought. There is no one who can put an end to it [to thought], not its own gods, its own ideals, beliefs, dogmas. Every thought, however wise or petty, shapes the response to the challenge of limitless life and this response of time breeds sorrow. Thought is mechanical and so it can never be free; only in freedom there is no sorrow. The ending of thought is the ending of sorrow.

4th

It had been threatening to rain but it never rained; the blue hills were heavy with clouds; they were always changing, moving from one hill to another but there was a long white-grey cloud, stretching west over many hills to the horizon, which had its birth in one of the eastern hills; it seemed to begin from there, from the side of the hill, and went on to the western horizon in a rolling movement, alive with the light of the setting sun; it was white and grey but deep within it was violet, a fading purple; it seemed to be carrying on its way the hills it covered. In the western gap the sun was setting in a fury of clouds and the hills were getting darker and more grey and the trees were heavy with silence. There is a huge, unmolested banyan tree, many years old, by the

side of the road; is is really magnificent, huge, vital, unconcerned and that evening it was the lord of the hills, the
earth and the streams; it had majesty and the stars seemed
very small. Along that road, a villager and his wife were
walking, one behind the other, the husband led and the wife
followed; they seemed a little more prosperous than the
others that one met on the road. They passed us, she never
looking at us and he looked at the far village. We caught up
with her; she was a small woman, never taking her eyes off
the ground; she wasn't too clean; she had a green soiled sari
and her blouse was salmon coloured and sweat-stained. She
had a flower in her oily hair and was walking bare-footed.
Her face was dark and there was about her a great sadness.
There was a certain firmness and gaiety in her walk which in
no way touched her sadness; each was leading its own life,
independent, vital and unrelated. But there was great sadness and you felt it immediately; it was an irremediable
sadness; there was no way out, no way to soften it, no way
to bring about a change. It was there and it would be there.
She was across the road, a few feet away and nothing could
touch her. We walked side by side for a while and presently
she turned off and crossed the red river-bed of sand and
went on to her village, the husband leading, never looking
back and she following. Before she turned off, a curious thing
was taking place. The few feet of road between us disappeared and with it also disappeared the two entities;
there was only that woman walking in her impenetrable
sadness. It was not an identification with her, nor overwhelming sympathy and affection; these were there but they
were not because of the phenomenon. Identification with
another, however deep, still maintains separation and division; there are still two entities, one identifying with the
other, a conscious or an unconscious process, through affection or through hate; in it there is an endeavour of some
kind, subtle or open. But here there was none at all. She
was the only human being that existed on that road. She

was and the other was not. It was not a fancy or an illusion; it was a simple fact and no amount of clever reasoning and subtle explanation could alter that fact. Even when she turned off the road and was going away, the other was not on that straight road that went on. It was some time before the other found himself walking beside a long heap of broken stones, ready for renewing the road.

Along that road, over the gap in the southern hills, came that otherness with such intensity and power that it was with the greatest difficulty that one could stand up and continue the walk. It was like a furious storm but without the wind and the noise and its intensity was overwhelming. Strangely every time it comes, there is always something new; it is never the same and always unexpected. This otherness is not something extraordinary, some mysterious energy, but is mysterious in the sense that it is something beyond time and thought. A mind that is caught in time and thought can never comprehend it. It is not a thing to be understood, any more than love can be analysed and understood, but without this immensity, strength and energy, life, and all existence, at any level, becomes trivial and sorrowful. There is an absoluteness about it, not a finality; it is absolute energy; it is self-existent without cause; it is not the ultimate, final energy for it is all energy. Every form of energy and action must cease for it to be. But in it all action is. Love and do what you will. There must be death and total destruction for it to be; not the revolution of outward things but the total destruction of the known in which all shelter and existence is cultivated. There must be total emptiness and only then that otherness, the timeless, comes. But this emptiness is not to be cultivated, it is not the result whose cause can be bought and sold; nor is it the outcome of time and evolutionary process; time can only give birth to more time. Destruction of time is not a process; all methods and processes prolong time. Ending of time is the ending of total thought and feeling.

5th

Beauty is never personal. The hills were dark blue and carried the light of the evening. It had been raining and now great spaces of blue appeared; the blue was ablaze with white clouds surrounding it; it was the blue that made the eyes sparkle with forgotten tears; it was the blue of infancy and innocence. And that blue became a pale nile-green of early leaves of spring and beyond it was the fire-red of a cloud that was gathering speed to cross the hills. And over the hills were the rain clouds, dark, heavy and immovable; these clouds were piling up against the hills in the west and the sun was caught between the hills and the clouds. The ground was soaked, red and clear, and every tree and bush had deep moisture; there were already new leaves; the mango had long russet tender leaves, the tamarind had bright yellow small leaves, the rain-tree had a few shoots of fresh light green; after a long wait of many months of baking sun, the rains brought comfort to the earth; the valley was smiling. The poverty-ridden village was filthy, smelly and so many children were playing, shouting and laughing; they didn't seem to care for anything except the games they were playing. Their parents seemed so weary, haggard and forgotten; they would never know one day of rest, cleanliness and comfort; hunger, labour and more hunger; they were sad, though they smiled readily enough, their eyes forlorn, beyond recalling. Everywhere there was beauty, the grass, the hills and the crowded sky; the birds were calling and high in the air an eagle was circling. There were lean goats on the hills, devouring everything that grew; they were insatiably hungry and their little ones pranced from rock to rock. They were so soft to touch, their skin sparkling, clean and healthy. The boy who was looking after them was singing away, sitting on a rock and occasionally calling to them.

The personal cultivation of the pleasure of beauty is self-centred activity; it leads to insensitivity.

6th

It was a lovely morning, clear, every star was ablaze and the valley was full of silence. The hills were dark, darker than the sky and cool air had a smell of rain, the scent of leaves and some strong-scented flowering jasmine. Everything was asleep and every leaf was still and the beauty of the morning was magic; it was the beauty of the earth, heavens and of man, of the sleeping birds and the fresh stream in a dry river-bed; it was incredible that it was not personal. There was a certain austerity about it, not the cultivated which is merely the activities of fear and denial but the austerity of completeness, so utterly complete that it knew no corruption. There on the verandah, with Orion in the western sky, the fury of beauty wiped away the defences of time. Meditating there, beyond the limits of time, seeing the sky ablaze with stars and the earth silent, beauty is not the personal pursuit of pleasure, of things put together, of things known, or unknown images and visions of the brain with its thoughts and feelings. Beauty has nothing whatsoever to do with thought or sentiment or with the pleasurable feeling aroused by a concert or a picture or seeing a game of football; the pleasures of concert, poems, are perhaps more refined than football but they are all in the same field as the Mass or some puja in a temple. It is the beauty beyond time and beyond the aches and pleasures of thought. Thought and feeling dissipate energy and so beauty is never seen. Energy, with its intensity, is needed to see beauty—beauty that is beyond the eye of the beholder. When there is a seer, an observer, then there is no beauty.

There on the perfumed verandah, when dawn was still far away and the trees were still silent, what is essence is beauty. But this essence is not experienceable; experiencing must cease, for experience only strengthens the known. The known is never the essence. Meditation is never the further experiencing; it is not only the ending of experience, which is the response to challenge, great or small, but it is the opening of the door to essence, opening the door of a furnace whose fire utterly destroys, without leaving any ashes; there are no remains. We are the remains, the yes-sayers of many thousand yesterdays, a continuous series of endless memories, of choice and despair. The Big Self and the little self are the pattern of existence and existence is thought and thought is existence, with never ending sorrow. In the flame of meditation thought ends and with it feeling, for neither is love. Without love, there is no essence; without it there are only ashes on which is based our existence. Out of the emptiness love is.

7th
The owls started, very early this morning, calling to each other. At first they were in different parts of the valley; one was in the west and the other north; their hoots were very clear in the still air and carried very far. At first they were quite a distance from each other and gradually they came nearer and as they came, their hoots became hoarse, very deep, not so long drawn-out, shorter and more insistent. As they came nearer they kept calling to each other more frequently; they must have been large birds, one couldn't see them, it was too dark even when they were in the same tree quite close and the tone and quality of their hoots changed. They were talking to each other at so profound a depth that they could hardly be heard. They were there for considerable time, until dawn came. Then slowly a series of noises began, a dog barked, somebody called, a firecracker went off—for the last two days there was some kind of festival—a door opened and as it became lighter all the noises of the day began.

To deny is essential. To deny today without knowing what tomorrow will bring is to keep awake. To deny the social, economic and religious pattern is to be alone, which is to be sensitive. Not to be able to deny totally is to be mediocre. Not to be able to deny ambition and all its ways is to accept the norm of existence which breeds conflict, confusion and sorrow. To deny the politician and so the politician in us, the response to the immediate, to live with short vision, is to be free from fear. Total denial is the negation of the positive, the imitative urge, conformity. But this denial itself is positive, for it is not a reaction. To deny the accepted standard of beauty, past or present, is to discover beauty which is beyond thought and feeling; but, to discover it, energy is necessary. This energy comes when there is no conflict, contradiction, and action is no longer partial.

8th

Humility is the essence of all virtue. Humility is not to be cultivated, nor is virtue. The respectable morality of any society is mere adjustment to the pattern set by social, economic, religious environment, but such morality of changing adjustment is not virtue. Conformity and the imitative self-concern of security, called morality, is the denial of virtue. Order is never permanent; it has to be maintained every day, as a room has to be cleaned every day. Order has to be maintained from moment to moment, every day. This order is not personal, individual adjustment to the pattern of conditioned responses of like and dislike, pleasure and pain. This order is not a means of escape from sorrow; the understanding of sorrow and the ending of sorrow is virtue, which brings about order. Order is not an end in itself; order, as an end in itself leads to the dead end of respectability, which is deterioration and decay. Learning is the very essence of humility, learning from everything and from everybody. There is no hierarchy in learning. Authority denies learning and a follower will never learn.

There was a single cloud, aflame with the light of the setting sun, behind the eastern hills; no fantasy could build such a cloud. It was the form of all forms; no architect could have designed such structure. It was the result of many winds, of many suns and nights, of pressure and strains. Other clouds were dark without light; they had no depth or height but this one shattered space. The hill, beyond which the cloud was, appeared emptied of life and strength; it had lost its usual dignity and its purity of line. The cloud had absorbed all the quality of hills, their might and silence. Below the towering cloud lay the valley, green and rain-washed; there is something very beautiful in this ancient valley when it has rained; it becomes spectacularly bright and green, green of every shade and the earth becomes more red. The air is clear and the big rocks on the hills are polished red, blue, grey and pale violet.

There were several people in the room, some sitting on the floor and some on chairs; there was the quietness of appreciation and enjoyment. A man was playing on an eight-stringed instrument. He was playing with his eyes closed, delighted as the little audience. It was pure sound and on that sound one rode, far and very deep; each sound carried one deeper. The quality of sound that instrument produced made the journey infinite; from the moment he touched it till the moment he stopped, it was the sound that mattered not the instrument, not the man, not the audience. It had the effect of shutting out all other sound, even the fireworks that the boys were setting off; you heard them crash and crack but it was part of the sound and the sound was everything—the cicadas that were singing, the boys laughing, the call of a small girl and the sound of silence. He must have played for over half an hour and during that entire period the journey, far and deep, continued; it was not a journey that is taken in imagination, on the wings of thought or in the frenzy of emotion. Such journeys are short, with some meaning or pleasure; this had no meaning and no pleasure. There was only sound and nothing else, no thought, no feeling. That sound carried one through and beyond the confines of time, and quietly it went on into great immense emptiness from which there was no return. What is returning always is memory, a thing that has been, but here there was no memory, no experience. Fact has no shadow, memory.

9th

There wasn't a cloud in the sky as the sun went down behind the hills; the air was still and not a leaf moved. Everything seemed held tight, in the light of a cloudless sky. The reflection of the evening light on a little stretch of water by the roadside was full of ecstatic energy and the little wildflower, by the wayside, was all life. There is a hill that looks like one of those ancient and ageless temples; it was purple, darker than violet, intense and vastly unconcerned; it was alive with an inward light, without shadow, and every rock and bush was shouting with joy. A bullock cart with two oxen came along the road, carrying some hay; a boy was sitting on the hay and a man was driving the cart which made a lot of noise. They stood out clearly against the sky, especially the outlines of the boy's face; his nose and forehead were clean cut, gentle; it was the face that had no education and probably would never have; it was an unspoiled face, not yet used to hard work nor to any responsibility; it was a smiling face. The clear sky was reflected on it. Walking along that road, meditation seemed a most natural thing; there was a fervour and a clarity and the occasion suited the state. Thought is a waste of energy as also is feeling. Thought and feeling invite distraction and concentration becomes defensive self-absorption, like a child absorbed in his toy. The toy is fascinating and he is lost in it; remove it and he becomes restless. The same with the grown-ups; their toys are the many escapes. There on the road, thought, with its feeling had no power of absorption; it had no self-generating energy and so it came to an end. The brain became quiet, as the waters become quiet when there is no breeze. It was the stillness before creation takes place. And there on that hill, just close by, an owl started gently hooting but suddenly stopped and high up in the sky one of those brown eagles was crossing the valley. It is the quality of stillness that has significance; an induced stillness is stagnation; a stillness that is bought is a merchandise which has hardly any value; a stillness that is the outcome of control, discipline, suppression is clamorous with despair. There was not a sound in the valley nor in the mind, but the mind went beyond the valley and time. And there was no returning for it had not gone. Silence is the depth of emptiness.

At the bend of the road, the road gently goes down across a couple of bridges over dry red river-beds, to the other side of the valley. The bullock cart had gone down that road; some villagers were coming up it, shy and noiseless; there were children playing in the river-bed and a bird kept on calling. Just as the road turned east, that otherness came. It came pouring down in great waves of benediction, splendid and immense. It seemed as though the heavens opened and out of this immensity came the unnameable; it had been there all day, one realized suddenly and only now, walking alone, with the others a little way off, did one realize the fact, and what made it extraordinary was this thing that was happening; it was the culmination of what had been going on and not an isolated incident. There was light, not of the setting sun nor powerful artificial light; this makes shadows but there was light without shadow and it was light.

10th

A deep-throated owl was hooting in the hills; its deep voice penetrated the room and quickened hearing. Except for these hoots everything was still; there was not even the croak of a frog or the rustle of some passing animal. The silence intensified between the hoots which came from the southern hills; they filled the valley and the hills and the air throbbed with the call. It wasn't answered for a very long time and when it came, it was way down the valley to the west; between them, they held the silence and the beauty of the night. Dawn would come presently but now it was dark; you could see the outlines of the hill and that huge banyan tree. The Pleiades and Orion were setting in a clear, cloudless sky; the air was fresh by a short shower of rain; it had a perfume that comes of old trees, rain, flowers and very ancient hills. It was really a marvellous morning. What was outside was taking place inside and meditation is really a movement of both, undivided. The many systems of meditation merely trap the mind in a pattern offering marvellous escapes and sensations; it is only the immature that play with them, getting a great deal of satisfaction from them. Without self-knowing all meditation leads to delusion and to varying forms of self-deception, factual and fancied. It was a movement of intense energy, that energy which conflict will never know. Conflict perverts and dissipates energy, as ideals and conformity do. Thought was gone and with it feeling but the brain was alive and fully sensitive. Every movement, action with a motive is inaction; it is this inaction that corrupts energy. Love with motive ceases to be love; there is love without motive. The body was completely motionless and the brain utterly still and both were actually aware of everything but there was neither thought nor motion. It was not a form of hypnosis, an induced state because there was nothing to be gained by it, no visions, sensations, all that silly business. It was a fact and a fact has no pleasure or pain. And the movement was lost to all recognition, to the known.

Dawn was coming and with it came the otherness which is essentially part of meditation. A dog barked and the day had begun.

11th

There are only facts, not greater or lesser facts. The fact, the what is, cannot be understood when approached with opinions or judgments; opinions, judgments, then become the fact and not the fact that you wish to understand. In pursuing the fact, in watching the fact, the what is, the fact teaches and its teaching is never mechanical, and to follow its teachings, the listening, the observation must be acute; this attention is denied if there is motive for listening. Motive dissipates energy, distorts it; action with a motive is inaction, leading to confusion and sorrow. Sorrow has been put together by thought and thought feeding upon itself forms the I and the me. As a machine has life, so does the I and the me, a life which is fed by thought and feeling. Fact destroys this machinery.

Belief is so unnecessary, as are ideals. Both dissipate energy which is needed to follow the unfolding of the fact, the what is. Beliefs like ideals are escapes from the fact and in escape there is no end to sorrow. The ending of sorrow is the understanding of the fact from moment to moment. There is no system or method which will give understanding but only a choiceless awareness of a fact. Meditation according to a system is the avoidance of the fact of what you are; it is far more important to understand yourself, the constant changing of the facts about yourself, than to meditate in order to find god, have visions, sensations and other forms of entertainment.

A crow was cawing its head off; it was sitting on the branch with thick foliage. It wasn't visible; other crows came and went but it went on hardly stopping its sharp, penetrating croak; it was angry with something or complaining about something. The leaves shook around it and even the few drops of rain didn't stop it. It was so completely absorbed in whatever it was that was disturbing it. It came out, shook itself and flew away, only to resume its biting complaint; presently, it got tired and rested. And from the same crow, in the same place came a different caw, subdued, somewhat friendly and inviting. There were other birds on the tree, the Indian cuckoo, a bright yellow bird with black wings, a silvery grey fat bird, one of many who was scratching at the foot of the tree. One of those small striped squirrels came along and went up the tree. They were all there in that tree but the crow's call was the loudest and most persistent. The sun came out of the clouds and the tree cast a heavy shadow and across the small, narrow dip in the land came the sounds of a flute, strangely moving.

12th

It had been cloudy all day, heavy dark clouds but they brought no rain and if it didn't rain heavily and for many hours, the people would suffer, the land would be empty and there would be no voices in the river-bed; the sun would bake the land, the green of these few weeks would disappear, the earth would be bare. It would be a disaster and all the villages around here would suffer; they were used to suffering, to deprivation, to go with little food. Rain was a blessing and if it didn't rain now there would be no rain for the next six months and the soil was poor, sandy, rocky. The rice fields would be watered from the wells and there would be the danger that they they too might go dry. Existence was hard, brutal, with little pleasure. The hills were indifferent; they had seen sorrow from generation to generation; they had seen all the varieties of misery, the coming and the going for they were some of the most ancient hills in the world, and they knew and they couldn't do much. People cut down their forests, their trees for firewood and the goats destroyed their bushes and the people had to live. And they were indifferent; sorrow would never touch them; they were aloof, and though they were so close, they were far away. They were blue that morning and some were violet and grey in their greenness. They could offer no help though they were strong and beautiful with the sense of peace that comes, so naturally and easily, without deep inward intensity, complete and without roots. But there would be neither peace nor plenty if the rains didn't come. It is a terrible thing to depend for one's happiness on rain, and the rivers and irrigation canals were far away and government was busy with its politics and schemes. Water that is so alive with light and that dances tirelessly was needed, not words and hope.

It was drizzling and low on the hill was a rainbow, so delicate and fanciful; it circled just over the trees and across the northern hills. It didn't stay long for the drizzle was a passing thing but it had left so many drops on the mimosa-like leaves of the spreading tree close by. On these leaves, three crows were taking a bath, fluttering their black-grey wings to get the drops on the underpart of their wings and their bodies; they called to each other and there was pleasure in their caw; when there were no more drops, they moved to another part of the tree. Their bright eyes looked at you and their really black beaks were sharp; there is a little water running in one of the river beds close by and there is a leaky tap which forms a decent pool for birds; they were there often but these three crows must have taken a fancy to having their morning bath among the cool, refreshing leaves. It is a wide-spreading tree, beautiful in shape and many birds come to take shelter at noonday. There is always some bird in it, calling or chattering away or scolding. The trees are beautiful in life and in death; they live and have never thought of death; they are always renewing themselves.

How easy it is to degenerate, in every way, to let the body waste, become sluggish, fat; to allow feelings to wither away; the mind allowing itself to become shallow, petty and dull. A clever mind is a shallow mind and it cannot renew itself and so withers away in its own bitterness; it decays by the exercise of its own brittle sharpness, by its own thought. Every thought shapes the mind in the mould of the known; every feeling, every emotion, however refined becomes wasteful and empty and the body fed on thought and feeling loses its sensibility. It is not physical energy, though it is necessary, that breaks through the wearying dullness; it is not enthusiasm or sentiment which bring about sensitivity of one's whole being; enthusiasm and sentiment corrupt. It is thought which is the disintegrating factor; for thought has its roots in the known. A life based on thought and its activities, becomes mechanical; however smoothly it may run, it is still mechanical action. Action with motive dissipates energy and so disintegration sets in. All motives, conscious or unconscious, generate from the known. A life of the known, though projected into the future as the unknown, is decay; in that life there is no renewal. Thought can never bring about innocency and humility and yet it is innocency and humility that keep the mind young, sensitive, incorruptible. Freedom from the known is the ending of thought; to die to thought, from moment to moment, is to be free from the known. It is this death that puts an end to decay.

13th

There is a huge boulder which projects itself from the southern hills; it changes its colour from hour to hour, it is red, highly polished marble of deep rose, a dull brick red, a rain-washed, sunburnt terra cotta, a grey of mossy green, a flower of many hues and sometimes it seems just a block of rock without any life. It is all these things, and this morning, just as dawn was making the clouds grey, this rock was a fire, a flame among the green bushes; it is moody as a spoiled person but its moods are never dark, threatening; it has always colour, flamboyant or quiet, shouting or smiling, welcoming or withdrawn. It might be one of the gods that is worshipped but it is still a rock of colour and dignity. All these hills seem to have something special to each one of them, none of them is too high, they are hard in a hard climate, they seem to be sculptured and exploding. They seem to go with the valley, not too large, far away from towns and traffic, green when it rains and arid; the beauty of the valley is the trees in the green rice fields. Some of the trees are massive, big of trunk and branch and they are splendid in their shape; others are waiting, expectantly, for the rain, stunted but slowly growing; others are full of leaves and shade. There are not too many of them but those that survive are really quite beautiful. The earth is red and the trees are green and the bushes very close to the red earth. They all survive in the rainless harsh sunny days of many months and when it does rain, their rejoicings shatter the quietness of the valley; every tree and every bush is shouting with life and the green leaf is quite incredible; the hills too join and the whole earth becomes the glory that is.

There was not a sound in the valley; it was dark and there wasn't a leaf moving; dawn would come in an hour or so. Meditation is not self-hypnosis, by words or thought, by repetition or image; all imagination of every kind must be put aside for they lead to delusion. The understanding of facts and not theories, not the pursuits of conclusions and adjustments to them and the ambitions of visions. All these must be set aside and meditation is the understanding of these facts and so going beyond them. Self-knowing is the beginning of meditation; otherwise so-called meditation leads to every form of immaturity and silliness. It was early and the valley was asleep. On waking, meditation was the continuation of what had been going on; the body was without a movement; it was not made to be quiet but it was quiet; there was no thought but the brain was watchful, without any sensation; neither feeling nor thought existed. And a timeless movement began. Word is time, indicating space; word is of the past or the future but the active present has no word. The dead can be put into words but the living cannot. Every word used to communicate about the living is the denial of the living. It was a movement that passed through and between the walls of the brain but the brain had no contact with it; it was incapable of pursuit or of recognition. This movement was something that was not born out of the known; the brain could follow the known as it could recognize it but here no recognition, of any kind, was possible. A movement has direction but this had no direction; it was not static. Because it was without direction, it was the essence of action. All direction is of influence or of reaction. But action which is not the outcome of reaction, push, or pull, is total energy. This energy, love, has its own movement. But the word love, the known, is not love. There is only the fact, the freedom from the known. Meditation was the explosion of the fact.

Our problems multiply and continue; the continuation of a problem perverts and corrupts the mind. A problem is a conflict, an issue which has not been understood; such problems become scars and innocency is destroyed. Every conflict has to be understood and so ended. One of the factors of deterioration is the continued life of a problem; every problem breeds another problem, and a mind burnt with problems, personal or collective, social or economic, is in a state of deterioration.

14th

Sensitivity and sensation are two different things. Sensations, emotions, feelings always leave a residue, whose accumulation dulls and distorts. Sensations are always contradictory and so conflicting; conflict always dulls the mind, perverts perception. The appreciation of beauty in terms of sensation, of like and dislike, is not to perceive beauty; sensation can only divide as beauty and ugliness but division is not beauty. Because sensations, feelings, breed conflict, to avoid conflict, discipline, control, suppression, have been advocated but this only builds resistance and so increases conflict and brings about greater dullness and insensitivity. The saintly control and suppression is the saintly insensitivity and brutal dullness which is so highly regarded. To make the mind more stupid and dull, ideals and conclusions are invented and spread around. All forms of sensations, however refined or gross, cultivate resistance and a withering away. Sensitivity is the dying to every residue of sensation; to be sensitive, utterly and intensely, to a flower, to a person, to a smile, is to have no scar of memory, for every scar destroys sensitivity. To be aware of every sensation, feeling, thought as it arises, from moment to moment, choicelessly, is to be free from scars, never allowing a scar to be formed. Sensations, feelings, thoughts are always partial, fragmentary and destructive. Sensitivity is a total of body, mind and heart.

Knowledge is mechanical and functional; knowledge, capacity, used to acquire status, breeds conflict, antagonism, envy. The cook and the ruler are functions and when status is stolen by either, then begin the quarrels, snobbery and the worship of position, function and power. Power is always evil and it is this evil that corrupts society. The psychological importance of function breeds the hierarchy of status. To deny hierarchy is to deny status; there is hierarchy of function but not of status. Words are of little importance but fact is of immense significance. Fact never brings sorrow but words covering the fact and escapes from it, do breed untold conflict and misery.

A whole group of cattle were feeding on the green land; they were all brown of different shades and when they moved together it was as though the earth moved. They are quite big, indolent and pestered by flies; these are specially cared for, well fed, unlike the village cattle; those are bone-thin small, yielding very little, rather smelly and seem to be everlastingly hungry. There is always some boy or a little girl with them, shouting at them, talking to them, calling them. Everywhere life is hard, there is disease and death. There is an old woman who goes by every day, carrying a little pot of milk or food of some kind; she seems to be shy, without teeth; her clothes are dirty and there is misery on her face; occasionally she smiles but it is rather forced. She is from the village nearby and always barefooted; they are surprisingly small feet and hard but there is fire in her; she is a wiry old lady. Her gentle walk is not at all gentle. Everywhere there is misery and a forced smile. The gods have gone except in the temples and the powerful of the land never have eyes for that woman. But it rained, a long and heavy shower and the clouds hold the hills. The trees follow the clouds and the hills were pursuing them and man is left behind.

15th

It was dawn; the hills were in clouds and every bird was singing, calling, screeching, a cow was bellowing and a dog howled. It was a pleasant morning, the light was soft and the sun was behind the hills and clouds. And a flute was being played under the old, big banyan tree; it was accompanied by a small drum. The flute dominated the drum and filled the air; by its very soft, gentle notes, it seemed to penetrate into your very being; you listened to it though other sounds were coming to you; the varying throbs of the little drum came to you on the waves of the flute and the harsh call of the crow came with the drum. Every sound penetrates, some you resist and others you welcome, the unpleasant and the pleasant and so you lose. The voice of the crow came with the drum and the drum rode on the delicate note of the flute and so the whole sound was able to go deeply beyond all resistance and pleasure. And in that there was great beauty, not the beauty which thought and feeling know. And on that sound rode the exploding meditation; and in that meditation, the flute, the throbbing drum, the harsh caw of the crow and all the things of the earth joined in and thereby gave depth and vastness to the explosion. Explosion is destructive and destruction is the earth and life, as love is. That note of the flute is explosive, if you let it be, but you won't for you want a safe, secure life and so life becomes a dull affair; having made it dull, then you try to give significance, purpose to the ugliness, with its trivial beauty. And so music is something to be enjoyed, arousing a lot of feeling, as football or some religious ritual does. Feeling, emotion, is wasteful and so easily turned to hate. But love is not sensation, a thing captured by feeling. Listening completely, without resistance, without any barrier is the miracle of explosion, shattering the known, and to listen to that explosion, without motive, without direction is to enter where thought, time, cannot pursue.

The valley is probably about a mile wide at its narrowest point, where the hills come together and they run east and west, though one or two hills prevent the others from running freely; they are to the west; where the sun comes from is open, hill after hill. These hills fade into the horizon with precision and height; they seem to have that strange quality of blue-violet that comes with vast age and hot sun. In the evening these hills catch the light of the setting sun and then they become utterly unreal, marvellous in their colour; then the eastern sky has all the colour of the setting sun, you might think that the sun went down there. It was an evening of light pink and dark clouds. The moment one stepped out of the house, talking with another of quite different things, that otherness, that unknowable, was there. It was so unexpected, for one was in the midst of a serious conversation and it was there with such urgency. All talk came to an end, very easily and naturally. The other did not notice the change in the quality of the atmosphere and went on saying something which needed no reply. We walked that whole mile almost without a word and we walked with it, under it, in it. It is wholly the unknown, though it comes and goes; all recognition has stopped for recognition is still the way of the known. Each time there is "greater" beauty and intensity and impenetrable strength. This is the nature of love too.

16th

It was a very quiet evening, the clouds had gone and were gathering around the setting sun. The trees made restless by the breeze were settling down for the night; they too had become quiet; the birds were coming in, taking shelter for the night among the trees that had thick foliage. There were two small owls, sitting high up on the wires, with their unblinking eyes, staring. And as usual, the hills stood alone and aloof far away from every kind of disturbance; during the day they had to put up with the noises of the valley but now they withdrew from all communication, and darkness was closing in upon them, though there was the feeble light of the moon. The moon had a halo of vaporous clouds round it; everything was preparing to go to sleep save the hills. They never slept; they were always watching, waiting, looking and communing amongst themselves, endlessly. Those two little owls on the wire made rattling noises, stones in a metal box; their rattling was far louder than their little bodies, like large fists; you would hear them in the night, going from tree to tree, their flight as silent as the big ones. They flew off the wire flying low, just above the bushes, rising again to the lower branches of the tree, and from a safe distance they would watch and soon lose interest. On the crooked pole further down was a large owl; it was brown with enormous eyes and with a sharp beak that seemed to come out between those staring eyes. It flew off with a few beats of its wings, with such a quietness and deliberation that it made you wonder at the structure and the strength of those graceful wings; it flew off into the hills and lost itself in darkness. This must be the owl, with its mate that has the deep hoot, calling to the other in the night; last night they must have gone into the other valleys beyond the hills; they would come back, for their home was in one of those northern hills where you could hear their early evening calls if you happened to pass by quietly. Beyond these hills were more fertile lands, with green, luscious rice fields.

Questioning has become merely a revolt, a reaction to what is and all reactions have little meaning. The communists revolt against the capitalists, the son against the father; the refusal to accept the social norm, to break through the economic and class bondage. Perhaps, these revolts are necessary but yet they are not very deep; instead of the old, a new pattern is repeated and in the very breaking of the old a new one is, closing in the mind and so destroying it.

The endless revolt within the prison is the questioning reaction of the immediate, and remodelling and redecorating the prison walls seems to give us such intense satisfaction that we never break through the walls. The questioning discontent is within the walls, which doesn't get us very far; it would take you to the moon and to the neutron bombs but all this is still within the call of sorrow. But the questioning of the structure of sorrow and going beyond it is not the escape of reaction. This questioning is far more urgent than going to the moon or to the temple; it is this questioning that tears down the structure and not the building of a new and more expensive prison, with its gods and saviours, with its economists and leaders. This questioning destroys the machinery of thought and not the substitution of one by another thought, conclusion, theory. This questioning shatters authority, the authority of experience, word and the most respected evil power. This questioning, which is not born of reaction, of choice and motive, explodes the moral, respectable self-centred activity; it is this activity that is always being reformed and never smashed. This endless reformation is the endless sorrow. What has cause and motive inevitably breeds agony and despair.

We are afraid of this total destruction of the known, the ground of the self, the me and the mine; the known is better than the unknown, the known with its confusion, conflict and misery; freedom from this known may destroy what we call love, relationship, joy and so on. Freedom from the known, the explosive questioning, not of reaction, ends sorrow, and so love then is something that thought and feeling cannot measure.

Our life is so shallow and empty, petty thoughts and petty activities, woven in conflict and misery and always journeying from the known to the known, psychologically demanding security. There is no security in the known however much one may want it. Security is time and there is no psychological time; it is a myth and an illusion, breeding fear. There is nothing permanent now or in the hereafter, in the future. By right questioning and listening, the pattern moulded by thought and feeling, the pattern of the known, is shattered. Self-knowing, knowing the ways of thought and feeling, listening to every movement of thought and feeling, ends the known. The known breeds sorrow, and love is the freedom from the known.

17th

The earth was the colour of the sky; the hills, the green, ripening rice fields, the trees and the dry, sandy river-bed were the colour of the sky; every rock on the hills, the big boulders, were the clouds and they were the rocks. Heaven was the earth and the earth heaven; the setting sun had transformed everything. The sky was blazing fire, bursting in every streak of cloud, in every stone, in every blade of grass, in every grain of sand. The sky was ablaze with green, purple, violet, indigo, with the fury of flame. Over that hill it was a vast sweep of purple and gold; over the southern hills a burning delicate green and fading blues; to the east there was a counter sunset as splendid in cardinal red and burnt ochre, magenta and fading violet. The counter sunset was exploding in splendour as in the west; a few clouds had gathered themselves around the setting sun and they were pure, smokeless fire which would never die. The vastness of this fire and its intensity penetrated everything and entered the earth. The earth was the heavens and the heavens the earth. And everything was alive and bursting with colour and colour was god, not the god of man. The hills became transparent, every rock and boulder was without weight, floating in colour and the distant hills were blue, the blue of all the seas and the sky of every clime. The ripening rice fields were intense pink and green, a stretch of immediate attention. And the road that crossed the valley was purple and white, so alive that it was one of the rays that raced across the sky. You were of that light, burning, furious, exploding, without shadow, without root and word. And as the sun went further down, every colour became more violent, more intense and you were completely lost, past all recalling. It was an evening that had no memory.

Every thought and feeling must flower for them to live and die; flowering of everything in you, the ambition, the greed, the hate, the joy, the passion; in the flowering there is their death and freedom. It is only in freedom that anything can flourish, not in suppression, in control and discipline; these only pervert, corrupt. Flowering and freedom is goodness and all virtue. To allow envy to flower is not easy; it is condemned or cherished but never given freedom. It is only in freedom the fact of envy reveals its colour, its shape, its depth, its peculiarities; if suppressed it will not reveal itself fully and freely. When it has shown itself completely, there is an ending of it only to reveal another fact, emptiness, loneliness, fear, and as each fact is allowed to flower, in freedom, in its entirety, the conflict betwen the observer and the observed ceases; there is no longer the censor but only observation, only seeing. Freedom can only be in completion not in repetition, suppression, obedience to a pattern of thought. There is completion only in flowering and dying; there is no flowering if there is no ending. What has continuity is thought in time. The flowering of thought is the ending of thought; for only in death is there the new. The new cannot be if there is no freedom from the known. Thought, the old, cannot bring into being the new; it must die for the new to be. What flowers must come to an end.

20th

It was very dark; the stars were brilliant in a cloudless sky and the mountain air was cool and fresh. The headlights caught the tall cacti and they were polished silver; the morning dew was upon them and they shone; the little plants were bright with the dew and the headlights made the green sparkle and flash with a green that was not of the day. Every

tree was silent, mysterious and dreaming and unapproachable. Orion and the Pleiades were setting among the dark
hills; even the owls were far away and silent; except for the
noise of the car, the country was asleep; only the nightjars,
with red sparkling eyes, caught by the headlights, sitting on
the road, stared at us and flutteringly flew away. So early in
the morning, the villages were asleep and the few people on
the road had wrapped themselves up just showing their faces
and were walking wearily from one village to another; they
looked as though they had been walking all night; a few
were huddled around a blaze, throwing long shadows across
the road. A dog was scratching itself in the middle of the
road; it wouldn't move and the car had to go around it.
Then suddenly, the morning star showed itself; it was easily
as large as a saucer, astonishingly bright and seemed to hold
the east in sway. As it climbed, Mercury appeared, just below
her, pale and over-powering. There was a slight glow and far
away was the beginning of dawn. The road curved in and
out, hardly ever straight and trees on either side of the road
held it from wandering off into the fields. There were large
stretches of water, to be used for irrigation purposes in the
summer when water would be scarce. The birds were still
asleep, except for one or two and as dawn came closer, they
began to wake up, crows, vultures, pigeons and the innumerable small birds. We were climbing and went over a long
wooded range; no wild animals crossed the road. And there
were monkeys on the road now, a huge fellow, sitting under
the large trunk of the tamarind; it never moved as we
passed by though the others scampered off in every direction.
There was a little one, it must have been a few days old, clinging to the belly of her mother who looked rather displeased
with things. Dawn was yielding to day and the lorries that
crashed by had turned off their lights. And now the villages
were awake, people sweeping their front steps and throwing
dirt in the middle of the road; mangy dogs still fast asleep
right in the middle of the road; they seemed to prefer the

very centre of the road; lorries went around them, cars and people. Women were carrying water from the well, with little children following them. The sun was getting hot and glary and the hills were harsh and there were fewer trees and we were leaving the mountains and going towards the sea in a flat, open country; the air was moist and hot and we were coming nearer the big, crowded, dirty city* and the hills were far behind.

The car was going fairly fast and it was a good place to meditate. To be free of the word and not to give too much importance to it; to see that the word is not the thing and the thing is never the word; not to get caught in the overtones of the word and yet use words with care and understanding; to be sensitive to words and not to be weighed down by them; to break through the verbal barrier and to consider the fact; to avoid the poison of words and feel the beauty of them; to put away all identification with words and to examine them, for words are a trap and a snare. They are the symbols and not the real. The screen of words acts as a shelter for the lazy, the thoughtless and the deceiving mind. Slavery to words is the beginning of inaction which may appear to be action and a mind caught in symbols cannot go far. Every word, thought, shapes the mind and without understanding every thought, mind becomes a slave to words and sorrow begins. Conclusions and explanations do not end sorrow.

Meditation is not a means to an end; there is no end, no arrival; it is a movement in time and out of time. Every system, method, binds thought to time but choiceless awareness of every thought and feeling, understanding their motives, their mechanism, allowing them to blossom is the beginning of meditation. When thought and feeling flourish and die, meditation is the movement beyond time. In this

* Madras. He went to stay in a house in seven acres of ground on the north bank of the Adyar River. This river flows into the Bay of Bengal, south of Madras.

movement there is ecstasy; in complete emptiness there is love, and with love there is destruction and creation.

21st

All existence is choice; only in aloneness there is no choice. Choice, in every form, is conflict. Contradiction is inevitable in choice; this contradiction, inner and outer breeds confusion and misery. To escape from this misery, gods, beliefs, nationalism, commitment to various patterns of activities become compulsive necessities. Having escaped, they become all important and escape is the way of illusion; then fear and anxiety set in. Despair and sorrow is the way of choice and there is no end to pain. Choice, selection, must always exist as long as there is the chooser, the accumulated memory of pain and pleasure, and every experience of choice only strengthens memory whose response becomes thought and feeling. Memory has only a partial significance, to respond mechanically; this response is choice. There is no freedom in choice. You choose according to the background you have been brought up in, according to your social, economic, religious conditioning. Choice invariably strengthens this conditioning; there is no escape from this conditioning, it only breeds more suffering.

There were a few clouds gathering around the sun; they were far down on the horizon and were afire. The palm trees were dark against the flaming sky; they stood in golden-green rice fields stretching far into the horizon. There was one all by itself, in a yellowing green of rice; it was not alone, though it looked rather forlorn and far away. A gentle breeze from the sea was blowing and a few clouds were chasing each other, faster than the breeze. The flames were dying and the moon strengthened the shadows. Everywhere there were shadows, quietly whispering to each other. The moon was just overhead and across the road the shadows deep and deceptive. A water snake might be crossing the road; quietly slithering across, pursuing a frog; there was water in the rice fields and frogs were croaking, almost rhythmically; in the long stretch of water beside the road, with their heads up, out of the water, they were chasing each other; they would go under and come up to disappear again. The water was bright silver, sparkling and warm to the touch and full of mysterious noises. Bullock carts went by, carrying firewood to the town; a cycle bell rang, a lorry with bright glaring lights screeched for room and the shadows remained motionless. It was a beautiful evening and there on that road so close to town, there was deep silence and not a sound disturbed it, not even the moon and the lorry. It was a silence that no thought, no word could touch, a silence that went with the frogs and the cycles, a silence that followed you; you walked in it, you breathed it, you saw it. It was not shy, it was there insisting and welcoming. It went beyond you into vast immensities and you could follow it if your thought and feeling were utterly quiet, forgetting themselves and losing themselves with the frogs in the water; they had no importance and could so easily lose themselves, to be picked up when they were wanted. It was an enchanting evening, full of clarity and fast-fading smile.

Choice is always breeding misery. Watch it and you will see it, lurking, demanding, insisting and begging, and before you know where you are you are caught in its net of inescapable duties, responsibilities and despairs. Watch it and you will be aware of the fact. Be aware of the fact; you cannot change the fact; you may cover it up, run away from it, but you cannot change it. It is there. If you will let it alone, not interfering with it with your opinions and hopes, fears and despairs, with your calculated and cunning judgements, it will flower and show all its intricacies, its subtle ways and there are many, its seeming importance and ethics, its hidden motives and fancies. If you will leave the fact alone, it will show you all these and more. But you must be choicelessly aware of it, walking softly. Then you will see that choice, having flowered, dies and there is freedom, not that you are free but there is freedom. You are the maker of choice; you have ceased to make choice. There is nothing to choose. Out of this choiceless state there flowers aloneness. Its death is never ending. It is always flowering and it is always new. Dying to the known is to be alone. All choice is in the field of the known; action in this field always breeds sorrow. There is the ending of sorrow in aloneness.

22nd*

In the opening of masses of leaves was a pink flower of three petals; it was embedded in green and it too must have been surprised by its own beauty. It grew on a tall bush, struggling to survive among all that greenery; there was a huge tree towering over it and there were several other bushes, all fighting for life. There were many other flowers on this bush but this one among the leaves had no companion, it was all by itself and so more startling. There was a slight breeze among the leaves but it never got to this flower; it was motionless and alone and because it was alone, it had a strange beauty, like a single star when the sky is bare. And beyond the green leaves was a black trunk of the palm; it wasn't really black but it looked like the trunk of an elephant. And as you watched it, the black turned to a flowering pink; the evening sun was upon it and all the treetops were afire, motionless. The breeze had died down and patches of the setting sun were upon the leaves. A small bird was sitting on a branch, preening itself. It stopped to look around and presently flew off into the sun. We were sitting facing the musicians who were facing the setting sun; there were very few of us and the little drum was being played with remarkable skill and pleasure; it was really quite extraordinary what those fingers did. The player never looked at his hands; they seemed to have a life of their own, moving with great rapidity and firmness, striking the taut skin with precision;

* That morning he gave the first of eight talks in Madras, continuing until December 17th.

there was never hesitation. What the right hand did the left hand never knew for it was beating out a different rhythm but always in harmony. The player was quite young, grave with sparkling eyes; he had talent and was delighted to be playing to that small, appreciative audience. Then a stringed instrument joined in and the small drum followed. It was no longer alone.

The sun had set and the few wandering clouds were turning pale rose; at this latitude there is no twilight and the moon, nearly full, was clear in a cloudless sky. Walking on that road, with the moonlight on the water and the croaking of many frogs, became a blessing. It is strange how far away the world is and into what great depth one has travelled. The telegraph poles, the buses, the bullock carts and the worn-out villagers were there beside you but you were far away, so deep that no thought could follow; every feeling stayed far away. You were walking, aware of everything that was happening around you, the darkening of the moon by masses of clouds, the warning of the cycle bell, but you were far away, not you but great, vast depth. This depth went on more profoundly within itself, past time and the limits of space. Memory couldn't follow it; memory is tethered, but this wasn't. It was total complete freedom, without root and direction. And deep, far from thought there was bursting energy which was ecstasy, a word that has pleasurable gratifying significance to thought but thought could never capture it or travel the spaceless distance to pursue it. Thought is a barren thing and could never follow or communicate with that which is timeless. The thundering bus, with its blinding lights, nearly pushed one off the road, into the dancing waters.

The essence of control is suppression. The pure seeing puts an end to every form of suppression; seeing is infinitely more subtle than mere control. Control is comparatively easy, it doesn't need much understanding; conformity to a pattern, obedience to established authority, fear of not doing the right

thing, of tradition, the drive for success, these are the very
things that bring about suppression of what is or the sublimation of what is. The pure act of seeing the fact, whatever the
fact be, brings its own understanding and from this, mutation
takes place.

25th

The sun was behind the clouds and the flat lands stretched
far into the horizon which was turning golden brown and red;
there was a little canal over which the road went among the
rice fields. They were golden yellow and green, spreading on
both sides of the road, east and west to the sea and to the
setting sun. There is something extraordinarily touching and
beautiful to see palm trees, black against the burning sky,
among the rice fields; it was not that the scene was romantic
or sentimental or picture post-cardish; probably it was all
this but there was an intensity and a sweeping dignity and
delight in the earth itself and in the common things that one
passed by every day. The canal, a long, narrow strip of water
of melting fire, went north and south among the rice fields.
silent and lonely; there was not much traffic on it; there were
barges, crudely made, with square or triangular sails carrying
firewood or sand and men sitting huddled together, looking
very grave. The palm trees dominated the wide green earth;
they were of every shape and size, independent and carefree,
swept by the winds and burnt by the sun. The rice fields were
ripening golden yellow and there were largish white birds
among them; they were flying now into the sunset, their long
legs stretched out behind, their wings lazily beating the air.
Bullock carts, carrying casuarina firewood to the town, went
by, a long line of them, creaking and the men walking and
the load was heavy. It was none of these common sights that
made the evening enchanting; they were all part of the
fading evening, the noisy buses, the silent bicycles, the croaks
of the frogs, the smell of the evening. There was a deep widening intensity, an imminent clarity of that otherness, with its

impenetrable strength and purity. What was beautiful was now glorified in splendour; everything was clothed in it; there was ecstasy and laughter not only deeply within but among the palms and the rice fields. Love is not a common thing but it was there in the hut with an oil lamp; it was with that old woman, carrying something heavy on her head; with that naked boy, swinging on a piece of string a piece of wood which gave out many sparks for it was his fireworks. It was everywhere, so common that you could pick it up under a dead leaf or in that jasmine by the old crumbling house. But everyone was occupied; busy and lost. It was there filling your heart, your mind and the sky; it remained and would never leave you. Only you would have to die to everything, without roots, without a tear. Then it would come to you, if you were lucky and you forever ceased to run after it, begging, hoping, crying. Indifferent to it, but without sorrow, and thought left far behind. And it would be there, on that dusty, dark road.

The flowering of meditation is goodness. It is not a virtue to be gathered bit by bit, slowly in the space of time; it is not morality made respectable by society nor is it the sanction of authority. It is the beauty of meditation that gives perfume to its flowering. How can there be joy in meditation if it is the coaxing of desire and pain; how can it flower if you are seeking it through control, suppression and sacrifice; how can it blossom in the darkness of fear or in corrupting ambition and in the smell of success; how can it bloom in the shadow of hope and despair? You will have to leave all these far behind, without regret, easily, naturally. You see, meditation has not the strain of building defences, to resist and to wither; it is not fashioned out of a sustained practice of any system. All systems will inevitably shape thought to a pattern and conformity destroys the flowering of meditation. It blossoms only in freedom and the withering of that which is. Without freedom there is no self-knowing and without self-knowing there is no meditation. Thought is always petty and shallow however far it may wander in search of knowledge; acquiring expanding knowledge is not meditation. It flowers only in the freedom from the known and withers away in the known.

26th

There is a palm tree, all by itself, in the middle of a rice field; it is no longer young, there are only a few palms. It is very tall and very straight; it has the quality of righteousness with the fuss and noise of respectability. It is there and it is alone. It has never known anything else and it would continue to be that way until it died or is destroyed. You suddenly came upon it at the turn of the road and you are startled to see it among the rich rice fields and flowing water; the water and the green fields were murmuring to each other which they always have been doing from ancient days and these gentle mutterings never reached the palm; it was alone with the high heaven and flashing clouds. It was by itself, complete and aloof and it would be nothing else. The water was sparkling in the evening light and away from the road towards the west was the palm tree and beyond it were more rice fields; before coming upon it you had to go through some noisy, dirty, dusty streets, full of children, goats and cattle; the buses raised clouds of dust which nobody seemed to mind and the mangy dogs crowded the road. The car turned off the main thoroughfare which went on, past many small houses and gardens, past rice fields. The car turned left, went through some pompous gates, and a little further on, there in the open, were deer, grazing. There must have been two or three dozen; some had tall heavy antlers and some of the young ones were already showing, sharply, what they would be; many of them were spotted white; they were nervous, flicking their large ears but they went on grazing. Many crossed the red road into the open and there were several more waiting among the bushes to see what was going to happen; the little car had stopped and presently all of them crossed over and joined the others. The evening was clear and the stars were coming out, bright and clear; the trees were withdrawing for the night and the impatient chattering of the birds had come to an end. The evening light was on the water.

In that evening light, along that narrow road, the intensity of delight increased and there was no cause for it. It had begun while watching a small jumping spider which jumped with astonishing rapidity on flies and held them fiercely; it had begun while watching a single leaf fluttering while the other leaves were still; it had begun while watching the small striped squirrel, scolding something or other, its long tail bobbing up and down. The delight had no cause, and joy that is a result is so trivial anyway and changes with the change. This strange, unexpected delight increased in its intensity and what is intense is never brutal; it has the quality of yielding but still it remains intense. It is not the intensity of all energy, concentrated; it is not brought about by thought pursuing an idea or occupied with itself; it is not a heightened feeling, for all these have motives and purposes. This intensity had no cause, no end, nor was it brought into being through concentration which really bars the awakening of the total energy. It increased without something being done about it; it was, as something outside of you, over which you had no control; you had no say in the matter. In the very increasing of intensity, there was gentleness. This word is spoilt; it indicates weakness, sloppiness, irresolution, uncertainty, a shy withdrawal, a certain fear and so on. But it was none of these things; it was vital and strong, without defences and so, intense. You couldn't cultivate it, if you wished; it didn't belong to the category of the strong and the weak. It was vulnerable as love is. The delight with its gentleness increased in intensity. There was nothing else but that. The coming and the going of people, the drive in the car and the talk, the deer and the palm tree, the stars and the rice fields were there, in their beauty and freshness, but they were all inside and outside this intensity. A flame has a form, a line, but inside the flame there is only intense heat without form and line.

27th

The clouds were piling up to the south-west driven by a strong wind; they were magnificent, great billowing clouds, full of fury and space; they were white and dark grey, rain-bearing, filling the sky. The old trees were angry with them and the wind. They wanted to be left alone, though they wanted rain; it would wash them again clean, wash away all the dust and their leaves would sparkle again but they didn't like being disturbed, like old people. The garden had so many flowers, so many colours and each flower was doing a dance, a skip and a jump and every leaf was astir; even the little blades of grass on the little lawn were being shaken. And two old, thin women were weeding it; two old women, old before their age, thin and worn out; they were squatting upon the lawn, chatting and weeding, leisurely; they weren't all there, they were somewhere else, carried away by their thoughts, though they were weeding and talking. They looked intelligent, their eyes sparkling, but perhaps too many children and lack of good food had made them old and weary. You became them, they were you and the grass and the clouds; it wasn't a verbal bridge over which you crossed out of pity or out of some vague, unfamiliar sentiment; you were not thinking at all, nor were your emotions stirred. They were you and you were they; distance and time had ceased. A car came with a chauffeur and he entered into that world. His shy smile and salute were those of yours and you were wondering at whom he was smiling and whom he was saluting; he was feeling a little awkward, not quite used to that feeling of being together. The women and the chauffeur were you and you were they; the barrier which they had built was gone and as the clouds overhead went by, it all seemed a part of a widening circle, including so many things, the filthy road and the splendid sky and the passer-by. It had nothing to do with thought,

thought is such a sordid thing anyway and feeling was involved in no way. It was like a flame that burned its way through everything leaving no mark, no ashes; it wasn't an experience, with its memories, to be repeated. They were you and you were they and it died with the mind.

It is strange, the desire to show off or to be somebody. Envy is hate and vanity corrupts. It seems so impossibly difficult to be simple, to be what you are and not pretend. To be what you are is in itself very arduous without trying to become something, which is not too difficult. You can always pretend, put on a mask but to be what you are is an extremely complex affair; because you are always changing; you are never the same and each moment reveals a new facet, a new depth, a new surface. You can't be all this at one moment for each moment brings its own change. So if you are at all intelligent, you give up being anything. You think you are very sensitive and an incident, a fleeting thought, shows that you are not; you think you are clever, well-read, artistic, moral but turn round the corner, you find you are none of these things but that you are deeply ambitious, envious, insufficient, brutal and anxious. You are all these things turn by turn and you want something to be continuous, permanent, of course only that which is profitable, pleasurable. So you run after that and all the many other yous are clamouring to have their way, to have their fulfilment. So you became the battle-field and generally ambition, with all its pleasures and pain, gaining, with envy and fear. The word love is thrown in for respectability's sake and to hold the family together but you are caught in your own commitments and activities, isolated, clamouring for recognition and fame, you and your country, you and your party, you and your comforting god.

So to be what you are is an extremely arduous affair; if you are at all awake, you know all these things and the sorrow of it all. So you drown yourself in your work, in your belief, in your fantastic ideals and meditations. By then you have become old and ready for the grave, if you are not already dead inwardly. To put away all these things, with their contradictions and increasing sorrow, and be nothing is the most natural and intelligent thing to do. But before you can be nothing, you must have unearthed all these hidden things, exposing them and so understanding them. To understand these hidden urges and compulsions, you will have to be aware of them, without choice, as with death; then in the pure act of seeing, they will wither away and you will be without sorrow and so be as nothing. To be as nothing is not a negative state; the very denial of everything you have been is the most positive action, not the positive of reaction, which is inaction; it is this inaction which causes sorrow. This denial is freedom. This positive action gives energy, and mere ideas dissipate energy. Idea is time and living in time is disintegration, sorrow.

28th

There was a large opening in the thick closely-planted casuarina grove beside a quiet road; towards the evening it was dark, deserted and the opening invited the heavens. Further down the road there was a thin-walled hut with palm leaves, woven together, for its roof; in the hut was a dim light, a wick burning in a saucer of oil, and two people, a man and a woman, were sitting on the floor, eating their evening meal, chatting loudly, with occasional laughter. Two men were coming through the rice fields on a narrow path, dividing the fields and to hold water. They were talking volubly, carrying something on their heads. There was a group of villagers, laughing shrilly and explaining something to each other, with a great many gestures. A few days' old calf was being led by a woman, followed by the mother softly assuring the baby. A flock of white birds with long legs were flying north, their wings beating the air slowly and rhythmically. The sun had set in a clear sky and a rose-coloured ray shot across the sky, almost from horizon to horizon. It was a very quiet evening and the lights of the city were far away.

It was that little opening in the casuarina grove that held the evening, and as one walked past it, one was aware of its extraordinary stillness; all the lights and glare of the day had been forgotten and the bustle of men coming and going. Now it was quiet, enclosed by dark trees and fast-fading light. It was not only quiet but there was joy in it, the joy of immense solitude and as one went by it, that ever-strange otherness came, like a wave, covering the heart and the mind in its beauty and its clarity. All time ceased, the next moment had no beginning. Out of emptiness only is there love.

Meditation is not a play of imagination. Every form of image, word, symbol must come to an end for the flowering of meditation. The mind must lose its slavery to words and their reaction. Thought is time, and symbol, however ancient and significant, must lose its grip on thought. Thought then has no continuity; it is then only from moment to moment and so loses its mechanical insistency; thought then does not shape the mind and enclose it within the frame of ideas and condition it to culture, to the society, in which it lives. Freedom is not from society but from idea; then relationship, society, does not condition the mind. The whole of consciousness is residual, changing, modifying, conforming, and mutation is only possible when time and idea have come to an end. The ending is not a conclusion, a word to be destroyed, an idea to be denied or accepted. It is to be understood through self-knowing; knowing is not learning; knowing is recognition and accumulation which prevents learning. Learning is from moment to moment, for the self, the me, is ever-changing, never constant. Accumulation, knowledge, distorts and puts an end to learning. Gathering knowledge, however expanding its frontier, becomes mechanical and a mechanical mind is not a free mind. Self-knowing liberates the mind from the known; to live the entire life in the activity of the known breeds endless conflict and misery. Meditation is not personal achievement, a personal quest for reality; it becomes one when it is restricted by methods and systems and thereby deceptions and illusions are bred. Meditation frees the mind from the narrow, limited existence to the ever-expanding, timeless life.

29th

Without sensitivity there can be no affection; personal reaction does not indicate sensitivity; you may be sensitive about your family, about your achievement, about your status and capacity. This kind of sensitivity is a reaction, limited, narrow, and is deteriorating. Sensitivity is not good taste for good taste is personal and the freedom from personal reaction is the awareness of beauty. Without the appreciation of beauty and without the sensitive awareness of it, there is no love. This sensitive awareness of nature, of the river, of the sky, of the people, of the filthy road, is affection. The essence of affection is sensitivity. But most people are afraid of being sensitive; to them to be sensitive is to get hurt and so they harden themselves and so preserve their sorrow. Or they escape into every form of entertainment, the church, the temple, gossip and cinema and social reform. But being sensitive is not personal and when it is, it leads to misery. To break through this personal reaction is to love, and love is for the one and the many; it is not restricted to the one or to the many. To be sensitive, all the senses must be fully alive, active, and fear of being a slave to the senses is merely the avoidance of a natural fact. The awareness of the fact does not lead to slavery; it is the fear of the fact that leads to bondage. Thought is of the senses and thought makes for limitation but yet you are not afraid of thought. On the contrary, it is ennobled with respectability and enshrined with conceit. To be sensitively aware of thought, of feeling, of the world about you, of your office and of nature, is to explode from moment to moment in affection. Without affection, every action becomes burdensome and mechanical and leads to decay.

It was a rainy morning and the sky was heavy with clouds,

dark and tumultuous; it began raining very early and you could hear it among the leaves. And there were so many birds on the little lawn, big and little ones, light grey, brown with yellow eyes, large black crows and little ones, smaller than sparrows; they were scratching, pulling, chattering, restless, complaining and pleased. It was drizzling and they didn't·seem to mind but when it began to rain harder, they all flew off, complaining loudly. But the bushes and the large, old trees were rejoicing; their leaves were washed clean of the dust of many days. Drops of water were clinging to the ends of leaves; one drop would fall to the ground and another would form to fall; each drop was the rain, the river and the sea. And every drop was bright, sparkling; it was richer than all the diamonds and more lovely; it gathered to a drop, remained in its beauty and disappeared into the ground, leaving no mark. It was an endless procession and disappeared into the ground. It was an endless procession beyond time. It was raining now and the earth was filling itself for the hot days of many months. The sun was behind many clouds and the earth was taking rest from the heat. The road was very bad, full of deep pot-holes, filled with brown water; sometimes the little car went through them, sometimes dodged them but went on. There were pink flowers which crept up trees, along the barbed-wire fences, growing wildly over bushes and the rain was among them, making their colours softer and more gentle; they were everywhere and would not be denied. The road went past a filthy village, with filthy shops and filthy restaurants and as it turned, there was a rice field, enclosed among the palm trees. They surrounded it, almost holding it to themselves, lest men should spoil it. The rice field followed the curving lines of the palms and beyond it were banana groves whose large, shining leaves were visible through the palms. That rice field was enchanted; it was so amazingly green, so rich and wondrous; it was incredible, it took your mind and heart away. You looked and you disappeared, never to be again the same. That colour was god, was music, was the love of the earth; the heavens came to the palms and covered the earth. But that rice field was the bliss of eternity. And the road went on to the sea; that sea was pale green, with enormous rolling waves crashing on a sandy beach; they were murderous waves and angry with the pent-up fury of many storms; the sea looked furiously calm and the waves showed its danger. There were no boats on the sea, those flimsy catamarans, so crudely put together by a piece of rope; all the fishermen were in those dark, palm-thatched huts on the sands, so close to the water. And the clouds came rolling along carried by winds that you couldn't feel. And it would rain again, with the pleasant laughter.

To the so-called religious to be sensitive is to sin, an evil reserved for the worldly; to the religious the beautiful is temptation, to be resisted; it's an evil distraction to be denied. Good works are not a substitute for love, and without love all activity leads to sorrow, noble or ignoble. The essence of affection is sensitivity and without it all worship is an escape from reality. To the monk, to the sanyasi, the senses are the way of pain, save thought which must be dedicated to the god of their conditioning. But thought is of the senses. It is thought that puts together time and it is thought that makes sensitivity sinful. To go beyond thought is virtue and that virtue is heightened sensitivity which is love. Love and there is no sin; love and do what you will and then there is no sorrow.

30th

A country without a river is desolate. It is a small river, if it can be called a river, but it has a fairly large bridge of stone and brick;* it is not too wide and the buses and cars have to go slowly and there are always people on foot and the inevit-

---

* The Elphinstone Bridge over the Adyar River. The house where he was staying was on the north-west side of the bridge.

able bicycle. It pretends to be a river and during the rains it looks like a deep, full river but now when the rains are nearly over, it looks like a large sheet of water with a large island, with many bushes in the middle of it. It goes to the sea, due east, with a great deal of animation and joy. But now there is a wide sand-bar and so it waits for the next rainy reason. Cattle were fording on to the island and a few fishermen were trying to catch some fish; the fish were always small, about the size of a large finger and they smelt dreadful as they were being sold under the trees. And that evening, in the quiet waters, was a large heron, utterly frozen and still. It was the only bird on the river; in the evening crows and other birds would be flying across the river but there were none that evening, except for this single heron. You couldn't help seeing it; it was so white, motionless, with a sunlit sky. The yellow sun and the pale green sea were some distance and as the land went towards them, three large palm trees faced the river and the sea. The evening sun was upon them and the sea beyond, restless, dangerous and pleasantly blue. From the bridge, the sky seemed so vast, so close and unspoiled; it was far from the airport. But that evening, that single heron and the three palm trees were the whole earth, time past and present and life that had no past. Meditation became a flowering without roots and so a dying. Negation is a marvellous movement of life and the positive is only a reaction to life, a resistance. With resistance there is no death but only fear; fear breeds further fear and degeneration. Death is the flowering of the new; meditation is the dying of the known.

It is strange that one can never say, "I don't know". To really say it and feel it, there must be humility. But one never admits to the fact of never knowing; it is vanity that feeds the mind with knowledge. Vanity is a strange disease, ever hopeful and ever dejected. But to admit to not knowing is to stop the mechanical process of knowing. There are several ways of saying, "I don't know"—pretence and all its

subtle and underhand methods, to impress, to gain importance and so on; the "I don't know" which is really marking
time to find out and the "I don't know" which is not search-
ing out to know; the former state never learns, it only gathers
and so never learns, and the latter is always in a state of learning, without ever accumulating. There must be freedom to
learn and so the mind can remain young and innocent;
accumulation makes the mind decay, grow old and wither.
Innocency is not the lack of experience but to be free of
experience; this freedom is to die to every experience and not
let it take root in the soil of the enriching brain. Life is not
without experience but life is not when the soil is full of roots.
But humility is not conscious clearing of the known; that is
the vanity of achievement, but humility is that complete not
knowing which is dying. Fear of death is only in knowing, not
in not knowing. There is no fear of the unknown, only in the
changing of the known, in the ending of the known.

But the habit of the word, the emotional content of the
word, the hidden implications of the word, prevent the freedom from the word. Without this freedom you are a slave to
words, to conclusions, to ideas. If you live on words, as so
many do, the inward hunger is insatiable; it is forever ploughing and never sowing. Then you live in the world of unreality,
of make-believe, of sorrow that has no meaning. A belief is a
word, a conclusion of thought, made up of words and it is
this that corrupts, spoiling the beauty of the mind. To destroy
the word is to demolish the inward structure of security,
which has no reality in any way. To be insecure, which is not
the violent wrenching from security, leading to various forms
of illness, but that insecurity which comes from the flowering
of security, is humility and innocency whose strength the arro-
gant can never know.

December 1st, 1961
The road was muddy, deep rutted, full of people; it was outside the town and slowly a suburb was being built, but now

it was incredibly dirty, full of holes, dogs, goats, wandering cattle, buses, cycles, cars and more people; shops were selling coloured drinks in bottles, shops that had cloth to sell, food, wood for fire, a bank, a cycle-repair shop, more food, goats and more people. There was still country on either side of the road, palm trees, rice fields, and great puddles of water. The sun was among the clouds behind the palm trees bursting with colour and vast shadows; the pools were ablaze and every bush and tree was amazed by the vastness of the sky. The goats were nibbling at their roots, women were washing their clothes at a tap, children went on playing; everywhere there was activity and nobody bothered to look at the sky or at those clouds, bearing colour; it was an evening that would soon disappear never to appear again and nobody seemed to care. The immediate was all important, the immediate that may extend into the future beyond sight. The long vision is the immediate vision. The bus came hurtling along, never giving an inch, sure of itself, everyone giving way, but the heavy buffalo stopped it; it was right in the middle, moving at its own heavy gait, never paying attention to the horn and the horn stopped in exasperation. At heart everyone is a politician, concerned with the immediate and trying to force all life into the immediate. And later on there would be sorrow, round the corner, but it could be avoided; there was the pill, the drink, the temple and the family of immediacies. You could end it all if you believed in something ardently or drowned yourself in work or committed yourself to some pattern of thought. But you have tried them all and your mind was as barren as your heart and you crossed to the other side of the road and got lost in the immediate. The clouds were now heavy in the sky and there was only a patch of colour where the sun had been. The road went on, past the palm trees, the casuarinas, rice fields, huts and on and on and suddenly as ever unexpectedly, that otherness came with that purity and strength which no thought or madness could possibly ever formulate and it was there and your heart seemed to explode into the empty heavens, with ecstasy. The brain was utterly still, motionless, but sensitive, watching. It could not follow into emptiness; it was of time but time had stopped and it could not experience; experience is recognition and what it recognized would be time. So it was motionless, merely quiescent, without asking, seeking. And this totality of love or what you will, word is not the thing, entered into everything and was lost. Everything had its space, its place, but this had none and so it cannot be found; do what you will you will not find it. It is not on the market nor in any temple; everything has to be destroyed, not a stone left unturned, no foundation to stand on, but even then this emptiness must be without a tear, then perhaps the unknowable might pass by. It was there and beauty.

All deliberate pattern of change is non-change; change has motive, purpose, direction and so it is merely a continuity, modified, of what has been. Such change is futile; it is like changing clothes on a doll but it remains, mechanical, lifeless, brittle, to be broken and thrown away. Death is the inevitable end of change; economic, social revolution is death in the pattern of change. It is not a revolution at all, it is a continuity, modified, of what has been. Mutation, total revolution, takes place only when change, the pattern of time, is seen as false and in its total abandonment mutation takes place.

2nd

The sea was rough, with thunderous waves that came in from afar; nearby was a village built round a large, deep pond, a tank it is called, and a broken-down temple. The water of the tank was pale green and steps lead down to it, from all sides. The village was neglected, dirty and there were hardly any roads, and round about this tank were houses and on one side was the old temple in ruins and a comparatively new one, with red striped walls; the houses were dilapidated but that village had a familiar, friendly feeling about it. Beside the way that led to the sea a whole group of women were haggling over some fish at the top of their voices; everyone seemed so excited about everything; it was their evening entertainment for they were laughing too. And there were the sweepings of the road in a heap in the corner and the mangy village dogs were poking their noses into it and a shop close to it was selling drinks, things to eat, and a poor woman with a baby and torn rags was begging at the door of the shop. The cruel sea was close by, thundering away and the luscious green rice fields were beyond the village, peaceful, full of promise in the evening light. Clouds were coming across the sea, unhurriedly, with the sun upon them and everywhere there was activity and no one looked up at the sky. The dead fish, the noisy group, the green waters in that deep pond, the striped walls of the temple seemed to hold back the setting sun. If you walk on that road across the canal, beside the rice field and casuarina groves, every passer-by you know, they are friendly, they stop and talk to you, that you should come to live among them, that they would look after you, and the sky is darkening and the green of the rice fields is gone and the stars are very bright.

Walking on that road in the dark with the light of the city in the clouds, that inviolable strength comes with such abundance and with such clarity that it took literally your breath away. All life was that strength. It wasn't the strength of carefully built-up will, nor the strength of many defences and resistances; it was not the strength of courage nor the strength of jealousy and death. It had no quality, no description could contain it and yet it was there as those dark distant hills and those trees beside the road. It was too immense for thought to bring it about or speculate upon. It was a strength that had no cause and so nothing could be added to or taken away from it. It cannot be known; it has no shape, form, and cannot be approached. Knowing is recognition but it is always new, something that cannot be measured in time. It had been there all day, uncertainly, without insistence like a whisper but now it was there with an urgency and with such abundance that there was nothing but that. Words have been spoilt and made common; the word love is on the market but that word had a totally different meaning, walking on that empty road. It came with that impenetrable strength; the two were inseparable, like the colour of a petal. The brain, the heart and the mind were totally consumed by it and there was nothing left but that. But yet the buses rattled by, the villagers were talking loudly and the Pleiades were just over the horizon. It continued, walking alone or walking with others, and it went on during the night until the morning came among the palm trees. But it is there like a whisper among the leaves.

What an extraordinary thing meditation is. If there is any kind of compulsion, effort to make thought conform, imitate, then it becomes a wearisome burden. The silence which is desired ceases to be illuminating; if it is the pursuit of visions and experiences, then it leads to illusions and self-hypnosis. Only in the flowering of thought and so ending thought does meditation have significance; thought can only flower in freedom not in ever-widening patterns of knowledge. Knowledge may give newer experiences of greater sensation but a mind that is seeking experiences of any kind is immature. Maturity is the freedom from all experience; it is no longer under any influence to be and not to be. Maturity in meditation is the freeing of the mind from knowledge for it shapes and controls all experience. A mind which is a light to itself needs no experience. Immaturity is the craving for greater and wider experience. Meditation is the wandering through the world of knowledge and being free of it to enter into the unknown.

3rd

They are quarrelling in that little hut, with an oil lamp, on that pleasant road; in a high-pitched, screechy voice she was screaming something about money, there wasn't enough left over with which to buy rice; he in a low, cowed tone was mumbling something. You could hear her voice quite far away and only the crowded bus drowned it. The palm trees were silent and even the feathery tops of the casuarinas had stopped their gentle movement. There was no moon and it was dark, the sun having set among the gathering clouds, some time ago. Buses and cars passed, so many of them, for they all had been to see an ancient temple by the sea and again the road became quiet, isolated and far away. The few villagers that passed talked quietly, worn out after a day's labour. That strange immensity was coming and it was there with incredible gentleness and affection; as a tender, new leaf in spring, so easily destroyed, it was there utterly vulnerable and so everlastingly indestructible. Every thought and feeling disappeared and recognition ceased.

It is strange how important money has become, both to the giver and to the receiver, to the man in power and to the poor. They talk everlastingly of money or avoid talking of money, as it is bad form but are conscious of money. Money to do good work, money for the party, money for the temple, and money to buy rice. If you have money you are miserable and if you haven't you are in misery too. They tell you what he is worth as they tell you his position and the degrees he has taken, his cleverness, his capacity and how much he is making. The envy of the rich and the envy of the poor, the competition to show off, knowledge, clothes and the brilliancy of conversation. Everyone wants to impress somebody, the larger the crowd the better. But money is more important than anything else except power. These two things are a marvellous combination; the saint has power, though he has no money; he is influencing the rich and poor. The politician will use the country, the saint, the gods that be, to come to the top and tell you the absurdity of ambition and the ruth-lessness of power. There is no end to money and power; the more you have, the more you want and there is no end to it. But behind all money and power, there is sorrow which can-not be denied; you may put it aside, try to forget it but it is always there; you can't argue it away and it is always there, a deep wound that nothing seems to heal.

Nobody wants to be free of it, it is too complex to under-stand sorrow; it is all explained in the books, and the books, words, conclusions, become all important but sorrow is there still covered over with ideas. And escape becomes significant; escape is the essence of superficiality, though it may have varying depth. But sorrow is not easily cheated. You have to go into the very heart of it to end it; you have to dig very deep into yourself, never leaving a corner uncovered. You have to see every twist and turn of cunning thought, every feeling about everything, every move of every reaction, with-out restraint, without choice. It is like following a river to its source; the river will take you to it. You have to follow every threat, every clue to the heart of sorrow. You have only to watch, see, listen; it is all there open and clear. You have to take the journey, not to the moon, not to the gods but into yourself. You can take a swift step into yourself and so swiftly end sorrow or prolong the journey, idling, lazy and dispas-sionate. You need to have passion to end sorrow, and passion is not bought through escape. It is there when you stop escaping.

4th
Under the trees it was very quiet; there were so many birds calling, singing, chattering, endlessly restless. The branches were huge, beautifully shaped, polished, smooth and it was quite startling to see them and they had a sweep and a grace that brought tears to the eyes and made you wonder at the things of the earth. The earth had nothing more beautiful than the tree and when it died it would still be beautiful;

every branch naked, open to the sky, bleached by the sun and there would be birds resting upon its nakedness. There would be shelter for owls, there in that deep hollow, and the bright, screeching parrots would nest high up in the hole of that branch; woodpeckers would come, with their red-crested feathers sticking straight out of their heads, to drive in a few holes; of course there would be those striped squirrels, racing about the branches, ever complaining about something and always curious; right on the top-most branch, there would be a white and red eagle surveying the land with dignity and alone. There would be many ants, red and black, scurrying up the tree and others racing down and their bite would be quite painful. But now the tree was alive, marvellous, and there was plenty of shade and the blazing sun never touched you; you could sit there by the hour and see and listen to everything that was alive and dead, outside and inside. You cannot see and listen to the outside without wandering on to the inside. Really the outside is the inside and the inside is the outside and it is difficult, almost impossible to separate them. You look at this magnificent tree and you wonder who is watching whom and presently there is no watcher at all. Everything is so intensely alive and there is only life and the watcher is as dead as that leaf. There is no dividing line between the tree, the birds and that man sitting in the shade and the earth that is so abundant. Virtue is there without thought and so there is order; order is not permanent; it is there only from moment to moment and that immensity comes with the setting sun so casually, so freely welcoming. The birds have become silent for it is getting dark and everything is slowly becoming quiet ready for the night. The brain, that marvellous, sensitive, alive thing, is utterly still, only watching, listening without a moment of reaction, without recording, without experiencing, only seeing and listening. With that immensity, there is love and destruction and that destruction is unapproachable strength. These are all words, like that dead tree, a symbol of that which was and it never is. It has gone, moved away from the word; the word is dead which would never capture that sweeping nothingness. Only out of that immense emptiness is there love, with its innocency. How can the brain be aware of that love, the brain that is so active, crowded, burdened with knowledge, with experience? Everything must be denied for that to be.

Habit, however convenient, is destructive of sensitivity; habit gives the feeling of security and how can there be alertness, sensitivity, when habit is cultivated; not that insecurity brings alert awareness. How quickly everything becomes habit, sorrow as well as pleasure and then boredom sets in and that peculiar thing called leisure. After habit which has been working for forty years, then you have leisure or leisure at the end of the day. Habit had its turn and now it's the turn of leisure which again turns into habit. Without sensitivity there is no affection and that integrity which is not the driven reaction of contradictory existence. The machinery of habit is thought which is always seeking security, some comforting state from which it will never be disturbed. It is this search for the permanent that denies sensitivity. Being sensitive never hurts, only those things in which you have taken shelter cause pain. To be totally sensitive is to be wholly alive and that is love. But thought is very cunning; it will evade the pursuer, which is another thought; thought cannot pursue another thought. Only the flowering of thought can be seen, listened to, and what flowers in freedom comes to an end, dies without leaving a mark.

5th

This cuckoo which had been calling from dawn was smaller than a crow, greyer, with long tail and brilliant red eyes; it was sitting on a small palm tree half hidden, calling in clear soft tones; its tail and head were showing and there on a small tree was its mate. It was smaller, more shy, more hidden; then the male flew to the female who came out onto an open branch; they stayed there, the male calling and presently they flew away. There were clouds in the sky and a soft breeze was playing among the leaves; the heavy palms were still, their time would come, later in the day, towards the evening to do their heavy dancing but now they were still, lethargic and indifferent. It must have rained during the night and the ground was wet and the sand was brittle; the garden was peaceful for the day had not yet begun; the heavy trees were somnolent and the little ones were all awake, and two squirrels were chasing each other playfully in and out of the branches. The clouds of early dawn were giving way to the clouds of day and the casuarinas were swaying.

Every act of meditation is never the same, there is a new breath, a new shattering; there is no pattern to be torn down for there is no building of another, a new habit covering the old. All habits, however recently acquired, are old; they are formed out of the old but meditation is not shattering the old for a new pattern. It was new and shattering; it was new, not in the field of the old; it had never entered into that ground; it was new as it had never known the old; it was shattering in itself; it was not breaking down something but it itself was destruction. It destroyed and so it was new and there was creation.

There is no toy in meditation which absorbs you or you absorb it. It is the destruction of all toys, visions, ideas, experience that goes to the making of meditation. You must lay the foundation for true meditation otherwise you will be caught in various forms of illusion. Meditation is purest negation, negation which is not the outcome of reaction. To deny and to remain with the denial in negation is action without motive, which is love.

6th

There was a grey speckled bird, nearly as large as a crow; it wasn't a bit shy and it could be watched as long as one liked; it was eating berries, choosing very carefully, which were hanging down in heavy bunches, green and silver. Presently two other birds, nearly as large as the speckled one, came to hang on to other bunches; they were the cuckoos of yesterday; there were no soft-throated calls this time, they were all eating busily. They generally are shy birds, these cuckoos, but they didn't seem to mind someone standing so close watching them, only a few feet away. Then the striped squirrel came to join them but all the three flew off and the squirrel set to and was eating away ravenously when a crow came cawing and this was too much for it and it raced away. The crow didn't eat any of the berries but probably didn't like others enjoying themselves. It was a cool morning and the sun was coming up slowly behind the thick trees; there were long shadows and the soft dew was still on the grass, and in the little pond there were two blue lilies with heart of gold; it was light golden in colour and the blue was the blue of spring skies and the pads were round, very green and a small frog was sitting on one of them, motionless, eyes staring. The two lilies were the delight of the whole garden, even the large trees looked down upon them without shadow; they were delicate, soft and quiet in their pond. When you looked at them, all reaction ceased, your thoughts and feelings faded away and only they remained, in their beauty and their quietness; they were intense, like every living thing is, except man who is so everlastingly occupied with himself. As you watched these two, the world was changed, not into some better social order, with less tyranny and more freedom or poverty eliminated, but there was no pain, no sorrow, the coming and going of anxiety and there was no toil of boredom; it was changed because those two were there, blue with golden hearts. It was the miracle of beauty.

That road was familiar with us all now, the villager, the long line of bullock carts with a man walking beside each one of them, fifteen or twenty of them in a long line, with the dogs, goats and the ripening rice fields, and that evening it was smilingly open and the skies were very close. It was dark and the road shone with the light of the sky and night was closing in. Meditation is not the way of effort; every effort contradicts, resists; effort and choice always breed conflict and meditation then only becomes an escape from fact, the what is. But on that road, meditation yielded to that otherness, utterly silencing the already quiet brain; the brain was merely a passage for that immeasurable; as a deep wide river between two steep banks, this strange otherness moved, without direction, without time.

7th

Out of the window you could see a young palm tree and a tree full of large, pink-petalled flowers among the green leaves. The palm leaves were waving in every direction, heavily and clumsily and the flowers were motionless. Far away was the sea and you heard it all night, deep and penetrating; it never varied its heavy sound which kept rolling in; in it there was threat, restlessness and brutal force. With the dawn the roar of the sea faded and other noises took over, the birds, cars and the drum. Meditation was the fire that burned away all time and distance, achievement and experience. There was only vast, boundless emptiness but in it there was movement, creation. Thought cannot be creative; it can put things together, on a canvas, in words, in stone or in a marvellous rocket; thought, however polished, however subtle is within the boundaries of time; it can only cover space; it cannot go beyond itself. It cannot purify itself; it cannot pursue itself; it can only flower, if it does not block itself, and die. All feeling is sensation and experience is of it, and feeling with thought builds the boundaries of time.

9th

From a long way you could hear the sea, thundering away, wave after wave, endlessly; these were not harmless waves; they were dangerous, furious, ruthless. The sea looked as though it was calm, dreaming, patient but the waves were huge, high and frightening. People were carried away, drowned and there was a strong current. The waves were never gentle, their high curves were magnificent, splendid to watch from a distance but there was brute force and cruelty. The catamarans, so flimsy, dark thin men on them, go through those waves, indifferent, careless, with never a thought of fear; they would go far out to the horizon and probably would come back late in the day, with their heavy catch. The waves that evening were particularly furious, high in their impatience and their crash on the shore was deafening; the shore stretched north and south, clean washed sand, yellowish, burnt by the sun. And the sun was not gentle either; it was always hot, burning and only in the early morning, just as it was coming up out of the sea or setting among the gathering clouds, was it mild, pleasant. The furious sea and the burning sun were torturing the land and the people were poor, thin, ever hungry; misery was there, ever present and death was so easy, easier than birth, breeding indifference and decay. The well-to-do were indifferent too, dull, except in making money or seeking power or in building a bridge; they were very clever at this kind of thing, getting more and more—more knowledge, more capacity—but always losing and there is always death. It is so final, it cannot be deceived, no argument, however subtle and cunning, can ward it off; it is always there. You cannot build walls against it but you can against life; you can deceive it, run away from it, go to the temple, believe in saviours, go to the moon; you can do anything with life and sorrow is there and death. You can hide from sorrow but not from death. Even at that distance you could hear the waves thundering away and the palm trees were against the red evening sky. The pools and the canal were flashing with the setting sun.

Every kind of motive drives us, every action has a motive and so we have no love. Nor do we love what we are doing. We think we cannot act, be, live without a motive and so make our existence a dull trivial thing. We use function to acquire status; function is only a means to something else.

Love for the thing itself doesn't exist and so everything becomes shoddy and relationship a dreaded affair. Attachment
is only a means to cover up our own shallowness, loneliness,
insufficiency; envy only breeds hate. Love has no motive and
because there is no love, every kind of motive creeps in. To
live without is not difficult; it requires integrity not conformity to ideas, beliefs. To have integrity is to be self-critic-
ally aware, aware of what one is from moment to moment.

10th

It was a very young moon that seemed to be hanging between
the palm trees; it wasn't there yesterday; it might have been
hiding behind the clouds, shyly avoiding, for it was just a slip
like a delicate golden curving line, and between the palm
trees, dark and solemn, it was a miracle of delight. Clouds
were gathering to hide her but she was there open, tender and
so close. The palm trees were silent, austere, harsh and the
rice fields were turning yellow with age. The evening was full
of talk among the leaves and the sea was thundering some
miles away. The villagers were unaware of the beauty of the
evening; they were used to it; they accepted everything, their
poverty, their hunger, the dust, the squalor and the gathering
clouds. One gets used to anything, to sorrow and to happiness; if you didn't get used to things you would be more
miserable, more disturbed. It is better to be insensitive, dull
than to invite more trouble; die slowly, easier that way. You
can find economic and psychological reasons for all this but
the fact remains, with the well-to-do and with the poor, that
it is simpler to get used to things, going to the office, factory,
for the next thirty years, the boredom and the futility of it
all; but one has to live, one has responsibility and so it is safer
to get used to everything. We get used to love, to fear and to
death. Habit becomes goodness and virtue and even escapes
and gods. A habit-ridden mind is a shallow, dull-witted
mind.

11th

Dawn was slow in coming; the stars were still brilliant and the trees were still withdrawn; no bird was calling, not even the small owls that rattled through the night from tree to tree. It was strangely quiet except for the roar of the sea. There was that smell of many flowers, rotting leaves and damp ground; the air was very very still and the smell was everywhere. The earth was waiting for the dawn and the coming day; there was expectation, patience and a strange stillness. Meditation went on with that stillness and that stillness was love; it was not the love of something or of someone, the image and the symbol, the word and the pictures. It was simply love, without sentiment, without feeling. It was something complete in itself, naked, intense, without root and direction. The sound of that far-away bird was that love; it was the direction and distance, it was there without time and word. It wasn't an emotion, that fades and is cruel; the symbol, the word can be substituted but not the thing. Being naked, it was utterly vulnerable and so indestructible. It had that unapproachable strength of that otherness, the unknowable, which was coming through the trees and beyond the sea. Meditation was the sound of that bird calling out of that emptiness and the roar of the sea, thundering against the beach. Love can only be in utter emptiness. The greying dawn was there far away on the horizon and the dark trees were more dark and intense. In meditation there is no repetition, a continuity of habit; there is death of everything known and the flowering of the unknown. The stars had faded and the clouds were awake with the coming sun.

Experience destroys clarity and understanding. Experience is sensation, response to various kinds of stimuli, and every experience thickens the walls that enclose, however expanding and wide the experience. Accumulating knowledge is mechanical, all additive processes are, and are necessary for mechanical existence, but knowledge is time-binding. The craving for experience is endless as all sensation is. The cruelty of ambition is the furthering of experience, in sensation of power and the hardening in capacity. Experience cannot bring about humility which is the essence of virtue. In humility alone there is learning and learning is not the acquisition of knowledge.

A crow began the morning and every bird in the garden joined in and suddenly everything was awake and the breeze was among the leaves and there was splendour.

13th
There was a long stretch of black clouds heavy with rain, from horizon to horizon, north, south, and white were the breakers; it was pouring in the north and slowly coming south, and from the bridge over the river there was a long white line of waves against the black horizon. Buses, cars, bicycles and naked feet were making their way across the bridge and rain was coming in a fury. The river was empty, as it generally is at that time and the water was as dark as the sky; there wasn't even that lovely heron and it was deserted. Across the bridge was part of the big town, crowded, noisy, dirty, pretentious, prosperous, and a little way further to the left were the mud huts, dilapidated buildings, small, unclean shops, a small factory and a crowded road, a cow lying right in the middle of it, the buses and cars going around it. There were streaks of bright red towards the west but they too were being covered up by the coming rain. Past beyond the police station, over a narrow bridge, is the road among the rice fields, going south, away from the noisy filthy town. Then it began to rain, heavy sharp downpour that made puddles in a second in the road and there was running water where there was dry land; it was a furious rain, an exploding rain that washed, cleansed, purified the earth. The villagers were soaked to the skin but they didn't seem to mind; they went on with their laughter and chatter, their naked feet in the puddles. The little hut with the oil lamp was leaking, the buses roared by, splattering everybody, and

the cycles, with their feeble lamps, passed with a tinkle, into the heavy rain.

Everything was being washed clean, the past and the present, there was no time, no future. Every step was time-less, and thought, a thing of time, stopped; it could not go further or go back, it had no existence. And every drop of that furious rain was the river, the sea and the unmelting snow. There was total, complete emptiness and in it were creation, love and death, not separate. You had to watch your step, the buses passed almost touching you.

15th
It was a beautiful evening; a few clouds had gathered around the setting sun; there were a few wandering clouds, heavy with burning colour and the young moon was caught among them. The roar of the sea came through the casuarina and the palm, softening the fury. The tall, straight palms were black against the bright, burning rose of the sky and a whole group of white water-birds were going north, group after group, their thin legs stretched out behind them, their wings moving slowly. And a long line of creaking bullock carts were making their way to the town, laden with the firewood, the felled casuarinas. The road was crowded for a while and became almost deserted as you went further on and as it got darker. Just as the sun sets, quietly there comes over the land a strange sense of peace, a gentleness, a cleansing. It is not a reaction; it is there in the town with all its noises, squalor, bustle and milling people; it is there in that little patch of neglected earth; it is there where that tree is with a coloured kite caught in it; it is there in that empty street, across the temple; it is everywhere, only one has to be empty of the day. And that evening, along that road, it was there, softly wooing you away from everything and everybody, and as it got darker, it became more intense and beautiful. The stars were among the palms and Orion was between them, coming out of the sea, and Pleiades was beyond their reach, already

three-quarters of the journey done. The villagers were getting to know us, wanted to talk to us, sell us some land, so that we would be among them. And as the evening advanced that otherness descended with exploding bliss and the brain was as motionless as those trees, without a single leaf stirring. Everything became more intense, every colour, every shape and in that pale moonlight all the wayside puddles were the waters of life. Everything must go, be wiped away, not to receive it but the brain must be utterly still, sensitive, to watch, to see. Like a flood that covers the dry parched land it came full of delight and clarity and it stayed.

*17th**

It was long before dawn when the sharp cry of a bird woke up the night for an instant and the light of that cry faded away. And the trees remained dark, motionless, melting into the air; it was a soft quiet night, endlessly alive; it was awake, there was movement; there was a deep stirring with utter silence. Even the village next door, with its many dogs, always barking, was quiet. It was a strange stillness, terribly potent, destructively alive. It was so alive and still that you were afraid to move; so your body froze into immobility and the brain, which had awakened with that sharp cry of the bird, had become still, with heightened sensitivity. It was a brilliant night with the stars in a cloudless sky; they seemed so close and the Southern Cross was just over the trees, sparkling in the warm air. Everything was very quiet. Meditation is never in time; time cannot bring about mutation; it can bring about change which needs to be changed again, like all reforms; meditation that springs out of time is always binding, there is no freedom in it and without freedom there is always choice and conflict.

18th

High up in the mountains, among the barren rocks with not

* The day of his last talk.

a tree or bush, was a little stream, coming out of massive, unapproachable rock; it was hardly a stream, it was a trickle. As it came down it made a waterfall, just a murmur, and it came down, down to the valley, and it was already shouting of its strength, the long way it would go, through towns, valleys, woods and open spaces. It was going to be an irresistible river, sweeping over its banks, purifying itself as it went along, crashing over rocks, flowing into far places, endlessly flowing to the sea.* It wasn't getting to the sea that mattered, but being a river, so wide, so deep, rich and splendid; it would enter the sea and disappear into the vast, bottomless waters but the sea was far away, many a thousand miles, but from now until then it was life, beauty and ceaseless merriment; none could stop that, not even the factories and dams. It was really a marvellous river, wide, deep, with so many cities on its banks, so carelessly free and never abandoning itself. All life was there upon its banks, green fields, forests, solitary houses, death, love and destruction; there were long, wide bridges over it, graceful and well-used. Other streams and rivers joined it but she was the mother of all rivers, the little ones and the big ones. She was always full, ever purifying herself, and of an evening it was a blessing to watch her, with deepening colour in the clouds and her waters golden. But the little trickle so far away, amongst those gigantic rocks which seemed so concentrated in producing it, was the beginning of life and its ending was beyond its banks and the seas.

Meditation was like that river, only it had no beginning and no ending; it began and its ending was its beginning. There was no cause and its movement was its renewal. It was always new, it never gathered to become old; it never

* He was now in Benares and was recalling the source of the Ganges which he had once visited. He stayed at Rajghat, just north of Benares, on the banks of the Ganges, where there is a Krishnamurti School. The Indians call Benares Banaras or Varanesi.

got sullied for it had no roots in time. It is good to meditate, not forcing it, not making any effort, beginning with a trickle and going beyond time and space, where thought and feeling cannot enter, where experience is not.

19th

It was a beautiful morning, fairly cool and dawn was far away still; the few trees and the bushes around the house seemed to have become a forest during the night and were hiding many serpents and wild animals and the moonlight with a thousand shadows deepened the impression; they were large trees, far above the house and they were all silent and waiting for dawn. And suddenly, through the trees and from beyond came a song, a religious song of devotion; the voice was rich and the singer was putting his heart into it and the song rode far into the moonlit night. As you listened to it, you rode on the wave of the sound and you were of it and beyond it, beyond thought and feeling. Then there was another sound of an instrument, very faint but clear.

26th

The river is wide and splendid here; it is deep and as smooth as a lake, without a ripple. There are a few boats, mostly fishermen's and a large boat, with a torn sail, carrying sand to the town, beyond the bridge. What is really beautiful is the stretch of the water towards the east and the bank on the other side; the river looks like an enormous lake, full of untold beauty and space to match the sky; it is a flat country and the sky fills the earth and the horizon is beyond the trees, far far away. The trees are on the other bank, beyond the recently sown wheat; there are the green spreading fields and beyond them are the trees, with villages among them. The river rises very high during the rains and brings with it rich silt and the winter wheat is sown as the river goes down; it is a marvellous green, so rich and plentiful, and the long, wide bank is a carpet of enchanting green. From this

side of the river the trees look like an impenetrable forest
but there are villages tucked among them. But there is one
tree, huge, its roots exposed, that is the glory of the bank;
there is a little white temple under it but its gods are as
the water that goes by and the tree remains; it has thick
foliage with long-tailed leaves and birds come across the
river for the night; it towers over other trees and you can
see it as far as you care to walk on this side down the river.
It has the presence of beauty, the dignity of that which is
alone. But those villages are crowded, small, filthy, and
human beings foul the earth around them. From this side, the
white walls of the villages among the trees look fresh, gentle
and of great beauty. Beauty is not man-made; the things of
man arouse feelings, sentiment, but these have nothing to
do with beauty. Beauty can never be put together, neither the
thing built, nor in the museum. One must go beyond all
this, all personal taste and choice, be cleansed of all emotion
for love is beauty. The river curves majestically as it flows
east,* past villages, towns, and deep woods but here, just
below the town and the bridge, the river and its opposite
bank is the essence of all rivers and banks; every river has
its own song, its own delight and mischief but here out of its
very silence, it contains the earth and the heavens. It is a
sacred river, as all rivers are, but again here, a part of the
long, winding river, there is a gentleness of immense depth
and destruction. Looking at it now, you would be enchanted
by its mellow age and tranquillity. And you would lose all
earth and heaven. In that quiet silence that strange otherness
came and meditation lost its meaning. It was like a wave,
coming from afar, gathering momentum as it came, crashing
on the shore, sweeping everything before it. Only there was
no time and distance; it was there with impenetrable strength,
with destructive vitality and so the essence of beauty which

---

* Although Rajghat is north of Benares it is downstream, for
the river curves north-east at this point before flowing south
again.

is love. No imagination could possibly conjure up all this, no deep hidden impulse can ever project this immensity. Every thought and every feeling, every desire and compulsion was totally absent. It was not an experience; experience implies recognition, an accumulating centre, memory and a continuity. It was not an experience; only the immature crave for experience and thereby are caught in illusion; it was simply an event, a happening, a fact, like a sunset, like death and the curving river. Memory could not catch it in its net and keep it and thereby destroy it. Time and memory could not hold it nor thought pursue it. It was a flash in which all time and eternity were consumed, without leaving any ashes, memory. Meditation is the complete and total emptying of the mind, not in order to receive, to gain, to arrive, but a denudation without motive; it is really emptying the mind of the known, conscious and unconscious, of every experience, thought and feeling. Negation is the very essence of freedom; assertion and positive pursuit is bondage.

30th

Two crows were fighting, they were viciously angry with each other; there was fury in their voices, both were on the ground but one had the advantage driving its hard, black beak into the other. Shouting at them from the window did no good and one was going to be killed. A passing crow dived in suddenly breaking its flight, calling, cawing more loudly than the two on the ground; it landed beside them, beating its black, shiny wings against them. In a second, half a dozen more crows came, all cawing away furiously and several of them with their wings and beaks separated the two who were intent on killing each other. They might kill other birds, other things, but there was going to be no murder amongst their own kind and that would be the end of them all. The two still wanted to fight it out but the others were telling them off and presently they all flew away and there was quietness in the little open space among the trees by the river.

It was late in the afternoon, the sun was behind the trees and the really bitter cold was gone and all the birds, all day were singing, calling and making all those pleasant sounds they do. Parrots were flying in crazily for the night; it was a bit early but they were coming in; the large tamarind tree could hold quite a lot of them; their colour was almost the colour of the leaves but their green was more intense, more alive; if you watched carefully you would see the difference and also you would see their brilliant curving beaks which they used to bite and to climb; they were rather clumsy among the branches, going from one to the other but they were the light of heavens in movement; their voices were harsh and sharp, and their flight never straight, but their colour was the spring of the earth. Earlier, in the morning, on a branch of that tree, two small owls were sunning themselves, facing the rising sun; they were so still you would not have noticed them, they were the colour of the branch, mottled grey, unless by chance, you saw them coming out of their hole in the tamarind tree. It had been bitterly cold, most unusual, and two golden green flycatchers dropped dead that morning from the cold; one was the male and the other female, they must have been mates; they died on the same instant and they were still soft to the touch. They were really golden green, with long, curving bills; they were so delicate, so extraordinarily alive still. Colour is very strange; colour is god and those two were the glory of light; the colour would remain, though the machinery of life had come to an end. Colour was more enduring than the heart; it was beyond time and sorrow.

But thought can never solve the ache of sorrow. You can reason in and out but it would be there still after the long, complicated journey of thought. Thought can never resolve human problems; thought is mechanical and sorrow is not. Sorrow is as strange as love, but sorrow keeps away love. You can resolve sorrow completely but you cannot invite love. Sorrow is self-pity with all its anxieties, fears, guilt but all this cannot be washed away by thought. Thought breeds the thinker and between them sorrow is begotten. The ending of sorrow is the freedom from the known.

31st
There were many fishing boats as the sun was deep in the west and the river suddenly was awake with laughter and loud talk; there were twenty-three of them and each boat held two or three men. The river is wide here and these few boats seemed to have taken charge of the waters; they were racing, shouting, calling to each other in excited voices, like children at play; they were very poor people, in dirty rags but just now they had no cares and loud talk and laughter filled the air. The river was sparkling and the slight breeze made patterns on the water. The crows were beginning now to fly back from across the river to their accustomed trees; the swallows were flying low, almost touching the water.

*January 1st, 1962**
A winding stream makes its way to the wide river; it comes through a dirty part of the town made filthy by everything imaginable and comes to the river almost exhausted; near where it meets the big one, there is a rickety bridge over it made up of bamboos, pieces of rope, and straw; when it is almost collapsing, they put a pole in the soft bed of the stream and more straw and mud and tie it up with not too thick a rope and the rope has many knots. The whole thing is a ramshackle affair; it must have been fairly straight once but now it dips almost touching the lazy stream and as you walk across it, you hear the mud and the straw dropping into the water. But somehow it must be fairly strong; it is a narrow bridge; it is rather difficult to avoid touching another coming the other way. Bicycles loaded with milk cans, happily go across it, without the least concern for

* On this day he gave the first of seven talks at Rajghat.

themselves or for others; it is always busy with villagers going to town with their produce and coming back in the evening to their villages, worn out, carrying something or other, tongs, kites, oil, a piece of wood, a slab of rock, and things they can't pick up in their own village. They are dressed in rags, dirty, ill and endlessly patient, walking, in naked feet, endless miles; they have not the energy to revolt, to chase all the politicians out of the country but then they themselves would soon become politicians, exploiting, cunning, inventing ways and means to hold on to power, the evil that destroys the people. We were crossing that bridge with a huge buffalo, several cycles and the crossing villagers; it was ready to collapse but somehow we all got across it and the cumbersome animal didn't seem to mind at all. Going up the bank following the well-worn sandy path, past a village with an ancient well, you came into the open, flat country. There are mangoes and tamarinds and fields of winter wheat; it is a flat country stretching away mile upon mile till it meets, far away, the foothills and the eternal mountains. The path is ancient, many thousand years and countless pilgrims have walked upon it, with ruined temples.* As the path turns, you catch the sight of the river, between trees in the distance.

It was a lovely evening, cool, silent and the sky was immense, no tree, no land could contain it; somehow, there was no horizon, the trees and the endless flat earth melted into the expanding sky. It was pale, delicate blue and the sunset had left a golden haze where the horizon should have been. Birds were calling from their sheltering trees, a goat was bleating and far away a train was whistling; some village folk, all women, were huddled around a fire and strangely they too had fallen silent. The mustard was in flower, a spreading yellow and from a village across the fields a column of smoke went straight up into the air. The silence was

* The pilgrims' path runs through the Rajghat estate, linking Kashi with Sarnath where the Buddha preached his first sermon after Enlightenment.

strangely penetrating; it went through you and beyond you; it was without a movement, without a wave; you walked in it, you felt it, you breathed it, you were of it. It was not that you brought this silence into being, by the usual tricks of the brain. It was there and you were of it; you were not experiencing it; there was no thought that could experience, that could recollect, gather. You were not separate from it, to observe, to analyse. Only that was there and nothing else. Time, by the watch, was getting late and, by the watch, this miracle of silence lasted nearly half an hour but there was no duration, no time. You were walking back in it, past the ancient well, the village, across the narrow bridge, into the room that was dark. It was there and with it was the otherness, overwhelming and welcoming. Love is not a word nor a feeling; it was there with its impenetrable strength and the tenderness of a new leaf, so easily destroyed. Pleiades was just overhead and Orion was over the tree-tops and the brightest star was in the waters.

2nd

The village boys were flying kites on the bank along the river; they were yelling at the top of their voices, laughing, chasing each other and wading into the river to get the fallen kites; their excitement was contagious, for the old people, higher up the bank, were watching them, shouting to them, encouraging them. It seemed to be the evening entertainment of the whole village; even the starved, mangy dogs were barking; everyone was taking part in the excitement. They were all half-starved, there wasn't a fat one among them, even among the old; the older they were the thinner they were; even the children were all so thin but they seemed to have plenty of energy. All of them had torn, dirty rags on, patched with different cloths of many colours. And they were all cheerful, even the old and ailing ones; they seemed to be unaware of their own misery, of their physical weakness, for many of them carried heavy bundles; they had amazing patience and they had to have it for death was there, very close and so also the agony of life; everything was there at the same time, death, birth, sex, poverty, starvation, excitement, tears. They had a place, under some trees higher up the bank, not far from a ruined old temple to bury their dead;* there were plenty of little babies who would know hunger, the smell of unwashed bodies and the smell of death. But the river was there all the time, sometimes threatening the village but now quiet, placid with swallows flying so low, almost touching the water, which was the colour of gentle fire. The river was everything, they occasionally bathed in it, they washed their clothes in it and their thin bodies, and they worshipped it and put flowers, when they could get them, in it to show their respect; they fished in it and died beside it. The river was so indifferent to their joy and sorrow; it was so deep, there was such weight and power behind it; it was terribly alive and so dangerous. But now it was quiet, not a ripple on it and every swallow had a shadow on it; they didn't fly very far, they would fly low for about a hundred feet, go up a little, turn and come down again and fly for another hundred feet or so, until darkness came. There were small water birds, their tails bobbing up and down, swift in their flight; there were larger ones, almost the colour of the damp earth, greyish-brown, wading up and down the water's edge. But the marvel of it all was the sky, so vast, boundless, without horizon. The late afternoon light was soft, clear and very gentle; it left no shadow and every bush, tree and bird was alone. The flashing river by day was now the light of the sky, enchanted, dreaming and lost in its beauty and love. In this light, all things cease to exist, the heart that was crying and the brain that was cunning; pleasure and pain went away leaving only light, transparent, gentle and caressing. It was light; thought and feeling had no part in it, they could never give light; they were not there, only this light when the

* These villagers were Moslems.

sun is well behind the walls of the city and not a cloud in the sky. You cannot see this light unless you know the timeless movement of meditation; the ending of thought is this movement. But love is not the way of thought or feeling.

It was very quiet, not a leaf was stirring and it was dark; all the stars that could fill the river were there and they spilled over into the sky. The brain was completely still but very alive and watching, watching without a watcher, without a centre from which it was watching; nor was there any sensation. The otherness was there, deep within at a depth that was lost; it was action, wiping away everything without leaving a mark of what has been or what is. There was no space in which to have a border nor time in which thought could shape itself.

3rd

There is something curiously pleasant to walk, alone, along a path, deep in the country, which has been used for several thousand years by pilgrims; there are very old trees along it, tamarind and mango, and it passes through several villages. It passes between green fields of wheat; it is soft underfoot, fine, dry powder, and it must become heavy clay in the wet season; the soft, fine earth gets into your feet, into your nose and eyes, not too much. There are ancient wells and temples and withering gods. The land is flat, flat as the palm of the hand, stretching to the horizon, if there is a horizon. The path has so many turns, in a few minutes it faces in all the directions of a compass. The sky seems to follow that path which is open and friendly. There are few paths like that in the world though each has its own charm and beauty. There is one [at Gstaad] that goes through the valley, gently climbing, between rich pasturage, to be gathered for the winter to be given to the cows; that valley is white with snow but then [when he was there] it was the end of summer, full of flowers, with snow mountains all around and there was a

noisy stream going through the valley; there was hardly any-
one on that path and you walked on it in silence. Then there
is another path [at Ojai], climbing steeply by the side of a
dry, dusty, crumbling mountain; it was rocky, rough and
slippery; there wasn't a tree anywhere near, not even a bush;
a quail with her small new brood, over a dozen of them,
was there and further up you came upon a deadly rattler,
all curled up, ready to strike but giving you a fair warning.
But now, this path was not like any other; it was dusty, made
foul by human beings here and there, and there were ruined
old temples with their images; a large bull was having its fill
among the growing grain, unmolested; there were monkeys
too and parrots, the light of the skies. It was the path of a
thousand humans for many thousand years. As you walked
on it, you were lost; you walked without a single thought
and there was the incredible sky and the trees with heavy
foliage and birds. There is a mango on that path that is
superb; it has so many leaves that the branches cannot be
seen and it is so old. As you walk on, there is no feeling at
all; thought too has gone but there is beauty. It fills the
earth and the sky, every leaf and blade of withering grass.
It is there covering everything and you are of it. You are
not made to feel all this but it is there and because you are
not, it is there, without a word, without a movement. You
walk back in silence and fading light.

Every experience leaves a mark and every mark distorts
experience; so there is no experience which has not been.
Everything is old and nothing new. But this is not so. All
the marks of all experiences are wiped away; the brain, the
storehouse of the past, becomes completely quiet and motionless, without reaction, but alive, sensitive; then it loses the
past and is made new again.

It was there, that immensity, having no past, no future;
it was there, without ever knowing the present. It filled the
room, expanding beyond all measure.

5th

The sun comes out of the trees and sets over the town and between the trees and the town is all life, is all time. The river passes between them, deep, alive and tranquil; many small boats go up and down it; some with large, square sails, which carry wood, sand, cut stone and sometimes men and women going back to their villages but mostly there are small fishing boats, with lean dark men. They appear to be very happy, voluble people, calling and shouting to each other though they are all clad in rags, with not much to eat, inevitably with many children. They cannot read and write; they have no outside entertainment, no cinemas etc., but they amuse themselves singing, in chorus, devotional songs or telling religious stories. They are all very poor and life is very hard, disease and death are always there, like the earth and the river. And that evening there were more swallows than ever, flying low, almost touching the water and the water was the colour of dying fire. Everything was so alive, so intense; four or five fat puppies were playing around their thin hungry mother; crows, many groups of them, were flying back to the other bank; parrots were flying back to their trees, in their flashing, screeching manner; a train was crossing the bridge and the noise of it came far down the river and a woman was washing herself in the cold river. Everything was struggling to live, a battle for its very life and there is always death, to struggle every moment of life and then to die. But between the rising of the sun and its setting behind the walls of the city, time consumed all life, time past and present ate man's heart away; he existed in time and so knew sorrow.

But the village men walking behind along the narrow path beside the river, strung out one by one, somehow were part of the man walking in front; there were eight of them and the old man directly behind was coughing and spitting all the time and the others were more or less walking silently. The man that was in front was aware of them, their silence, their coughs, their weariness after a long day; they were not agitated but quiet and if anything cheerful. He was aware of them as he was aware of the glowing river, of the gentle fire of the sky and the birds coming back to their home; there was no centre from which he was seeing, feeling, observing; all these imply the word, thought. There was no thought but only these things. They were all walking fast and time had ceased to be; those villagers were going back home to their hovels and the man was going with them; they were part of him, not that he was aware of them as being a part. They were flowing with the river, flying with the birds and were as open and wide as the sky. It was a fact and not imagination; imagination is a shoddy thing and fact is a burning reality. All those nine were walking endlessly, going nowhere and coming from nowhere; it was an endless procession of life. Time and all identity had ceased, strangely. When the man in front turned to walk back, all the villagers, especially the old man who was so close, just behind him, saluted as though they were age long friends. It was getting dark, the swallows had gone; there were lights on the long bridge and the trees were withdrawing into themselves. Far away a temple bell was ringing.

7th

There is a little canal, about a foot wide, that goes between the green fields of wheat. There is a path along it and you can walk along it for quite a while, without meeting a soul. That evening it was particularly quiet; there was a fat jay with startlingly bright blue wings that was having a drink in that canal; it was fawn coloured, with those sparkling blue wings; it wasn't one of those scolding jays; you could approach it fairly close without being called names. It looked at you in wonderment and you looked at it with exploding affection; it was fat and comfortable and very beautiful. It waited to see what you would do and when you did nothing, it grew calmer and presently flew away without a cry. You had met in that bird all the birds ever brought into being; it was that explosion that did it. It was not a well planned, thought-out explosion; it just happened with an intensity and fury whose very shock stopped all time. But you went along that narrow path, past a tree which had become the symbol of a temple, for there were flowers and a crudely painted image and the temple was a symbol of something else and that something else was also a vast symbol. Words, symbols, have become, like the flag, so frighteningly important. Symbols were ashes which fed the mind and the mind was barren and thought was born out of this waste. It was clever, inventive, as all things are which come out of arid nothingness. But the tree was splendid, full of leaves, sheltering many birds; the earth around was swept and kept clean; they had built a mud platform around the tree and on it was the image, leaning against the thick trunk. The leaf was perishable and the stone image was not; it would endure, destroying minds.

8th

The early morning sun was on the water, shimmering, almost blinding the eyes; a fisherman's boat was crossing that brilliant path and there was a slight fog among the trees, on the opposite bank. The river is never still, there is always a movement, a dance of countless steps and this morning it was very alive, making the trees, the bushes heavy and dull, except the birds which were calling, singing, and the parrots as they screeched by. These parrots lived in the tamarind tree beside the house and they would be coming and going all day, restless in their flight. Their light green bodies shone in the sun and their red curving beaks were brighter as they flashed by. Their flight was fast and sharp and you could see them among the green leaves if you looked carefully, and once there they became clumsy and not so noisy as on their flight. It was early but all the birds had been out long before the sun was on the water. Even at that hour the river was awake with the light of the heavens and meditation was a sharpening of the immensity of the mind; the mind is never asleep, never completely unaware; patches of it were, here and there sharpened by conflict and pain, made dull by habit and passing satisfaction, and every pleasure left a mark of longing. But all these darkened passages left no space for the totality of the mind. These became enormously important and always breeding more immediate significance and the immensity is put aside for the little, the immediate. The immediate is the time of thought and thought can never resolve any issue except the mechanical. But meditation is not the way of the machine; it can never be put together to get somewhere; it is not the boat to cross to the other side. There is no shore, no arriving and, like love, it has no motive. It is endless movement whose action is in time but not of time. All action of the immediate, of time, is the ground of sorrow; nothing can grow on it except conflict and pain. But meditation is the awareness of this ground and choicelessly never letting a seed take root, however pleasant and however painful. Meditation is the passing away of experience. And then only is there clarity whose freedom is in seeing. Meditation is a strange delight not to be bought on the market; no guru or disciple can ever be of it; all following and leading have to cease as easily and naturally as a leaf drops to the ground.

The immeasurable was there, filling the little space and all space; it came as gently as the breeze comes over the water but thought could not hold it and the past, time, was not capable of measuring it.

9th

Across the river, smoke was going up in a straight column; it was a simple movement bursting into the sky. There wasn't a breath of air; there wasn't a ripple on the river and every leaf was still; the parrots were the only noisy movement as they flashed by. Even the little fisherman's boat did not disturb the water; everything seemed to have frozen in stillness, except the smoke. Even though it was going so straight up in the sky there was a certain gaiety in it and freedom of total action. And beyond the village and the smoke was the glowing sky of the evening. It had been a cool day and the sky had been open and there was the light of a thousand winters; it was short, penetrating and expansive; it went with you everywhere, it wouldn't leave you. Like perfume, it was in the most unexpected places; it seemed to have entered into the most secret corners of one's being. It was a light that left no shadow and every shadow lost its depth; because of it, all substance lost its density; it was as though you looked through everything, through the trees on the other side of the wall, through your own self. Your self was as opaque as the sky and as open. It was intense and to be with it was to be passionate, not the passion of feeling or desire, but a passion that would never wither or die. It was a strange light, it exposed everything and made vulnerable, and what had no protection was love. You couldn't be what you were, you were burnt out, without leaving any ashes and unexpectedly there was not a thing but that light.

12th

There was a little girl of ten or twelve leaning against a post in the garden; she was dirty, her hair had not been washed for many weeks, it was dusty and uncombed; her clothes were torn and unwashed too, like herself. She had a long rag around her neck and she was looking at some people who were having tea on the verandah; she looked with complete indifference, without any feeling, without any thought of what was going on; her eyes were on the group downstairs and every parrot that screeched by made no impression on her nor those soft earth-coloured doves that were so close to her. She was not hungry, she was probably a daughter of one of the servants for she seemed familiar with the place and fairly well-fed. She held herself as though she was a grown-up young lady, full of assurance and there was about her a strange aloofness. As you watched her against the river and the trees, you suddenly felt you were watching the tea party, without any emotion, without any thought, totally indifferent to everything and to whatever might happen. And when she walked away to that tree overlooking the river, it was you that was walking away, it was you that sat on the ground, dusty and rough; it was you who picked up the piece of stick and threw it over the bank, alone, unsmiling and never cared for. Presently you got up and wandered off around the house. And strangely, you were the doves, the squirrel that raced up the tree and that unwashed, dirty chauffeur and the river that went by, so quietly. Love is not sorrow nor is it made up of jealousy but it is dangerous for it destroys. It destroys everything that man has built around himself except bricks. It cannot build temples nor reform the rotting society; it can do nothing, but without it nothing can be done, do what you will. Every computer and automation can alter the shape of things and give man leisure which will become another problem when there are already so many problems. Love has no problem and that is why it is so destructive and dangerous. Man lives by problems, those unresolved and continuous things; without them, he wouldn't know what to do; he would be lost and in the losing gain nothing. So problems multiply endlessly; in the resolving of the one there is another, but death, of course, is destruction; it is not love. Death is old age, disease and the problems which no computer can solve. It is not the destruction that love brings; it is not the death that love brings. It is the ashes of a fire that has been carefully built up and it is the noise of automatic machines that go on working without interruption. Love, death, creation are inseparable; you cannot have one and deny the others; you cannot buy it on the market or in any church; those are the last places where you would find it. But if you don't look and if you have no problems, not one, then perhaps it might come when you are looking the other way.

It is the unknown, and everything you know must burn itself away, without leaving ashes; the past, rich or sordid, must be left as casually, without any motive as that girl throwing a stick over the bank. The burning of the known is the action of the unknown. Far away a flute is playing not too well and the sun is setting, a great big red ball behind the walls of the town, and the river is the colour of gentle fire and every bird is coming in for the night.

13th
Dawn was just coming and already, every bird seemed to be awake, calling, singing, endlessly repeating one or two notes; the crows were the loudest. There were so many of them, cawing to each other and you had to listen with care to catch the notes of other birds. The parrots were already screeching in their flight, flashing by and in that pale light their lovely green was already splendid. Not a leaf was stirring and the river was running silver, wide, expansive, deep with the night; the night had done something to it; it had become richer, deep with the earth and inseparable; it was alive with an intensity that was destructive in its purity. The other bank was still asleep, the trees and the wide green stretches of wheat were still mysterious and quiet and far away a temple bell was ringing, without music. Everything was beginning to wake up now, shouting with the coming sun. Every caw was more loud and every screech and the colour of every leaf and flower, and strong was the smell of the earth. The sun came over the leaves of trees and made a golden path across the river. It was a beautiful morning and its beauty would remain, not in memory; memory is shoddy; it is a dead thing and memory can never hold beauty or love. It destroys them. It is mechanical, having its use, but beauty is not of memory. Beauty is always new but the new has no relationship with the old, which is of time.

*14th**

The moon was quite young yet it gave enough light for shadows; there were plenty of shadows and they were very still. Along that narrow path, every shadow seemed to be alive, whispering amongst themselves, every shadowy leaf chattering to its neighbour. The shape of the leaf and the heavy trunk were clear on the ground and the river down below was of silver; it was wide, silent and there was a deep current which left no mark on the surface. Even the afternoon breeze had died and there were no clouds to gather around the setting sun; higher up in the sky, there was a solitary rose-coloured whisper of a cloud that remained motionless till it disappeared into the night. Every tamarind and mango was withdrawing for the night and all the birds were silent, taking shelter, deep among the leaves. A little owl was sitting on the telegraph wire and just when you were below it, it flew off on those extraordinary silent wings. After delivering milk, the cycles were coming back, the empty tins rattling; there were so many of them, single or in groups, but for all their chatter and noise that peculiar silence of the open country and immense sky remained. That evening nothing could disturb it, not even a goods train crossing the steel bridge. There is a little path to the right wandering among the green fields and as you walk on it, far away from everything, from faces, tears, suddenly, you are aware that something is taking place. You know it is not imagination, desire, taking to some fancy or to some forgotten experience or the revival of some pleasure and hope; you know well it is none of these things; you have been through this examination before and you brush all these aside, swiftly with a gesture and you are aware something is taking place. It is as unexpected as that big bull that comes through the darkening evening; it is there with insistency and immensity, that otherness, which no word or symbol

* He gave the last of his seven talks that morning.

can catch; it is there filling the sky and the earth and every little thing in it. You and that little villager who without a word passes you by, are of it. At that timeless time, only there is that immensity, neither thought nor feeling and the brain utterly quiet. All meditative sensitivity is over, only that incredible purity is there. It is the purity of strength, impenetrable and unapproachable but it was there. Everything stood still, there was no movement, no stir and even the sound of the whistle of the train was in the stillness. It accompanied you as you walked back to your room and it was there, too, for it had never left you.

16th

With the heavily-laden camel, we all crossed the new bridge across the little stream, the cyclists, the village women returning from town, a mangy dog and an old man with a long, white beard and haughty. The old, rickety bridge was taken away and there was this new bridge, made of heavy poles, bamboos, straw and mud; it was strongly built and the camel didn't hesitate to cross it; it was haughtier than the old man, its head right up in the air, disdainful and rather smelly. We all went over the bridge and most of the villagers went down along the river and the camel went the other way. It was a dusty path, fine dry clay and the camel left a big wide imprint and couldn't be coaxed to walk along any faster than it wanted to; it was carrying sacks of grain and it seemed so utterly indifferent to everything; it went past the ancient well and ruined temples and its driver did his best to make it walk faster, slapping it with his bare hands. There is another path that turns off to the right, past the flowering yellow mustard, flowering peas and rich green wheat fields; this path is not used much and it is pleasant to walk along there. The mustard had a slight smell but the pea was a little stronger, and the wheat, which was beginning to form its ear, had its own smell too and the combination of the three filled the evening air with a **fragrance** that was not too strong, pleasant but unobtrusive. It was a beautiful evening, with the setting sun behind the trees; on that path you were far away from anywhere, though there were scattered villages all around but you were far away and nothing could come near you. It was not in space, time or distance; you were far away and there was no measure. The depth was not in fathoms; there was a depth that had no height, no circumference. An occasional villager passed you by, carrying the few meagre things that he had bought in town and as he went by, almost touching you, he had not come near you. You were far away, in some unknown world that had no dimension; even if you wanted to know, you couldn't know it. It was too far away from the known; it had no relationship with the known. It wasn't a thing you experience; there was nothing to be experienced, and besides all experiencing is always in the field of the known, recognized by that which has been. You were far away, immeasurably far, but the trees, the yellow flowers and the ear of the wheat were astonishingly close, closer than your thought and marvellously alive, with intensity and beauty that could never wither. Death, creation and love were there and you didn't know which was which and you were part of it; they were not separate, something to be divided and argued over. They were inseparable, closely inter-related, not the relationship of word and action, expression. Thought could not shape it, nor feeling cover it, these are too mechanical, too slow, having their roots in the known. Imagination is within their ground and could never come near. Love, death, creation was a fact, an actual reality, as the body they were burning on the river-bank under the tree. The tree, the fire and the tears were real, were undeniable facts but they were the actualities of the known and the freedom of the known, and in that freedom those three are—inseparable. But you have to go very far and yet be very near.

The man on the bicycle was singing in a rather hoarse and tired voice, coming back with the rattling empty milk-cans from the city; he was eager to talk to someone and as he passed by he said something, hesitated, recovered and went on. The moon was casting shadows now, dark and almost transparent ones and the smell of the night was deepening. And around the bend of the path was the river; it seemed to be lighted from within, with a thousand candles; the light was soft with silver and pale gold and utterly still, bewitched by the moon. Pleiades was overhead and Orion was well up in the sky and a train was puffing up the grade to cross the bridge. Time had stopped and beauty was there with love and death. And on the new bamboo bridge there was no one, not even a dog. The little stream was full of stars.

20th
It was long before dawn, a clear starlit sky; there was a slight mist over the river and the bank on the other side was just visible; the train was chugging up the grade to cross the bridge; it was a goods train and these trains always puff up the incline in a special way, long, slow strokes of heavy puffs, unlike the passengers [trains], who have quick short bursts and are on the bridge almost immediately. This goods train, in that vast silence, made a rattling roar, more noisy than ever before but nothing seemed to disturb that silence in which all movements were lost. It was an impenetrable silence, clear, strong, penetrating; there was an urgency which no time could gather. The pale star was clear and the trees were dark in their sleep. Meditation was the awareness of all these things and the going beyond all these and time. The movement in time is thought and thought cannot go beyond its own bondage to time and is never free. Dawn was coming over the trees and the river, a pale sign as yet but the stars were losing their brilliancy and already there was a call of the morning, a bird in a tree quite close by. But that immense silence still persisted and it would always be there, though the birds and the noise of man would continue.

21st*

The cold had been too severe, it had been below freezing; the hedge had been burned brown, the brown leaves had fallen off; the lawn was grey-brown, the colour of the earth; except for a few yellow pansies and roses, the garden was bare. It had been too cold and the poor, as usual, were suffering and dying; population was exploding and people were dying. You saw them shivering, with hardly a thing on, in dirty rags; an old woman was shaking from head to foot, hugging herself, the few teeth chattering; a young woman was washing herself and a torn cloth by the cold river [the Jumna] and an old man was coughing deeply and heavily and children were playing, laughing and shouting. It was an exceptionally cold winter they said and many were dying. The red rose and the yellow pansy were intensely alive, burning with colour; you couldn't take your eyes off them and those two colours seemed to expand and fill the empty garden; even though the children were shouting, that shivering old woman was everywhere; the incredible yellow and red and the inevitable death. Colour was god and death was beyond the gods. It was everywhere and so was colour. You could not separate the two and if you did then there was no living. Neither could you separate love from death and if you did it was no longer beauty. Every colour is separated, made much of but there is only colour and when you see every different colour as only colour, then only is there splendour in colour. The red rose and the yellow pansy were not different colours but colour that filled the bare garden with glory. The sky was pale blue, blue of a cold, rainless winter but it was the blue of all colour. You saw it and you were of it; the noises of the city faded but colour, imperishable, endured.

Sorrow has been made respectable; a thousand explana-

* He was now in New Delhi where he gave eight talks, from January 21st to February 14th. He must have flown from Benares to Delhi on January 20th.

tions have been given to it; it has been made a way to virtue, to enlightenment, it has been enshrined in churches and in every house it is made much of and given sanctity. Everywhere there is sympathy for it, with tears and blessing. And so sorrow continues; every heart knows it, abiding with it or escaping from it, which only gives to it greater strength, to flourish and darken the heart. But sorrow is the way of self-pity, with its immeasurable memories. Sorrow has its root in memory, in the dead things of yesterday. But yesterday is always very important; it is the machinery that gives significance to life; it is the richness of the known, the things possessed. The source of thought is in the yesterday, the yesterdays that give meaning to a life of sorrow. It is yesterday that is sorrow and without cleansing the mind of yesterday there will always be sorrow. You cannot clean it by thought for thought is the continuation of yesterday and so also are the many ideas and ideals. The loss of yesterday is the beginning of self-pity and the dullness of sorrow. Sorrow sharpens thought but thought breeds sorrow. Thought is memory. The self-critical awareness of this whole process, choicelessly frees the mind from sorrow. Seeing this complex fact, without opinion, without judgment, is the ending of sorrow. The known must come to an end, without effort, for the unknown to be.

22nd
The surface was highly polished; every line, every curl of the hair was studied and had its place, every gesture and smile was contained and all movement was examined before the glass. She had several children and the hair was turning grey; she must have money and there was a certain elegance and aloofness. The car was highly polished too; the chromium was bright and sparkling in the morning sun; the white-walled tyres were clean, without any mark and the seats spotless. It was a good car and could go fast, taking the corners very well. This intense and expanding progress was bringing

security and superficiality, and sorrow and love could so easily be explained and contained and there are always different tranquillizers and different gods and new myths replacing the old. It was a bright, cold morning; the slight fog was gone with the rising sun and the air was still. The fat birds, with yellowish legs and beak, were out on the little lawn, very pleased, inclined to be talkative; they had black and white wings with dark fawn-coloured bodies. They were extraordinarily cheerful, hopping about, chasing each other. Then the grey-throated crows came and the fat ones flew off scolding noisily. Their long, heavy beaks shone and their black bodies sparkled; they were watching every movement you were making and nothing was going to escape them and they knew that big dog was coming through the hedge before he was aware of them but they were off cawing and the little lawn was empty.

The mind is always occupied with something or other, however silly or supposedly important. It is like that monkey always restless, always chattering, moving from one thing to another and desperately trying to be quiet. To be empty, completely empty, is not a fearsome thing; it is absolutely essential for the mind to be unoccupied, to be empty, unenforced, for then only it can move into unknown depths. Every occupation is really quite superficial, with that lady or with the so-called saint. An occupied mind can never penetrate into its own depth, into its own untrodden spaces. It is this emptiness that gives space to the mind and into this space time cannot enter. Out of this emptiness there is creation whose love is death.

23rd
The trees were bare, every leaf had fallen off, even the thin, delicate stems were breaking off; the cold had been too much for them; there were other trees which kept their leaves but they were not too green, some of them were turning brown. It was an exceptionally cold winter; there was heavy snow

all along the lower ranges of the Himalayas, several feet thick and in the plains a few hundred miles away it was quite cold; there was heavy frost on the ground and flowers were not blooming; the lawns were burnt. There were a few roses whose colour filled the little garden and the yellow pansies. But on the roads and public places you saw the poor, wrapped up in torn, filthy rags, bare-legged, their heads covered up, their dark faces hardly showing; the women had every kind of coloured cloth on them, dirty, with silver bangles or some ornament around their ankles and around their wrists; they walked freely, easily and with a certain grace; they held themselves very well. Most of them were labourers but in the evening as they went back to their homes, huts really, they would be laughing, teasing each other and the young would be shouting and laughing, far ahead of the older people. It was the end of the day and they had been labouring heavily all day; they would wear themselves out very quickly and they had built houses and offices where they would never live or ever work. All the important people went by there in their cars and these poor people never even bothered to look who went by. The sun was setting behind some ornate building, in a mist that had been hanging about all day; it had no colour, no warmth and there wasn't a flutter among the flags of different countries; these flags too were weary; they were just coloured rags but what importance they had assumed. A few crows were drinking out of a puddle and other crows were coming in to have their share. The sky was pale and ready for the night.

Every thought, every feeling was gone and the brain was utterly still; it was past midnight and there was no noise; it was cold and the moonlight was coming in through one of the windows; it made a pattern on the wall. The brain was very awake, watching, without reacting, without experiencing; there was not a movement within itself but it was not insensitive or drugged by memory. And of a sudden that unknowable immensity was there, not only in the room and beyond but also deep, in the innermost recesses, which was once the mind. Thought has a border, produced by every kind of reaction, and every motive shapes it as with every feeling; every experiencing is from the past and every recognition is from the known. But that immensity left no mark, it was there, clear, strong, impenetrable and unapproachable whose intensity was fire that left no ash. With it was bliss and that too left no memory for there was no experiencing it. It simply was there, to come and go, without pursuit and recall.

The past and the unknown do not meet at any point; they cannot be brought together by any act whatsoever; there is no bridge to cross over nor a path that leads to it. The two have never met and will never meet. The past has to cease for the unknowable, for that immensity to be.